AF290943

THE
VINEYARD
VENTURE

THE VINEYARD VENTURE

An English Family's Life in
SAUTERNES

NIGEL REAY-JONES

First published in Great Britain in 2026 by
Fonthill
An imprint of
Pen & Sword Books Ltd
Yorkshire – Philadelphia
www.fonthill.media

ISBN 978-1-03618-671-5

A CIP catalogue record for this book
is available from the British Library.

Typeset in SabonLTStd 10.5/14 by
SJmagic DESIGN SERVICES, India.
Printed and bound in the UK by CPI Group (UK) Ltd, Croydon, CR0 4YY

The Publisher's authorised representative in the EU for product
safety is Authorised Rep Compliance Ltd., Ground Floor,
71 Lower Baggot Street, Dublin D02 P593, Ireland.
www.arccompliance.com

For a complete list of Pen & Sword titles please contact
PEN & SWORD BOOKS LIMITED
George House, Units 12 & 13, Beevor Street, Off Pontefract Road,
Barnsley, South Yorkshire, S71 1HN, England
E-mail: enquiries@pen-and-sword.co.uk
Website: www.pen-and-sword.co.uk

or

PEN AND SWORD BOOKS
1950 Lawrence Rd, Havertown, PA 19083, USA
E-mail: uspen-and-sword@casematepublishers.com
Website: www.penandswordbooks.com

Foreword

This foreword is dedicated to the memory of my father, Nigel, the author of this book.

One of my fondest memories of my father is of watching him write this book—a labour of love punctuated by agonising moments of writer's block followed by sudden breakthroughs of inspiration, when he would find the right words or turn of phrase and laugh out loud, confident that the events unfolding on the page were true to the ups, downs and many unexpected mishaps that come with running a vineyard, a restaurant and a hotel in Southwest France. The joy that my father took in telling our story can be felt on every page, and we continue to laugh with him each time we re-read it.

Nigel never got to see his book in print. In the fifteen years since his death, much has changed in my life and in the lives of my mother and four brothers: seven grandchildren, countless house and job moves, life events small and big, and so much more in the world around us.

Throughout that time, this book has been a constant for us. A source of joy, laughter and comfort, a treasure trove of happy, loving and often hilarious family memories, and, above all, the most beautiful gift that Nigel could have left to us and to his grandchildren, whom he never met; a record of the life of fun, adventure and eccentricity that he gave us when, nearly forty years ago, he and our mother Georgea decided to up sticks, leave grey Middle England behind, and live the French dream with their five boys.

All that my father was can be found in these pages. His wit, humour and intelligence, his instinct for the sublime and the ridiculous in equal measure. His passion for biology, winemaking and the esoteric science of oenology. His sense of fun, adventure and optimism—but, perhaps above all, his wholehearted commitment to the joy of a family life lived on a road less travelled.

Nigel was a uniquely special man, and my mother, brothers and I are so pleased that his book is finally getting the wider readership that it deserves.

This short foreword is for my wonderful father, Nigel. This book is my father's love letter to his family, to France, to wine and winemaking, and to the adventure of life. We hope you enjoy reading it as much as we have and will continue to love and treasure it.

Robert Reay-Jones
October 2025

Preface

The backdrop is Sauternes, land of mists and golden wine, and an ancient château that started life as a medieval fortified farm.

Onto the scene of this idyllic corner of rural France comes an English couple with five small children, bent on fulfilling that dream, cherished by so many … of owning a vineyard. It isn't as simple as that! Vineyards are expensive and the Reay-Joneses aren't rich. But sensible advice like, 'Don't do it!' is ignored, and safe, cosy Britain is abandoned for Château de Commarque. To balance the books, they open a hotel-restaurant, an activity about which they know even less than they do about vineyards. The resulting life is as unpredictable and unimaginable as it is hilarious and catastrophic. The rose-tinted vision becomes reality, a reality which includes natural disasters, bureaucratic nightmares, triumphs in the restaurant—'She can't be English; *une Anglaise* would not be able to cook like that!'—and eventually, success in the vineyard.

Scores of characters pass across the stage of hotel and restaurant and others play their roles among the vines: an accident-prone and hypochondriac chef, a serving brigadier working as a grape picker, a pyjama-clad stranger playing snooker with the children before breakfast, a row of veterans from the Algerian war peeing against the oak trees behind the restaurant, a non-driving, non-French-speaking wine and travel writer, the Marquis de Lur-Saluces and the Comte de Vaucelles, the shifty previous owner, Freddie the Brie shepherd dog, to whom every bent female form is an invitation to copulate, and Monsieur Saint-Martin, black belt at Judo and Karate and vigneron extraordinaire. Owls live under the arches, hoopoes feed on the lawns, deer wander through the park and there are bats and toads in the cellar.

Vineyard Venture is a family biography, a vineyard saga and a book on Sauternes wine. It is also the story of a dream become reality, a comedy of errors and a not-too-serious commentary on French education and administration.

If you want to find out what it's really like, read on.... If you don't, you could always pour yourself a glass of Sauternes and dream about a château in France.

Contents

1

How to Commit a Folly

It all started at Cesco's fortieth birthday dinner. The idea had seemed, on that buoyant evening, both logical and, yes, plausible. It still seemed that way the following day and the feeling of (slightly) advancing years lent an urgency to our desire to pursue it.

Cesco and I had been D.Phil. students together at Oxford. We both had jobs without career prospects, we both had wives interested in France, we all liked wine, none of us was entirely satisfied with British state education.

'Wouldn't it be wonderful for the children?' We were both biologists, or anyway ex-biologists, so there was the logic—why not run a vineyard?

Bergerac seemed a good place to start; we had visited it often, indeed we claim to have discovered it before the regular British wine trade, a 'lesser' wine area, overshadowed by Bordeaux, whose vineyards touch its own. Surely the land would be less expensive than that of its illustrious neighbour? Moreover, Bergerac had prospects. Production was improving. There was new blood in the area's governing body, the Conseil Interprofessionel. But the most interesting thing for us was the presence of an Englishman, Henry 'Nick' Ryman, at the height of his powers at Château la Jaubertie. His is one of the few, the very few, success stories among British settlers in France. Nick Ryman had sold a stationery chain, a household name in England, and sunk the proceeds into his vineyard and winery. His wine was simply much better than others from the area, the result of application of modern methods derived from the New World and an obsessive attention to detail. He was plainly the man to talk to, especially as the conversation would be in English.

'Are you men of substance?' he asked when I telephoned him.

'No,' I replied.

'Well don't do it,' he said. Then added, 'You'd better come and see me.'

Cesco and I went to see him. He showed us his *chai*, the place where he made his wine, and the results of being a man of substance were evident. If this was what was needed then we were more seriously underfunded than we had thought! Nick Ryman, however, was encouraging in a way totally at odds with his 'well don't do it' remark, but he had found kindred spirits and was even, may I dare suggest of such a consummate businessman, carried away by his own enthusiasm.

He had been busy on our behalf before we arrived. His next-door neighbour wanted to retire and Château la Rayre might be just what we were looking for. With 17 hectares of vines in excellent condition it was big enough to be profitable, there was adequate equipment for serious winemaking, Monsieur Revol had a decent reputation and a portfolio of customers, and there was potential for improvement. Nick Ryman sounded like a headmaster making a qualified recommendation of a candidate for Oxbridge entrance.

'Don't worry about the price, he's bound to pump it up because you're with me.' The property was exactly as he had described it. Monsieur Revol was extremely hospitable with his wine, tasting it himself with sufficient gusto not to notice the extent to which noses had been thrust into his affairs when I injudiciously produced the carefully annotated map of his property which Nick Ryman had obtained from the local *mairie*— the mayor's office.

The price quoted was suitably high and we left in an alcoholic haze, swearing future contact and, for all I can remember, eternal friendship. The visit had been tremendous fun, spiced as it was with the possibility that we might end up actually owning the place. Sober calculation in the hours that followed showed clearly that this was not to be. Even allowing for a most generous drop in the price, we would still have to sell more bottles of wine in the first year than Monsieur Revol had ever done in order to pay for the borrowed money. There was also the question of a second house for whichever family did not occupy that of Monsieur Revol.... We told ourselves that it was the first property we had seen and anyway, did we really want to be in the shadow, both literally and figuratively, of the great Ryman?

We saw others the following day: 85 hectares of mud with vines stuck in it and the biggest *chai* I have ever seen filled with the rustiest collection of machinery. Seven hectares of perfect vines, with 15 hectares of maize and a tiny house with an outside loo. We seemed far from finding anything in Bergerac, so we drove home.

Cesco's career then took a sharp upswing. His company was taken over and taken over again. The new bosses could spot a good man and he was made Director of Research. The interest and stimulation previously lacking were now present in full measure and as Cesco started to receive invitations to join pioneering trade missions and to advise foreign governments, Georgea and I, whom nobody had spotted, continued to search alone.

One might think that the haze of imprudence in which this project had been launched would have cleared with the departure of Cesco from the scene. There was now no safety in numbers. We could not fall back on Cesco's highly relevant experience of agricultural industry, likely to be a lot more useful than my highly theoretical knowledge of winemaking!

So why didn't we come to our senses? The problem was that by now the scheme was too clearly imaginable to go away. Both Georgea and I needed something to dream about. Georgea had had four children under school age, while keeping on her job as a peripatetic classical guitar teacher, and now Edward was on the way. I had drifted into my career-less job in an Oxford tutorial college more or less by chance. You see! Already a fundamental lack of responsibility had been revealed and no properly directed ambition. At best, this job would stay the same until retirement. In fact it would probably have disappeared, as it did a few years later for the rest of the staff when the recession struck in earnest. It wasn't that daft to get out, just daft to try and buy a vineyard instead.

The whole idea of it suited us and the argument about benefiting the children gave it respectability. Our eldest son, Thomas, had already had a taste of state education and we had been so unimpressed with it that he, together with the twins, Francis and William, had gone off to a tiny private school in the middle of a field to learn some serious reading and writing. The trouble with this solution was that it could only be temporary. For most of the pupils at the Francis Eyre School this was but the first step in an entirely private school career which we could not possibly afford for five children. We reckoned the French state education system could not be worse than what we had seen in Oxfordshire, and rumour had it that it might well be a lot better. The acquisition of a second language would be inevitable. We were convinced of the benefits for the children and who knows? We might even be successful!

Georgea admits freely that she felt a certain pride in being able to say, 'We're going to France to live in a château and run a vineyard.' It felt like a step up and it met with admiring reactions: 'Are you really? How wonderful! We'd love to do something like that!'

How many people claim this dream? We were foolishly proud to be doing something about it, foolishly proud to be turning the dream into a quite undreamt-of reality.

So it was that a year later we were outside yet another abandoned vineyard, this time with all the children and ... the ever-patient Nick Ryman. It was, we agreed, a nice spot and he thought the *chai* was 'workable', while awaiting, inevitably, the essential re-equipment, but he didn't like some of the vines.

'You should have the soil analysed, there's something wrong here but I don't know what. My seven-year-old vines are this size,' and he indicated a girth about three times greater than that of the slender, small-leaved specimens in front of us. Whatever the problem was it was relatively minor compared with that announced by the agent of SAFER* who was responsible for selling the property.

'You understand, *bien sûr, monsieur*, that under the improvement scheme for the Bergerac area all these vines,' and he gestured at the whole vineyard, apart from the problem vines, 'are scheduled to be grubbed up and replaced with high-grown, wide-spaced vines in parcels aligned with those of the adjoining properties. *Evidemment* there are grants to help you do this.'

Unfortunately, it appeared that there were no grants to help beginners with no stock while they passed several years without income, watching their fine new vines grow high and widely spaced. Of course, it was all thoroughly logical and economic, the fruit of the new dynamism in the Conseil Interprofessionnel. Properties could share large, labour-saving machines, too expensive for all but the biggest vineyards, and so benefit from the economies of scale. It works, even if it damages a little our rosy view of the artisan grower fashioning his wine from grapes lovingly produced by his own skilled hands. It sunk us anyway. We needed a vineyard in production.

The only hope in Bergerac then was a smallish vineyard that had already been 'realigned'. Big would be too expensive, too small meant not enough stock of a wine with a fairly low value. Bergerac wines are not expensive. It seemed improbable that the perfect specimen would ever be available. We had already counted out the Cahors district as too expensive and the Savoie for the same reason, despite the fact that few people know the wines of the Savoie and they are hard to find outside the areas of production. But places surrounded by mountains must conduct their affairs in the valleys and these take on an importance out of

---

* A government agency responsible, among other things, for the sale of unwanted farms.

proportion with their size, and are valued accordingly. All the classic areas like Burgundy and Bordeaux had been ruled out on grounds of cost, and Provence and the South West were far too hot for us Brits. We reckoned to work in the vines ourselves. The prospects looked dim indeed.

The solution was as unexpected as it was lucky and was found appropriately, if unintentionally, by Nick Ryman. He thought a couple of Bergerac vineyards had been advertised in *Decanter* magazine a few months previously. He couldn't remember exactly when, but the advertising department would be able to find them, if they existed. It appeared that they did not. The helpful lady from the magazine searched many months of advertisements to no avail. I asked if anything else had appeared during this time.

'Well not much. You understand we don't handle much in the way of vineyard sales. Oh! but there was one, a couple of months ago: in Sauternes. A vineyard with a small hotel. The owner's English, Mr Jenkin-Lee, which should make things easier for you. It's called Château de Commarque and the asking price...' It was much too high for us of course.

And that seemed to be that. But we couldn't help thinking about the vineyard-hotel—if only because there was so little else to think about.

We had certainly not considered places like Sauternes, anyway everyone knows Sauternes is the hardest wine in the world to make. But in the spirit of leaving no stone unturned I telephoned the number given to me by the lady at *Decanter*. Mr Jenkin-Lee's voice was a little hesitant and he sounded ill at ease. The information he gave me was only mildly interesting. The vineyard, it seemed, ran to 8 hectares and was not yet in production. The vines were two and three years old. The oldest ones would therefore be allowed to start producing next year.

Presumably there was no *chai* yet? Yes, there was a little one. This struck me as a peculiar description. Did he mean too small for the vineyard? Just temporarily small until production increased? An inconveniently small building? However, the call was at peak time and the conversation moved on. There were fourteen hotel rooms and a restaurant. The buildings were described as 'very, very old'. Would I like a write-up with some pictures? I said 'Yes please', and the conversation was finished.

While waiting for the write-up, expectations were aroused. Château de Commarque appeared to have certain advantages: the vineyard was small enough not to require much expensive labour but the wine that came from it would be valuable, much more so than the wines of Bergerac. The yield of Sauternes is very low and the grapes are picked gradually over a relatively long period of time, the time needed for the Noble Rot to prepare each bunch of grapes. The result is that your *chai* requires only modest equipment compared with those of similar sized vineyards elsewhere. The hotel could provide the income needed to fill the gap so clearly visible in any forecasts based purely on sales of wine from a Bergerac-type vineyard, and there was the interesting possibility of selling the wine produced, both in the restaurant and to hotel guests. One could see the two enterprises developing hand in hand: the better the hotel did the more wine we could flog on site at high price—and we could even run wine tour holidays! We worked up a sufficient lather of enthusiasm to decide that the matter needed taking further. A visit was necessary. A glance at the pictures that arrived in the post provided confirmation.

This was February 1986 and the weather was awful. Our village was more or less cut off by snow. The journey to Château de Commarque promised to be difficult. At Heathrow it was announced that Bordeaux was snowbound. There might be a diversion to Biarritz. I telephoned Mr Jenkin-Lee and, yes indeed, he knew all about it. Bordeaux had 4 inches of snow. His voice expressed incredulity. Bordeaux airport was *never* affected by the weather. Nobody could remember when it had last happened! What extraordinary bad luck! I recognised in his shocked tones the salesman's desire to maintain a good image of Southwest France in the mind of a possible customer flying out of freezing, fog-bound England.

The plane arrived late, but it did at least arrive in Bordeaux. Mr Jenkin-Lee was not at all like his voice. Tall, bearded and charming, he drove at a most alarming speed and, as we approached Sauternes, he provided a running commentary on the passing scenery.

'We'll take the scenic route past the back of Château Yquem. And this one here is Château Lafaurie-Peyraguey. D'you know it was built by the same architect who did Commarque?' That was a real masterstroke but he managed to continue at the same level of virtuosity. 'There's Château Filhot, our immediate neighbour. The Comte de Vaucelles has been most helpful over the years…' etc., etc. It was so obvious what he was doing but I was hooked nonetheless!

The roads got narrower. The landscape closed in and he was still driving so fast that I was unable to take in all the twists and turns of the road. Then he braked sharply and we were on a track with vines to the right, then on both sides and ahead … ahead, high walls, a round tower at the right-hand end, a battlemented gateway with wrought-iron gates, trees over the wall, a glimpse of a courtyard with white buildings facing the gate, another tower behind the first. Then we were in the courtyard and the hook was fatally embedded.

It was lovely, even on a cold, dark February afternoon, even with peeling paint, patchy gravel and mossy roofs. This was what we had been looking for and we would have to make an all-out effort to get it. It quickly became apparent, however, that there might be more to this than I had imagined. All was not quite as it had been made out to be.

The first indication came when we stepped out into the gathering gloom for a look at the vineyard. Even I could tell that what I was being shown did not amount to 8 hectares, about twenty acres. Mr Jenkin-Lee explained that instead of 8 hectares of vines, I should have understood 4 hectares planted with vines and 4 hectares that *could* be planted with vines, so making 8 hectares of vineyard. It seemed churlish to point out the difference between hypothetical vineyard and actual vines in the soil, so I concentrated instead on the matter of the unplanted hectares. What did Mr Jenkin-Lee mean by saying that there were 4 hectares that *could* be planted? He replied that they were in the area demarcated for Sauternes—the term he used was that they were in the area of the Sauternes Appellation Contrôlée. But this is not enough. Droits de Plantation (Plantation Rights) are required, even though your land is in the right place. Any vineyard whose vines have been pulled up gives rise to Droits, which last for ten years and are then lost for ever. Normally they are used at once, to replant the same vineyard when the old vines have worn out, but the rights may be transferred elsewhere, even to a different kind of vineyard. These days, the distances they can be taken are severely limited. New planting rights are granted each year but the areas involved are tiny. This is partly a matter of Common Market politics: the vineyard area must not be allowed to grow in an unlimited way and so create unwanted surpluses ... or perhaps too much competition for the other producing nations. I must say that, in either case, the danger appears slight for Sauternes, with just 2,000 hectares to supply the whole world! The story Mr Jenkin-Lee had already told fostered the notion that Commarque's unplanted hectares came fully garnished with rights; in the 1950s the vineyard had covered 15 hectares but had, like the whole of Sauternes, fallen on hard times and been sold off in bits and pieces. He had bought the property totally abandoned and pulled up the remaining vines, smothered as they were in twelve feet of scrub.

'Do you have planting rights for the whole four hectares?' I asked, feeling rather pleased with my grasp of the subject.

'Not quite,' he replied.

'How much *do* you have then?'

'About a third of a hectare,' he said, and had the grace to look a little sheepish.

We then moved on to the *chai*. It was neither too small for the vineyard nor in an inconveniently small building. It simply wasn't a *chai*. That is to say: a place designed and equipped for the making of wine; but, in the same way that the unplanted land was not a vineyard but could *become* one, so this building could become a *chai*. At present it was a hypothetical *chai* and it was filled with a mass of old iron pipes, wood and, above all straw, which Mr Jenkin-Lee insisted on calling manure, saying that it was for fertilising the next patch of vineyard to be planted. I searched the pile in vain for traces of dung. Far from fertilising a vineyard, the decomposition of this stuff would probably cause the death by starvation of most baby vines! I began to suspect that Mr Jenkin-Lee knew less about viticulture than he should.

It also dawned on me that when Mr Jenkin-Lee seemed hesitant, that was the moment to wake up and start asking questions, for hesitancy indicated that Mr Jenkin-Lee was not telling the whole truth. His hesitancy would continue at least until the story of the moment was well launched. No wonder he had sounded odd on the telephone!

By now it was too dark and too cold to continue the tour so we went into the house. This was more like it. The kitchen was huge with an immense fireplace, great logs burning, bread, cheese, bottles of wine. I was introduced to Mr Jenkin-Lee's fiancée. We retired to the sitting-room where there was another fire, a bit smoky this time, but it was an attractive room with exposed beams and beautiful furniture. Sauternes was served. It came from the vines next to those of Commarque, said Mr Jenkin-Lee. It may have done, but as only 10 per cent of the vineyard of Château Lamourette is near Commarque, it may well not have done. The other 90 per cent is at Bommes, a good 2 miles away.

Apart from the kitchen and the sitting-room the house was very cold. I realise now that the sitting-room fire had been lit for my benefit and the stove in the kitchen, which was to save our skins later on, had been allowed to go out in favour of the more appealing log fire.

My bedroom was magnificent. 'The Blue Room' measured, still does measure, 24 feet in each direction and is a good 12 feet high. It had a fireplace with tiny exposed bricks, two double beds and immense wall cupboards from floor to ceiling. Standard lamps and oil paintings completed the impression of rustic opulence. It was freezing cold. Mr Jenkin-Lee had given me an electric heater but it might as well have been out in the courtyard. I got up at 1.00 am and dressed. At 2.30 am I put on my coat. At breakfast next morning, needless to say, Mr Jenkin-Lee earnestly assured me that he hadn't ever known a night like it all the time he had been in France. He presumably had something resembling a blast furnace in his own room, which I now know to be the coldest in the house.

He showed me the rest of the property that morning. The restaurant was beautiful. It was in the former *chai* and Mr Jenkin-Lee had cleverly converted a concrete *cuve* (a wine vat) into a small bar. There was a raised fireplace across one corner and across another were the entrances to one of the round towers. A staircase led to its upstairs room. A muddle of balloons and streamers lay in one corner, left over from the revelries of New Year's Eve, Mr Jenkin-Lee explained. This was the last time the restaurant had been used. He had 'let go' the hotel and restaurant activity, he said, since the previous summer, but by popular request he had opened for New Year's Eve. How many people had he had? I enquired.

'About eighty,' he replied. 'Four hundred francs a head. It's the way to set yourself up for the winter, then you don't need to worry about trying to stay open when there aren't any tourists around.'—Oh Mr Jenkin-Lee! Mr Jenkin-Lee!

I have since heard about that New Year's Eve party from a couple of people who worked there. It ended *before* midnight—and it ended with a fight. There were forty people, not eighty, and they were brought along by a friend of Mr Jenkin-Lee. Dissatisfaction was rife among the guests within minutes of their arrival. Mr Jenkin-Lee had lit the fire at 4.00 pm. There was no other form of heating except two electric wall heaters and this room is 38 feet long, 20 feet wide and 18 feet high. The fur coats came off and went back on quickly. The food, which sounded magnificent from the menu left pinned up under the arch outside, had been cooked some forty miles away and shipped to Commarque in Mr Jenkin-Lee's car. When it was served it was about as cold as the restaurant itself! I doubt very much if Mr Jenkin-Lee collected a single 400F. that night. Of course, all of this only came to light much later and I have got ahead of myself. For the moment, I was more interested in Commarque's potential than in its recent history. It looked as though it would be wonderful in summer.

The hotel rooms were simple but charming. They occupied the long white building that faced the gate and were on two levels. Downstairs there was a little sitting-room with bathroom behind, and a steep staircase led to the bedroom above. Outside, three enormous plane trees would cast shade in the summer and it was easy to imagine tables and chairs on the gravel terrace, leisurely breakfasts, couples strolling across the courtyard to the swimming pool. Yes! There was a swimming pool too! It was not very big and, at this time of the year, brownish green. In itself it was unalluring, but the situation was perfect. Separated from the courtyard by a long wall, it was approached through double wrought iron gates, flanked by worn stone pillars to one of which was attached an ancient bell frame, used to summon the workers to lunch in the old days. A semi-circular stone staircase led down to the pool area. This was enclosed on the far side by a laurel hedge, by pampas grass at each end, a banana plant, bamboo. Beyond this enclosure the vines stretched away to the woods. It faced south, a veritable suntrap, I was told, and for once this was no less than the truth.

There was no avoiding the fact that the place exerted a powerful attraction but, equally, that the lure had to be resisted until the manifold problems that came with it were resolved. For example, I had seen five two-level hotel rooms in the white building and a two-bedroomed cottage—the gîte—which formed the end of it. The gîte was equipped with a kitchen and was intended for self-catering holidays.

'A sure-fire source of income,' said Mr Jenkin-Lee.

But the particulars had indicated fourteen hotel rooms. So where were the other nine? Mr Jenkin-Lee became hesitant again.

'I counted the bedrooms of the gîte. After all you can't really separate it from the hotel.'

Fair enough! That makes seven.

'There's another gîte over by the front gateway.'

There was indeed. When the door was opened a wave of cold and damp hit us. The odour of mould was overwhelming. Across a corner stood a brownish sofa with large grey patches on it.

'Roof needs a bit of attention, I think,' muttered Mr Jenkin-Lee.

Upstairs there were two interconnecting bedrooms with damply wilting furniture in each. That made nine rooms.

'In the season we use all the bedrooms in the house,' Mr Jenkin-Lee assured me.

This seemed reasonable. The one I had occupied the night before would certainly make a handsome family room when it had thawed out, and I had seen another behind it equally well set up. A mental add-up gave four bedrooms in the house including Mr Jenkin-Lee's.

'Where do you sleep in the summer then?' I asked.

'Oh, we use the caravan down the back—I've fixed it up with running water, mains electricity and everything. It's very comfortable.'

I looked at it later. It was more than adequate, but through the window I could see a wasp's nest hanging from a corner that had most certainly grown for a whole season. It didn't look as though Mr Jenkin-Lee had used the caravan during the previous summer at any rate—and then there was still the matter of a fifth bedroom in the house, necessary to make up the total of the hotel rooms to fourteen.

'It's up that staircase,' said Mr Jenkin-Lee, indicating the shabby flight that started outside his bedroom and seemed to disappear into the roof.

As I started to climb it he added, 'It's not finished yet.'

He really was a master of understatement. It was, in fact, another hypothetical creation; a potential bedroom—on condition that it was provided with a door and floor, plus walls to separate it from the rest of the roof space. I looked at Mr Jenkin-Lee reproachfully.

'Well you know how it is,' he said. 'You have to make the most of what you've got when you're trying to sell something.'

I replied that I didn't mind that but objected to him making so much of what he *hadn't* got. He was quite unabashed and drove me back to the airport in high good humour at the same breakneck speed as he had brought me from it. 'Flexibility' over the price was possible. He would, of course, answer all my questions. His notary would be only to willing to help, etc.

Even allowing for halving of the vineyard, halving of the hotel, an almost certain lack of customers and the stone-cold certain need for investment, the figures added up better than those of the vineyards we had seen before. A very modest performance from the hotel and restaurant would see to that. The vineyard was about to become productive. We could just about bridge the gap until we had bottles to sell and there was the added appeal that we could enormously increase the value of the place by planting the rest of the vineyard. In 1986 it was still possible to obtain planting rights, on the small scale that we required, and at a price that would add only a modest percentage to the total cost of bringing new hectares into production. There were all those empty buildings into which the hotel could expand. We planned another trip to Commarque, and this time Georgea and the children would come.

We drove down at the beginning of April. This time I did the running commentary for Georgea's benefit. She was less impressed by mine than I had been by Mr Jenkin-Lee's, remarking that she was more interested in whether Sauternes had a school, a doctor or a chemist than in the elevation of the Commarque plateau and its relationship with the Crus Classés—Classed Growths, the best vineyards of Sauternes. She was, quite rightly, steeling herself against over enthusiasm but her resolve failed as we sat behind the house that evening watching the sun set gloriously beyond the giant oaks that grew at the back of the hotel buildings.

The children loved it. We were staying in the gîte at the end of the hotel rooms and they thought it was the most wonderful adventure. There was constant running up and down the stairs and a Lego town rapidly developed all over their bedroom floor. They were not interested in exploring, only enjoying their new den. So it was that we were able to sit in the sunshine—don't forget this was the very beginning of April—sipping, inevitably, Sauternes and telling each other how perfect it all was. Well, it was! I have since seen many hotel guests sitting where we sat that evening doing nothing but admire the sunset. It performs with gratifying regularity beyond an immense horizon composed of the pine trees of the Forêt des Landes.

Meanwhile Mr Jenkin-Lee was preparing a feast. In honour of our presence he was barbecuing, over the kitchen fire, the lamb he received annually from a neighbour in exchange for use of the field which adjoined the property. A lamb from the same flock which was to eat the vines on the other side of the valley the following year and so give rise to the vineyard's first revenue: an insurance claim. The lamb in question, however, was quite blameless—but slow to cook. The kitchen fire was sluggish and the children did not have French habits. They were used to supper at 6.30 and pyjamas by 7.30! By 10 o'clock that night desperation was in the air! Robert, aged nearly 6, almost fell off his chair several times as sleep got the upper hand over hunger. When the lamb was finally served the children barely touched it. For them the evening stopped there. We carried them up the steep staircase of the gîte and put them to bed on the other side of Legotown, then returned to the lamb and the entertaining company of Mr Jenkin-Lee, for once safely removed from his sales pitch.

The serious business started the following day. Prices were discussed, well below the asking price, but still too high. The vineyard diminished by a further hectare, following a careful inspection of the Plan Cadastral at the Mairie. (This is a list of all the parcels of land belonging to every proprietor in the commune with their areas and the use to which they are put, an essential reference in any property transaction.) This time even Mr Jenkin-Lee seemed taken aback, 'I could have sworn I planted four hectares.'

We drove back to England with nothing concluded and with several questions for Mr Jenkin-Lee's notary. But Mr Jenkin-Lee's notary was something of a problem.

For the British, the involvement of notaries in property deals always takes some getting used to. One notary acts for both parties and there is therefore no one, as it were, rooting for your side. In the majority of cases this probably doesn't matter and the notary *does* see fair play and *does* deal properly with the legal formalities. It has, however, often been said that in practice he acts for nobody but himself and is extremely well paid for doing so. In theory, the system should make conveyancing easier than it is in the UK, but when you are coming from abroad the notary always seems to be 'in place' and therefore to have been chosen by the vendor, or else by the estate agent, whose fees you, the buyer, will pay. In either case the arrangement gives rise to the niggling suspicion that these are forces marshalled by the vendor to ensure that your purchase is made as difficult and as expensive as possible. I have said that Mr Jenkin-Lee's notary was a problem; he was in fact almost hypothetical.

'Oh come off it,' I hear you say. 'Don't exaggerate. Either he's got a notary or he hasn't, in which case *you* can organise one.'

I promise you there is no need to exaggerate, none whatsoever; Mr Jenkin-Lee had a struck-off notary! He had been, we discovered, erased from the list of notaries for persistent wickedness associated with drink and consequent incompetence but his office, or *étude*, as notaries like to call their place of work, was still open. All transactions were carried out by the chief clerk, a friend of Mr Jenkin-Lee. A minor additional inconvenience was that the *étude* was situated a long way from Sauternes, on the far side of the Entre-deux-Mers. As Mr Jenkin-Lee said, you didn't want one too close to home or everyone would know all about your affairs. I could well imagine that he would not be keen on that. Anyway, his friend the chief clerk was not a fully-fledged notary and could not, therefore, pass the *acte* of purchase. This had to be, as it were, rubber-stamped by another notary, one with a right to his title. The one chosen also lived far from Sauternes, and in the opposite direction, so he knew nothing of the details of the affair. We were perhaps even less protected by the officers of the law than was usual!

To add to the difficulty, the independent valuer that we take so much for granted in Britain is a rare bird in France—and very expensive. This may have something to do with the absence of a longstanding, universal mortgage system. After all, the livelihoods of many valuers in the UK depend on the building societies and the banks. Whatever the reason, the kind of impartial advice to which we are accustomed is not the norm in France. It seemed prudent, to say the least, to have a slice of the French system on our side.

But how do you go about finding an honest notary? The simple answer, 'by recommendation', does not work when you don't know anybody whose recommendation you can take. The actual answer was, 'ask an honest solicitor'. We can all, of course, lay our hands on lots of these! I was recommended to the Cabinet (not an Etude this time) de Chambrun in Paris: 'Absolutely straight and they do a lot of work in England so there'll be no language problem.' A warning was given however: 'I can recommend the quality of their work but not so much the size of their fees. They say you can pay an arm and a leg just for a telephone call.'

It seemed to me that Mr Jenkin-Lee would get at least an arm and a leg if I did not enlist their help so I telephoned the Cabinet de Chambrun.

The urbane voice at the other end of the line spoke perfect English with just the trace of an accent: Maître Allain was expecting my call and had been briefed on the general situation. He felt he could be useful; he would scrutinise the *acte* of purchase for pitfalls and would push the other side to complete the formalities with a minimum of delay. We were mildly reassured. We also started to make progress. A further flight to Commarque resulted in agreement on the price. I thought I was being very severe with Mr Jenkin-Lee and was pleased with myself. I took the opportunity to check on the state of the vines, which seemed to be developing leaves properly. The necessary finance was raised and our house was put on the market. It appeared, though, that the sale of Commarque could not possibly be completed much before the end of the year. There were simply too many formalities to go through. Privately we thought there were also too many of Mr Jenkin-Lee's affairs to unscramble. Meanwhile the pound started to slip against the franc....

We were plainly about to miss any summer season we might have had in the hotel and quite probably the grape harvest as well. Yet Mr Jenkin-Lee was fidgeting to go as much as we were to get in. Subsequent events suggested that he really needed to go. Sundry creditors, legitimate and, well, less reputable, were at his heels and he required at least the promise of money to come to stave off even more energetic pursuit.

The normal procedure in purchases like this is for the parties concerned to sign a Compromis de Vente or Sous-Seing (a private treaty) accompanied by the payment of a non-returnable deposit, which binds both sides to the sale and sets out a timetable for the signing of the final *acte* of purchase and any intervening stage payments that may be agreed. I suggested to Mr Jenkin-Lee that he should move out and we should move in as soon as this document was signed. He agreed readily. I believe his continued presence at Commarque was becoming an embarrassment to him.

Maître Allain at the Cabinet de Chambrun was audibly perturbed when I put this scheme to him.

'Do you realise the risk that you take? You would have no security of tenure until the final *acte* is signed. I cannot recommend you to expose yourself and your family to the risk of eviction in the event of a creditor foreclosing on the present proprietor.

'What we shall do,' he continued more calmly, 'is to draw up a formal rental agreement, a *bail commercial*, in which the vendor will undertake to let the whole of the property to you for a nominal sum until completion of the sale. In this way you cannot be turned out and we shall write in numerous safeguards against interference by the proprietor. If he does not agree to sign this document then you will not agree to sign the Compromis de Vente!'

Well played Maître Allain! This was just the kind of advice I had been hoping for. It seemed worth at least a good slice of arm and leg!

We followed this plan to the letter. In addition, Mr Jenkin-Lee was persuaded to come to Paris to sign the documents, as it were, on our territory. So it was that on 27 June 1986, after two-and-a-half years of plotting, we finally crossed the Rubicon, by which I mean I crossed the Channel to Paris and signed the Compromis de Vente. It all passed off without a hitch at the magnificent offices of the Cabinet de Chambrun—in the middle of the Champs Elysées. For those on whom the significance of this is lost I should say that in the French version of the game of Monopoly the Champs Elysées replaces Park Lane. That alone is enough to add a percentage to any invoice rendered by the organisation. It is absolutely vast. When I pushed open the front door, which was big enough and thick enough to guard Bluebeard's Castle, all I could see was a great corridor stretching, it seemed, almost out of sight. There were no signs to direct me so I marched resolutely along it. At the end the only turning was to the right and then I was in another even bigger corridor. This one was entirely panelled from the floor to the ceiling 20 feetabove and at intervals immense bookcases housed thousands of uniform fat books. Open doors revealed palatial but empty offices and at the end of this corridor was the reception. The place seemed to be staffed by the entire line-up of the Miss France competition. Why such an august and also silent place, for I saw but a single notary, Maître Allain, should attract such a collection of beautiful women I have never understood, and I did not have the nerve to ask!

2

Emigration and a Little History

We were now ready to leave England and we were going to do so separately. One object of this unromantic departure was to break the first vicious circle set up by the French authorities whereby, in order to import your furniture into France, you have to have moved already. This was 1986 and things became simpler in later years (at least whilst the UK was part of the EU), but one should never underestimate the capacity of the French authorities to complicate your plans. The French themselves never do.

The problem, as perceived by the authorities, is this: the French love antique furniture almost as much as they adore royalty and, having destroyed the greater part of both during the Revolution, they cannot get their hands on enough of them. Subsequent wars on French soil have further diminished the supply of the home-grown product (antiques that is, not royalty); so there is an ever-present danger that enterprising dealers will flood the market with sought-after foreign antiques, especially English ones of which the French are particularly fond. There have been some unlikely claims made for lorry loads of furniture stopped by the motorway police. It requires an improbable suspension of disbelief on the part of the gendarmes to let through six dozen silver candelabra, twenty-five bow fronted chests of drawers and fifteen grandfather clocks without asking the whereabouts of the château vast enough to contain them all.

Before you can take your own precious furniture to your house in France an import licence is required, issued by the French Consulate in London. The consular officials will certainly not believe your story that you have bought a dream house in the Dordogne, Provence or even Sauternes. Documentary evidence is needed, French documentary evidence: a Cértificat de Domicile signed and sealed by the mayor of the commune wherein lies your house. So, you have to have moved, or at least have made a special journey, in order to get your furniture to move with you. Our solution was for me to go first and send back the Cértificat de Domicile to Georgea, who would go to London for the import licence and give it to the removal firm before setting out herself, on her own, with all five children, three weeks later. She is made of stern stuff, that one!

* * *

Our emigration got off to a bad start. The elderly van we had bought for the purpose, full of beds, chests of drawers, etc., to furnish the gatehouse gîte at the château, the contents of which, you may recall, had succumbed to the effects of damp, simply had not the clutch to climb our steep drive out into the lane and away to the New Future beckoning from across the Channel. After ten minutes and a nasty smell of burning it was time to switch off the engine and rethink my exit. This furniture, by the way, was being transported without the benefit of an import licence, but it was of no great value.

I went back into the house to give the clutch time to cool down. Georgea had gone shopping with Edward (the youngest, nearly 2). The other children were at school. It would be embarrassing if I was still there when she got back. I reversed the van until it rested against the garage door where the slope was more gentle, warmed the engine thoroughly and revved the motor to a roar. The van shot up the garden and leapt out into the lane, a one way street with no visibility in the direction from which the traffic comes. I opened my eyes in time to stop at the T-junction. Things had gone marginally better than Adrian Mole's school outing. It had only taken twenty-five minutes to reach the garden gate.

On looking back, this episode strikes us as symptomatic of much that was to come—a great deal of effort expended for not much result. But ... *ça c'est la vie*! One cannot really complain when travelling hopefully is done without the benefit of hindsight.

I went first to London to say goodbye to my mother. She was losing her children to the wide world at a high rate that year: my sister went to Hong Kong at nearly the same time as we left. However, she was certainly not the sort to discourage our enterprise and had even bought a small stake in Château de Commarque.

That night I dined in Arras at a restaurant with sentimental associations. I shall not mention its name for it is not what it was, and Georgea was badly treated when she went there with the children three weeks later.

The restaurant was busy and five omelettes and chips and one *plat du jour* did not make a sufficiently attractive table-full of customers to warrant much attention from the waiters. The family was ignored. Partly as a result of this experience we later swore an oath to be nice to children in our restaurant. There is a practical aspect to this: children are accompanied by their parents and their parents may well be planning to spend a lot of money. You can never be sure that two *petits menus* and a *menu enfant* do not represent a reconnaissance for a baptism, a confirmation, or even a wedding.

The following afternoon I was rattling round Bordeaux and down the A62 to Sauternes. Like many people before and since, I got lost between the motorway and Sauternes, a distance of about 6 kilometres. The Sauternes district (the Sauternais) is well known to be a maze and even the wine courtiers, the people who arrange the sales of wine between the châteaux and the *negociants* (merchant shippers) lose themselves in the hinterland of Preignac and Barsac. It took me half an hour to get from Illats to Pujols-sur-Ciron, about 3½ kilometres away, and it was very hot. I was therefore not in a good mood by the time I found the bumpy track that leads to Commarque. I was in an even worse one by the time I entered the courtyard. Mr Jenkin-Lee appeared to have 'let go' the vines as comprehensively as he had 'let go' the hotel and restaurant the previous year. He had sworn, over the phone, that he had had 'the gypsies' in to weed them. He may have done, but since very few of the vines were actually visible beneath the luxuriant jungle into which the vineyard had turned, my immediate reaction was to disbelieve him. In fact it took a year to realise how quickly things grow round here. During the spring and early summer, when there is moisture in the soil, the performance of grass and vegetables, let alone weeds, is quite spectacular compared with the moderate rates of growth which satisfy us in the UK, even in ground much richer than the sandy, pebbly or rock-solid apologies for soil which characterise the vineyards. So Mr Jenkin-Lee may have done what he said, but no amount of hand-weeding was going to get rid of everything in the rich community which had developed where our monoculture was supposed to be. I was therefore understandably grumpy when I got out of the van, but Mr Jenkin-Lee had organised a combined reception and farewell party, so, apart from a muttered oath in his ear (we were on very good terms by now), I was obliged to swallow my indignation, not for the first time, and rush upstairs to put on a tie.

Mr Jenkin-Lee had assembled a selection of people for me to meet, most of whom he himself had found useful during his time at Commarque, and with some of whom he was actually friendly. He wanted to give me some helpful introductions, and in fact gave me much useful advice before he left, plus numerous *bon tuyeaux*—literally, 'good tubes'. Handy tips is a better translation—to suppliers, employees, customs, organisations, etc. He was certainly not obliged to do this and had every right to collect his affairs and depart to his new château in the Dordogne without another word. I believe that his frequently swashbuckling treatment of the truth was sometimes less cynical than might have been supposed. He lived, and from what I have heard he still does live, on the edge of a semi-make-believe world in which his creations become real and attacks on them create genuine, if short-lived distress. So he really did believe that he had planted 4 hectares of vines and not three, and I remember him earnestly counselling me not to advertise the hotel-restaurant as under new ownership but just to announce its reopening 'so as not to put off my old customers'. He had nothing to gain from this piece of advice—and no more did we—because, of course, there were no old customers, unless you count the man who turned up some months later and explained that he came to the restaurant from time to time for a good laugh. You could never tell what was going to be done to you next. He announced that he was disappointed now that it had become quite normal. Oh well! you can't win 'em all. That's enough about Mr Jenkin-Lee for the moment. What about Château de Commarque?

* * *

It started life as a medieval fortified farm. It was never a grand château, the house of a feudal war lord, but more a place of refuge for relatively modest folk in the dangerously unstable environment of the Hundred Years' War. It would have been a square of low buildings with a squat, round tower at each corner, enclosing a large courtyard with a well in the centre. One complete side of the square remains, attached to two incomplete sides, making a U open to the south. The two surviving towers are at either end of the complete side which makes up the northern flank of the ensemble and is now pierced by a quite unwarlike and unguarded entrance large enough to allow a gas tanker, or even a removal lorry, to pass through. The track ends at the gateway in the eastern side. The hotel building facing it makes up the westerly wing of the U and this side is completed by the main house, a solid unfussy building, a so-called Maison de Maître. At the other end the restaurant makes an 'L' with the hotel and stops at the northern entrance. The rest of the original quadrangle is represented merely by a low wall with a gateway in the southern face giving access to the swimming pool. The house must surely have been constructed of what is missing from the original four sides.

The place got its name in 1742 when a gentleman from Bazas, a town about 15 miles away, one Mathias de Commarque, described as a Cavalier and as Sieur de Fita, came to Sauternes and married a lady of that commune. The family did not survive here long. Mathias, who must by then have been an old man, had his head cut off in the Revolution. Apparently the bloodshed was intended to stop there but Mathias's two sons defended him stoutly and duly lost their heads as well, and that was the end of the Commarque dynasty in Sauternes.

We are told that the house was originally much grander than it is now, with a third storey and a Mansard roof. Some accident, perhaps a less than entirely accidental fire during the Revolution, destroyed it and it was rebuilt in its present form in about 1800.

I do not know how one could deduce the existence of a Mansard roof by looking at the existing structure, or if there is documentary evidence for it somewhere, but there are clear signs of a third storey: a staircase, the one leading to Mr Jenkin-Lee's hypothetical fourteenth hotel room, stops abruptly under the eaves and led nowhere until we converted the hypothetical room into an actual fifth bedroom for the house. The roof beams are also a peculiar hotch-potch that look more like a major repair job than part of an original construction.

The space enclosed by the buildings and walls measures 60 metres by 40 metres. There is room for lawns, shrubs and trees. The biggest tree in the neighbourhood, a youthful giant Wellingtonia, stands outside the house, halfway along the southern wall. It bends and groans ominously in storms. If it ever fell it would go straight across the gatehouse gîte as that is the direction in which every storm blows, but we are assured it will not fall. The fact of being alone gives it a stable root system and knowledgeable Californians have told us that such trees only ever fall when the mountainside on which they are growing collapses! The rest of the courtyard is gravelled and the central well is now a shrubbery.

Outside the walls the vines occupy three sides. To left and right of the track to the château, on the northern flank, 'the restaurant vines', and below the swimming pool, 'the swimming pool patch'. The château occupies a plateau and the land falls away to a stream, the Ruisseau de Commarque, on the south side before rising to the cluster of houses called Labouray where we have a further half hectare of vines. Between the swimming pool vines and the Ruisseau is a field to gladden the hearts of all who mourn the uncut, unsprayed meadows of yesteryear. In May and June it hums, quite literally, with insect life and if you have ever wondered what Swallow-Tailed Butterflies or Clouded Yellows look like when they are not displayed in a glass case transfixed by pins, then this is the place to come.

To the west, the land falls steeply into the valley of the river Ciron and there are fine views across rolling countryside. To the north and east, the horizon is largely occupied by acacia woods beyond a landscape of vines; only one house is visible from the courtyard, the one at the start of the bumpy track.

Commarque's recent history has not been a happy one. What I know about it I have heard from Papy Dartigues, our neighbour to the west, out of sight because of the fall of the land but not entirely out of hearing, as his son Bernard runs a woodyard, making thousands and thousands of vine posts for the surrounding châteaux. Bernard is a good-natured man, and well-equipped with the heavy machinery needed to bale the incompetent British next door out of their difficulties. This he has done freely over the years and one could not ask for a better neighbour, even though it was Papy Dartigues's sheep who ate the vines at Labouray. Thus, Bernard has pulled my tractor out of the mud with his own immense forest tractor, and he has smashed through the screen of trees beyond the oaks with his caterpillar digger to provide us with trenches for new drains. He taught me how to keep a chainsaw in good condition and when a violent storm blew a large, ornamental conifer outside the courtyard flat across the vines, he was there the following morning with three other men to dispose of it. A memorable characteristic of Papy Dartigues is his driving: he must be the slowest man on four wheels in the Gironde. Even a win on the Loterie Nationale resulting in a brand-new Renault van failed to lift his top speed above 25mph!

Old Monsieur Dartigues has known no fewer than eleven different owners at Commarque. It is not, he told me, a lucky place. Many of the owners had not been good *viticulteurs* and for much of the time the vineyard had been too small to be profitable. 'They did not understand the need to combine vine growing with the *élevage* of cows.' He advanced the sound, if old fashioned, view that the two activities should go together because cow manure is the best fertiliser in the world for vineyards and the cows themselves provide a fall-back in lean years of spring frosts and autumn rain. I have since understood how right, historically, he was. After the great frost of 1956, which destroyed large areas of vineyard and left others unproductive for several years, many small producers were quite literally close to starvation. Marc Belis, of the Graves vineyard Clos Tourmillot outside Langon, told me that ever since then he has kept cows 'just in case', although they brought in virtually nothing, because they had saved him during that terrible time when he had watched so many of his friends and neighbours being driven off the land. However, the economics of farming have changed and anyway, Commarque does not have enough suitable grazing to maintain a worthwhile herd. Papy agreed that no one had yet tried to combine viticulture with the running of a hotel!

The last serious wine-makers at Commarque were the Tracous, and their wine, said Monsieur Dartigues, was *comme ça* and he made a vigorous thumbs up gesture. But they fell on hard times in the sixties when a succession of poor vintages, plus it is now admitted, some indifferent wine-making, put Sauternes completely out of fashion. Quite a number of producers saved their skins by planting red grape varieties, despite the fact that the resulting wine is usually undistinguished. It is a sign of the times that this practice is now banned throughout the area of the Sauternes *appellation*. Anyway, Commarque had six years of stock in its cellars and the Tracous retired as gracefully as they could. Their son is manager of the Maison de Sauternes and not one of our greatest fans. I think he is bitter about losing his heritage and he has been heard to remark that if he had understood how to make Sauternes at the time when his parents sold up he would never have let them do it. This seems rather feeble for a man born and bred in a Sauternes vineyard.

Things went from bad to worse after the Tracous left; the next owner, who had better remain nameless, has been described to me as 'a bandit, I mean a *vrai* bandit'. Not the least of his crimes was his total lack of interest in the vineyard. He liked racehorses, the kind that trot in front of minute, lightweight carts bearing their drivers on spindly frames. Under his reign the vineyard was abandoned and the barrel store converted into stables. It was he who, in a fit of pique, filled in the well in the centre of the courtyard with a digger. Apparently he kept hitting it with his horseboxes.

This gentleman had a transport company in Paris which went down spectacularly after the French tax authorities investigated the non-payment of years and years of tax due on the fuel used by his lorries. He told me this himself one day on one of his periodic visits in search of escaped horses. He looked wistfully at the house and said, 'Of course, you know I lost all this, so stupid of me.'

According to him he had failed to supervise his employees closely enough and had not realised until too late that they had been cheating him for years. He lives just across the valley at Labouray and still trots his horses at great speed along the local byways. One is struck by how strained and anxious he looks when he is doing it.

So the château went into receivership and was bought for a song by Mr Jenkin-Lee. By now the vines were lost forever and the roof of the house had a great hole in it. The previous owner had developed a scrap-yard among the oak trees behind his stables and the whole place was on the point of tumbling into ruin. Mr Jenkin-Lee's main interest was the restoration of such buildings and he did do an enormous amount of work here. There was, you may be sure, a great deal more to do when we arrived but we knew that and, as the French say, '*Il faut faire avec.*'

3

The First Days

The question was what exactly should I do first? A matter for reflection that evening after the departure of Mr Jenkin-Lee's guests. The most pressing task, apart from sending the mayor's piece of paper to Georgea, seemed to be to save the vines from further decline, they were, after all, the primary reason for being in France. In fact, of course life was to be much more complicated than that. There were numerous minor things to deal with, like learning to look after the swimming pool, we had never had one before; learning to serve breakfast to the people who did occasionally turn up for hotel rooms; finding out what to do about getting our *cartes de séjour*, without which we would not even be allowed to stay in France; arranging insurance for the property; changing the telephone and electricity supply to our account; organising the doctor; re-registering the cars—and all the hundred and one other things that we do so easily in our own country but which are dealt with slightly differently elsewhere and in a foreign language. There were also major considerations, apart from the vineyard, like how to reopen the restaurant, how to register our new company, how to find suitable employees—a cook and a waitress for starters—and when Georgea and the children arrived, what to do about schooling. Life was to become both hectic and complicated and the allocation of time to these numerous activities almost impossible to decide. There were good days when progress was made on several fronts, and then there were bad days; the worst were the ones spent chasing from office to office in Bordeaux, in the burning heat, on some administrative formality which contributed absolutely nothing (in our opinion) to the progress of the venture.

That first evening the vineyard got the decision and at 6.30 the following morning I sallied forth into the restaurant vines. An hour and a half (and one and a third rows) later the scale of the problem was becoming apparent, and when Mr Jenkin-Lee sauntered out with his hands in his pockets and a grin on his face, I had seen enough to know that help was needed immediately. The plants showed no obvious signs of disease—even of the ordinary kind, caught if they are not regularly sprayed with fungicide—just a touch of mildew here and there which was not too *méchant*. The weather had been fine and anyway the plants were too young to catch some of the worst horrors that can afflict vines. They were, however, in danger of choking to death because of the weeds, and of being broken by wind or tractor. For they had not been attached to their posts, nor had their branches been tucked into the wires that support and restrain them. In fact, the essential middle pair of wires which should hold them all in place had not even been installed. A brief calculation based on my achievements between 6.30 and 8.00 am showed that it would take two days to attach and tuck in the fourteen rows of vines in the restaurant patch. There were sixty rows on either side of the track, twenty- one beyond the swimming pool and forty at Labouray.

Mr Jenkin-Lee now gave me perhaps his best ever *tuyau*: Monsieur André Saint-Martin from Budos, the village just visible on the hillside to the west beyond the valley of the Ciron, had sprayed the vines once or twice and earthed them up for the winter. He and his brother had done the pruning. Would I like his phone number? He was not at home when I called, he was out in the vines. Would I please phone back later, at lunchtime? The last sentence represents a summary of the conversation. It is a precis in twenty words of an exchange that lasted several minutes, and ran to many hundreds of words, 98 per cent of which were not understood. Madame Saint-Martin was defeated by my accent, hesitancy, and inability to reply to what were probably questions. I was floored by her abrupt opening: '*Oui, j'écoute.*' You imagine saying this in English! Instead of, 'Budos, six-two-five-one-seven-eight, Madame Saint-Martin speaking,' you get: 'Yes, I'm listening'!

Of course, it's not at all rude in French and is commonly used, but I didn't even grasp what she had said and things went downhill from then on. A few minutes into the 'conversation' I managed to catch her murmured, '*Oh là! là! qu'est-ce qu'il veut, ce monsieur?*'—more or less, 'What on earth does this fellow want?'

The telephone continued to be a daily nightmare for some months. You cannot claim to speak a language until you are capable of carrying on a telephone conversation. The first landmark is reached when you can pick up enough to recognise a word you do not know, as distinct from failing to recognise a single word in a whole sentence!

Monsieur Saint-Martin would for the moment, I hoped, fill the need for machinery, but the vines also required manual work. Where was I to find some *vignerons* (vineyard workers) quickly? I need not have worried. They appeared shortly before midday, unannounced and without my having lifted a finger to find them. They had been sent by Comte Henri de Vaucelles, the owner of our great neighbour Château Filhot, to whom I had been introduced the previous evening.

This extraordinary man had at first appeared rather forbidding, if not grim, but he had been extremely talkative—and equally difficult to understand in both French and English. He had seemed very keen on Château de Commarque and my presence there, which was as encouraging as it was mystifying. It took some time to realise that there were large historical reasons for this, as there are for many of the opinions held so passionately by this intriguing personality. His enthusiasm for us stems from the fact that we represent a little surge of activity at the southern end of Sauternes, which has known little but decline over the last half century and more. He has shown me old books listing twenty or thirty small properties no longer in existence, or anyway in wine production. Some of this is due to periodic frost damage. The vineyard of Filhot itself has varied from zero to 120 hectares over the last century and a bit, in accordance with variations in the severity of the climate plus some assistance from the disease Phylloxera. It appears, then, that the survival or extinction of vineyards can be a matter of delicate balance. But some of the local decline, Monsieur de Vaucelles assures me, results from the dead weight of disapproval emanating from Château Yquem! For these little properties were incapable of producing wine like Yquem's and they were therefore bad for the Image de Marque—the brand image. It seems surprising that such a grand property should have such a mean-minded outlook, but Monsieur de Vaucelles has shown me other old books illustrating the wine area of Sauternes cut off abruptly just south of Yquem itself—no Filhot, no Lamothe, and even Château Guiraud is chopped in half and left unnamed. This was Yquem propaganda. Of course, Château Filhot and Château Yquem are centuries old rivals and it has to be admitted that Yquem has long since won the struggle for supremacy. But Henri de Vaucelles wants a flourishing commune around him and not just a few grand châteaux, and for him the good fight goes on. Long may he remain mounted on his charger!

The first *vigneron* to arrive was a great bear of a man who rose out of a small, battered car that had fairly hurtled down the track, straight through the front gate and skidded to a halt in a shower of pebbles.

He shambled towards me tucking his shirt in and doing up his trousers. I wondered what on earth this slightly menacing figure wanted, but I need not have worried. Daniel introduced himself with great politeness, and indeed respect (I hadn't thought of myself until then as *le patron*), and explained that he had been 'sent' by Monsieur de Vaucelles. Inevitably, the exchange was more complicated than this. In fact, Daniel quite justifiably concluded that I was more or less cretinous and from that moment on never spoke a word to me without an elaborate accompanying mime to help my feeble understanding.

In the early stages of our acquaintance I admit this was a great help, especially as Daniel had a habit of speech which is very common in this region, and perhaps elsewhere in France, but which I had never encountered until then: the regular interjection of the word *con* into his sentences. This word has a number of meanings, none of them exactly polite. To call someone a *con* is roughly equivalent to calling them a 'bloody idiot', and to say something is *con* means that it is stupid, but its meaning is more forceful and impolite than that. The word is also slang for the vagina. When Daniel uses it, it means none of these things and either has no force at all, as in: '*Allez, je te paie un coup à boire, con!*' (Come on, I'll buy you a drink) or adds a slight emphasis, '*Il a complètement raté le but, con!*' (He totally missed the goal). It is a kind of verbal knee-jerk, a bit like, 'He kicked the f...ing ball right out of the f...ing ground!' If I have laboured this point, my excuse is that it is an example of 'real' everyday French of the kind one never learns at school or in a BBC language course.

The effect of Daniel's use of the word *con* was simply to add to the confusion. It was another small defeat. Straining after this word inevitably caused the start of the next sentence to blur into the general fog of incomprehension. However, Daniel forced me to understand, with the help of his mime, that he would be there the following morning with his wife Jacqueline and a friend. First they would lift up and tie the vines, and afterwards they would attack the weeds. Here he made vigorous hoeing movements and then did something more obscure which I grasped was meant to be the swinging of a scythe. His friend was very expert at this. As Daniel was about to leave, another car shot down the track and into the courtyard. A tough-looking young man with a moustache introduced himself as a tractor driver and told me he could do 'everything' concerning the vines. I did not have much machinery and was in any case pinning my hopes on Monsieur Saint-Martin, so I thanked him very much and took his telephone number. Daniel whispered as he got into his car, 'You don't want him. He's much too expensive!'—'*Trop cher! trop cher!*' shaking his hand in that vivid French gesture as though it has been burnt. So much for worker solidarity!

Monsieur Saint-Martin was at home the next time I phoned. He talked like a machine-gun, both fast and loudly and the effect was inevitable, although I did manage to catch his way of addressing me, '*M'sieur de Commarque.*' I did like that! The solution he adopted was to prune his speech of every superfluous word. Verbs, adjectives and pronouns vanished, so that his intention to come to the château that afternoon to see what needed doing was reduced to, '*Commarque, rendez-vous, dix-huit heures.*' Very effective.

Some weeks later, Jacqueline (Daniel's wife) phoned to say that she and Daniel could, or could not, come that day, and when she'd hung up I turned triumphantly to Georgea and announced that I now knew the name of their house. It was La Pareille. Georgea looked at me pityingly and asked, 'Are you sure she didn't say "this is Jacqueline *à l'appareil?*"'

'Well, yes. That's exactly what she said.'

'That means, "it's Jacqueline here", you twit! "*A l'appareil*" means "on the phone".'

The first morning had gone well after a difficult start. The afternoon seemed to go even better. I presented myself at the Mairie at 3.30 to collect our Certificat de Domicile and was told by the secretary that Monsieur le Maire would like to meet me. The mayor was none other than the Marquis Alexandre de Lur Saluces, owner of the great Château Yquem. He was perfectly charming and very encouraging. We were coming to Sauternes at just the right time. Did I realise how well it had been doing recently? He showed me a publication that listed the current wholesale prices of every wine in the region, and there was Sauternes rising from F18,000 a *tonneau* to F24,000 over the past six months. This situation would continue, he assured me, as he handed over the completed Certificat, at last Sauternes was starting to become profitable. Privately, I thought he looked as though he had been profitable for rather more than the last few months, but it was a churlish thought when he was being so kind and I repressed it. As we rose to say goodbye he looked at me squarely and said, 'I know a great many people in every walk of life. If ever you need help, of whatever sort, do not hesitate to contact me.'

What more could one ask of one's mayor? That was the last time I ever saw him, except from the pavement as he passed through Sauternes in his chauffeur-driven BMW, but I'm sure he meant what he had said. At the next election the Marquis was roundly defeated after a bad-tempered campaign in which he was accused of running Sauternes from his flat in Bordeaux, and of totally ignoring the parish council. There is no doubt some truth in this, but I must say that if I was mayor I would definitely want to ignore certain members of the parish council.

Monsieur Saint-Martin arrived dead on *dix-huit heures*. His punctuality, which has continued unfailingly over the years, may seen perfectly normal to us northerners but it is rare in the southern half of France—south of the Loire, as the bank manager put it. I was loitering on the edge of the vines at the end of the track waiting for him when his car crawled into sight. Monsieur Saint-Martin was not worried about the potholes; he was inspecting the vines and from the look on his face as he drew closer he didn't much like what he saw. He positively bounced out of his car and greeted me with a bone-crushing handshake before I had had time to take him in. Then he brushed past me and stood glaring at the vines as though they were a personal insult. I heard him mutter, '*Merde, il y a du boulot là*'—more or less, 'Christ, there's some work here'—and while he glared and then dashed energetically into the rows to pull, push and peer at the vines I had a chance to look at him, while checking the bones of my right hand. He was short and squat, clad in sandals, jeans and a T-shirt with a pork pie hat on his head, tanned to a deep leathery brown and prodigiously muscular.

He had been, I discovered later, a black belt in both judo and karate and was still as hard as nails, quite definitely a man to have on your side. There are legends in the neighbourhood about the fate which has befallen *voyous* (yobbos) unwise enough to try and interfere with him. He was to become an essential element in the life of Commarque and I cannot think of a better 'friend of the firm'. He has a reputation for being *sec*, a word which means more than just 'dry' in this context, more like 'a little unyielding', perhaps even intolerant. It is easy to see how this opinion might develop, for André Saint-Martin has a northerly rigour in his outlook which must occasionally clash with the more laissez-faire attitude of his neighbours.

That afternoon neither of us realised that a long-term arrangement was being set up. As I watched him rummaging and muttering in the vines I thought he looked sufficiently affronted by their state to want to redeem them, but only until I had bought the basic machinery and learned how to work it. After all, he had no need to trouble himself with my vines; together with his brother he was proprietor of eleven good hectares of Graves on the slopes facing us across the valley of the Ciron. Finally, he straightened up with an explosive '*bon!*' and strode back down the row. The first thing to do was to spray against the *mauvais champignons* (fungal diseases) a *sulfatage* was required, so-called because in the old days sulphur was the principal ingredient of the spray. It is still used, but so are many other products. The machine that carries out a *sulfatage* is called a *sulfateuse*. He would be here 'very early' the following morning and he would bring the necessary products which I could replace later. We had some mites and he would deal with them at the same time. After that we had to do something about all this *saloperie*, and he indicated the weeds. I explained about Daniel and his troops and Monsieur Saint-Martin nodded approval. He would follow them at least with a rotavator and possibly with a herbicide, but the vines were so small and feeble that much care would be needed. We would in any case have to wait until we could see a bit more of them. He looked across at my row and a bit of tying up and asked who had done it. I owned up apprehensively, but he just said, '*C'est très bien fait,*' and my cup was for the moment full.

There was just one last thing to discuss: the cost. Monsieur Saint- Martin looked very serious and regretted that he could not undertake a *sulfatage* for less than F250! I refrained, just, from blurting out, 'is that all?'

At six o'clock the next morning Monsieur Saint-Martin returned, sitting on and pulling £25,000 worth of equipment which he proceeded to work for an hour and a half before driving back the way he had come, a journey which takes about twenty-five minutes on a tractor. He did all this for F250. A few weeks later, while an elderly *sulfateuse* was being demonstrated to me by an agricultural supplier outside Barsac, it dawned on me what an uneconomic and pointless purchase it would be if Monsieur Saint-Martin could be persuaded to go on spraying the vines. I did not like the machine anyway. All the spray came out of the top; there were no jets close to the ground to blast the bunches of grapes like those on Monsieur Saint-Martin's 'Thomas'. In fact he was both ready and willing not only to continue spraying but to undertake all the mechanical operations in the vineyard. As a result, we never bought a single piece of machinery.

After Monsieur Saint-Martin's first *sulfatage* I just had time to reach Langon station to meet Stephen off the train from Bordeaux. The son of the solicitor who put us on to the Cabinet de Chambrun, Stephen was 18 years old and between school and art college. He turned out to be useful beyond my wildest dreams. He knew all about swimming pools— well every solicitor has one I suppose! He had done some waiting and therefore served breakfast, with great aplomb, in dazzling white shorts and T-shirt. He could speak French and he could drive, he could iron sheets and pillowcases, he could empty the hypothetical *chai* of its straw and spread it across a field in the boiling heat. Later he played ferocious games of rounders with the children and generally helped to make their first summer in France just like an extended holiday. Mr Jenkin-Lee moved out—I caught him unscrewing the ornamental glass door handles upstairs—and I remember sitting in the emptied kitchen eating breakfast with Stephen and planning the day's problem-solving activities. The only furniture was a plastic garden table and two garden chairs which we pulled close to the French windows opening onto the courtyard. The bread was beyond belief, from Léogeats, cooked in a wood-burning stove, not from Sauternes (flabby and flavourless), the weather was flawless, the vines were becoming visible under Daniel's vigorous care, the furniture, Georgea and the children would arrive shortly. As the days passed things really didn't look too bad. In fact they looked quite idyllic.

Back in England, however, Georgea was having forebodings about the 'idyll' aspect of Commarque, even before getting here. For example, I told her once over the phone that I had just spent all day ironing sheets. 'Oh, we do the laundry do we?'

She was made more uneasy by our English bank manager when she went, alone, to sign various papers before leaving the country. He had swivelled towards her in his black leather chair, looked her straight in the eye and said, 'You do realise that you are selling everything you own here, cutting yourself off completely from England and all you know and possess. Are you clear what you are doing if you sign these documents?'

Naturally she said 'yes' and signed, but perhaps for the first time the reality of what we were doing struck her. Even booking the removal men, organising the packing on her own, informing schools of our departure and leaving family and friends had not jolted her into a realisation of the enormity of what she was about to do in the way the bank manager's question had done.

There was another incident, relatively trivial in its way, which had the same effect on her, perhaps because it involved one of the children. Thomas was, and still is, an excellent swimmer and had just completed his bronze, silver and gold swimming awards within a year, passing them all with flying colours. As he finished his gold examination, the local swimming club trainer, prospecting for talent, stepped down from his high chair, congratulated him and invited him to join the club. Georgea, watching from the spectators' lounge, suffered a pang of guilt as she saw Thomas shake his head, explain his imminent departure and then turn sadly away to the changing rooms.

She found her spirits lifting when she set out on her journey. It felt like going on holiday, despite the evidence of that totally denuded house and the very final, final farewells. The children felt the same way. Driving through northern France she listened to the BBC commentary on Prince Andrew's wedding and a fleeting nostalgia for *mon pays qui me manque* passed over her, but it faded with the fading of the 'Beeb' south of Paris. France in summer—those long straight roads, sleepy villages, fields burnt by the summer sun—dissolved her feelings of doubt. The holiday mood took resolute hold. There were baguettes, Camembert and wine to look forward to. Tomorrow there would be pâté, peaches and pâtisserie. Who needs Bovril, Golden Syrup and Grape-Nuts?

So Georgea arrived, the day after the furniture, losing herself briefly, more briefly than I had, after navigating correctly to the very threshold of the Sauternais, where our famous wine district proclaims itself by the roadside as 'Sauternes, Vin Blanc Unique au Monde'. The children tumbled out of the car under the interested gaze of the English family in the gîte. Thomas was then nearly 10 years old, the twins, Francis and William, were 8, Robert was 6, and Edward was 1¾. It was baking hot and they all jumped into the pool without even undressing. Edward sank like a stone, was rescued by a couple of big brothers and reminded to put on his rubber ring! That evening the holiday feeling was perfected with a barbecue *au sarments de vignes*, the vine prunings which transform humble beefburgers and even those inferior French sausages into delicious treats, holiday treats and uniquely French. Georgea will learn that those vine prunings are gathered each winter at the cost of roughened, scratched and blistered hands, but all that is for the future. Tonight we are reunited, we have all of this around us and more than enough wine to go with it. Let reality wait for tomorrow ...

* * *

It arrived soon enough. William found a heavy iron wheel in the courtyard the very next day and dropped it on his foot, fracturing a toe. So while his brothers spent long periods in the swimming pool throughout the weeks that followed, William was obliged to sit forlornly by the side watching them play happily with the succession of English families that occupied the gîtes that summer. Later we got him sitting forlornly *in* the pool, on an inflatable boat, by tying up the injured foot in a plastic bag. The gîtes are plural, by the way, because we sorted out the one by the gate in time to get some use out of it that year.

William's misfortune with the wheel provided our first experience of French medicine. I had already located the doctor's house in Sauternes and we went there at once, leaving Stephen in charge, with William sobbing in the back of the car. Inevitably Dr Daubech was out. The only person there was Madame Daubech, in her dressing gown and looking, if anything, worse than William. She was recovering from a hip operation and in no fit state to help us herself. What she did do was telephone the hospital in Langon and warn them we were coming, then gave us detailed but incomprehensible instructions on how to find it. Fortunately, hospitals always seem to be well signposted in France and the Clinique Sainte-Anne was no exception.

From the moment we arrived we were cocooned in competence and reassurance. What's more, the whole performance was achieved almost without the use, or misuse, of language, so smoothly oiled was the machinery of the hospital. Would French immigrants in the UK receive such a good impression in the same situation?

A nurse was waiting at the door with a wheelchair. Someone else rang a bell and a doctor arrived almost instantly, accompanied by no fewer than three other people in white uniforms pushing a theatre trolley. The resources available to deal with one injured toe seemed adequate for an entire ambulance-full of motorway injuries and we were left to reflect on the likely cost of it all as William's anxious face disappeared behind swing doors. For we were not allowed to go with him.

He reappeared the way he had left forty minutes later, sitting in a wheelchair and looking much more cheerful. The doctor was talking to him animatedly and Georgea swears she saw William nod and smile although he did not speak a word of French and the doctor was definitely not speaking English.

The matter of the bill and the fact that we had, as yet, no medical insurance were airily brushed aside by the receptionist. '*Rien à payer*,' she repeated several times, with one of those gestures of distaste at which the French excel. '*Plus tard, plus tard*'—Later, later. The bill would be sent to us. Perhaps it required all the resources of the extensive computer set up behind the desk to calculate it. Our thanks were met with numerous *je vous en pries* (don't mention its) and farewells to William and we drove away with a little knot of people waving from the door.

4

Two Big Problems

If the vineyard had won the battle for attention on the first day, by the second other problems were clamouring for a solution. We needed income. It was July; the tourists were arriving and the opening of the restaurant was a priority if we were to catch at least a few of them before they all vanished again for the winter.

Watching them drive down the track, examine the menu with its *fermé* sign and drive out again was frustrating. On the other hand, this happened often enough to suggest that we would have some customers if we could ever get the place open. I put an advert for a cook in the paper called the *Sud-Ouest*, highly recommended as the marketplace for labour in the region. The problem was that by mid-July any competent cook should be fixed up. The seaside resorts were in full swing at least until the end of August and even in the interior, which purports to be a tourist region, every restaurant was at the height of its season and therefore employing. In the peculiarly temporary, itinerant world of seasonal catering one can always expect oddballs to answer an advertisement, but in mid-July that was about *all* we got.

The first encounter was particularly depressing. A man with a strong local accent phoned up on behalf of his wife. She had cooked in various châteaux but he was non-committal about which ones and uninformative as to the kind of cooking she had done in them. We arranged an interview.

From the Olympian heights of my ignorance about restaurants, I had decided that one way to sort the wheat from the chaff was to ask the prospective cooks to suggest dishes for menus at different prices. We were going to ask them to do just that if they came to work for us and it appeared to be a reasonable first test of their knowledge, imagination and confidence. The qualities of diligence, honesty and organisational skill would have to be tested, so far as they could be, by other means, but first things first! At that time we did not even know the names of the diplomas awarded to French cooks when they have finished their training, and there was nothing whatever in the kitchen with which they could demonstrate their skills. We have since learned the importance of a demonstration. No matter where a cook says they have worked (they may well have been the potato-peeler), no matter what dishes they claim to have cooked (it may well have been the packet version), no matter how many covers they claim to be able to manage single-handed (the other five members of the *équipe* probably did the cooking and then knocked off while all the cook did was dish it up (be especially cautious if they say they can serve it as well)), and no matter how abjectly their last *patron* is said to have begged them to stay, make the guy cook for you before you sign the Contrat de Travail.

The lady who turned up that day failed the first test and did so spectacularly. Mr Jenkin-Lee was still in residence and his fiancée, Marie-Louise, had kindly offered to sit in on the interview and she did most of the talking. The lady had done every kind of cooking: traditional, regional, *nouvelle cuisine*; she had cooked gastronomic banquets and had cooked simple meals for grape pickers. There was nothing in the kitchen to which she could not turn her hand, and what is more she had forty years' experience. Her husband chipped in at this point to announce that he would do *grillades* on the open fire for us. The matter for them was concluded. It was just a question of deciding the starting date.

At this point Marie-Louise asked the question: *what would Madame put in our bottom-priced menu at F65?* The lady cook assumed a look of grave concentration and rocked backwards and forwards in her chair for perhaps half a minute. There were *plein de choses* she could do, a menu like that was no problem. *What could she suggest then?* persisted Marie-Laure.

'Well! There were crudités and ... there were crudités.'

'And, of course, a *grillade* to follow.' This was the husband helping out.

'What would Madame put in the crudités?' Marie-Louise asked sweetly.

Again there were, '*Plein de choses, plein de choses* ... there were grated carrots ... and, of course, radishes and lots of other things: *eh! beh!* grated carrots and, and....'

I was feeling sorry for her by now and Marie-Louise had caught my eye. She was in the middle of suggesting that, in a restaurant like this one, carrots and radishes would not..., when the mood changed abruptly. The lady cook began to shout and swear. At least, I deduced she was swearing from her tone of voice and the look of horror on Marie-Louise's face; what's more, I caught the word *con* several times!

Marie-Louise rose to her feet. The lady cook rose with her. I understood when Marie-Louise said, 'You are not at all polite, Madame. That is quite enough, kindly leave!'

Her husband took her arm and, grinning and nodding nervously at us, he pulled her backwards through the door while she gesticulated violently and continued shouting at the top of her voice.

The only subsequent occasions on which I have heard such a stream of vituperation are when Monsieur Saint-Martin got his tractor stuck in the mud at the bottom of the vines. He could be seen bouncing up and down in the seat, barefoot and caked in mud to the knees, as the rich flow of invective rose above the unavailing roar of the tractor. But the spirit was different. When Monsieur Saint-Martin emerges from the mud he has a broad grin on his face. I am afraid the lady cook was extremely disappointed, even if her disappointment was unjustified from any reasonable point of view, and her swearing was focused whereas Monsieur Saint-Martin's was general. Marie-Louise would not tell me what she had been saying but there had definitely been some reflections on foreigners.

Charles Sellier was at the other end of the culinary scale: he had his own restaurant on the Ile de Ré, off La Rochelle, which functioned for the month and a half of the tourist season and was closed for the rest of the year. A glance at his press cuttings indicated that there was no need to ask him for menu suggestions. If this man came to Commarque it would be a real coup! And his pretty wife would be doing some course or other which would leave her time to help out with the waiting. They liked the little flat set aside for the cook and Monsieur Sellier had not been put off by the kitchen. He found the whole idea of trying to relaunch Château de Commarque a challenge and he would have no trouble finding one or more people to replace him during his brief season on the Ile de Ré. Three days later he took a job as sous-chef at a great restaurant in Paris. The salary was three times what I had been able to offer him and it was obviously a much better place for an ambitious cook who wanted to remain in touch with the 'scene'.

Another lesson was learned: when a cook says, '*Oui* I accept the post', what he means is, '*Oui*, I accept the post for the moment while I look at the six other jobs that interest me.' One cannot blame them. In the shifting world of cooking there is surprisingly little unemployment even in these depressed times. Good cooks can, to some extent, choose where they want to go and there are often hidden surprises for them if they choose badly: disagreeable patrons, appalling lodgings, or insanitary working conditions. We saw several cooks that summer who said they would come but never did. Monsieur Sellier was the only one whose non-arrival I regretted. After half-a-dozen abortive interviews it was apparent that we would have to wait until summer contracts came to an end and more cooks were released onto the market. There were plenty of other things to occupy us, most of which were not destined to contribute greatly to our income.

Trying to register the business came into this category. It was William's injured toe and our lack of medical insurance that brought the need for registration into sharp relief. The problem was part of a larger one which could not be ignored. In the absence of a national health system, medical insurance is obligatory; in fact, it *is* the national health system, but paid for more openly and directly than ours! Most people are insured through the social security system (the *sécu*) and pay their premiums as part of the stoppages out of their pay packets. But the *sécu* is not for the self-employed like us. We *travailleurs* (independents) have our own separate organisation for medical insurance, and old-age pension, but they will not allow us to belong unless we have a recognisable form of self-employment. Recognisable means registered— so that numbers can be attached to our names. It became apparent that many things followed from being registered and that lots of people wanted—no, demanded!—this registration. Without it regulations could not be observed, inspectors were incapable of inspecting, taxes remained uncollected and in general files could not be opened; the hungry dragon of French administration risked starvation. The minimum was the business *en cours d'immatriculation* (in the process of being registered) so that at least temporary numbers could be assigned. The process of *immatriculation* would take time and would be fraught with difficulty. The bank manager told me so, the insurance agent did as well, my accountant and the Clinique Sainte-Anne both agreed. It was almost as if, having demanded registration, the dragon did all in its power to prevent it happening.

The opening shots in the campaign were fired by the distant Notary's Clerk, the one in charge of the sale of Commarque; *'Je m'occupe de tout,'* he told me, but I think he had as little idea of what he was letting himself in for, as I did. The application form he sent to the Chamber of Commerce in Bordeaux was returned a week later scored all over in red and accompanied by a long list of *pièces manquantes* (missing papers).

The Notary's Clerk had made a grave initial blunder in trying to register the company which would eventually run the business when we had finished buying it. The company had no more official existence than the business: without statutes, directors and a leasing agreement with the other, equally embryonic, company that was to own Commarque, the jaws of the dragon had nothing concrete, or more accurately, paper, on which to chew and had duly spat out this first feeble offering. The only entity that could be registered was the business we had 'rented' from Mr Jenkin-Lee which provided security of tenure while we waited to buy the château. Pointing out that this rental agreement would expire before the registration was completed was no argument against starting the process. The dragon was perfectly capable of registering a business and then erasing it all on the same day.

A second application form was completed and despatched with every piece of paper available. The whole lot came back for a second time, marked all over once again in red. The Notary's Clerk admitted defeat so I told him I would have a go myself, believing that a personal visit to the Chamber of Commerce and the resulting human contact with officialdom would smooth away the difficulties.

Business formalities such as registration, changes in company statutes, deposition of accounts and so on are governed by the Greffe du Tribunal, the chief officer of which is the Maître Greffier. In a domain where much public attention has been focused on misuse of funds, false invoices, jobs for the boys, etc., the notion of an official title 'the Chief Grafter' strikes me as rather droll. The more prosaic translation is Chief Clerk, and his office was anything but amusing.

The Chamber of Commerce in Bordeaux is one of those huge, pomp-and-circumstance buildings of the kind found in most great cities, designed to testify permanently to the wealth and power of the community that built it. It dominates physically the quarter of Bordeaux in which it is situated, overlooking the River Garonne, no less than its contents dominate the business life of the Gironde. At the entrance stands an enterprising beggar, tolerated by the ever-present gendarmes, who greets visitors with unfailing courtesy and requests to know which public service they are seeking. He then gives brief, clear directions and accepts whatever coins are offered with a graceful expression of thanks. The place is complicated and he does a useful job. I suppose he saves the wages of a doorman or receptionist but he does look rather out of place in all that awesome nineteenth-century grandeur.

The office of the Greffe, at the top of the enormous flights of stairs to which the beggar had directed me, was a nightmarish place that could have created by George Orwell. I knocked on the 20 feet high door and went in. Dozens of pairs of eyes were on me and it was plain that I should have crept in silently. I hesitated briefly before a clear voice called out, '*Prenez un numéro, monsieur*', and I saw beside me on the wall a box full of numbered cards. I took one and sat down.

The place was divided into 'us' and 'them'. The 'us' part where I was sitting was bare except for mean seats all around the wall space not occupied by 'them'. 'They' were behind a counter facing the door, divided into separate desks by telephones, file cabinets and so on. At the desks were four ladies I thought of as receptionists until I met mine, and behind them was a large office space with all the usual trimmings. By far the most interesting things in the room were the people sitting waiting for the receptionists to call them.

There were perhaps a dozen men and three or four women. Most of them were of the type you see swinging confidently down the wealthier quarters of big towns, briefcase in hand, entering or emerging from smart restaurants or driving BMWs or Mercs. But there they sat, briefcase on their knees, anxious expressions on their faces, the Bordeaux executive classes looking for all the world like the more pathetic seekers after inaccessible benefits to be seen in welfare offices. The whole place spoke of authority and they were the underdogs. When their numbers were barked out they scuttled across the empty space to the reception desks like Wall Street Crash victims to the soup kitchens. It was truly bizarre and I am not exaggerating, but it is no longer like that. Last time I went, for some minor formality like a K-bis (an extract from the register, the sort of identity card of a business) it had all changed to open plan. Smiling girls in jeans directed visitors to their similarly clad colleagues. There were no barriers; all was light, air and welcome. Power still rests there but the iron fist is dramatically less evident.

The iron fist that 'welcomed' me belonged to a lady so small that she had two cushions to help her see over the desk. She did not bother to look up but kept on at whatever she was writing and snapped, '*Oui?*'

I started to explain that I wished to register a new business. She smacked down her biro, opened several drawers and started piling forms on the desk. In stumbling French I explained that I had already had the forms, at which she banged hers back where they belonged and slammed shut the drawers. She had still not even glanced at me. Where do they find people like this? She looked up at last and spat out, '*Que voulez-vous, monsieur?*' The tone implied: 'What the hell do you want?'

It occurred to me that she might be a very unhappy person so I determined to stay polite, also I was mindful of the more than respectful attitudes adopted by my fellow sufferers. Heaven knows what she might do if I showed hostility; there *were* all those gendarmes downstairs.

While she gazed at me with an expression of withering contempt I tried to explain that I needed help with some of the questions; my case did not always fit into the categories given. Then I really put my foot in it. I owned up to the fact that I did not yet have a *carte de séjour*.

There was a hissing intake of breath before she launched forth. Fear must have sharpened my wits because I understood most of the tirade. It started: '*Vous perdez votre temps*'—You're wasting your time. That was not news anyway. It continued: 'Under no circumstances will we register your business until you have a *carte de séjour*. Do you realise what has happened in the past when we have done this?'

There was a telling pause while I wracked my brains vainly for something to say; there was no need, she was going to tell me anyway.

'The Préfecture has refused *cartes de séjour* to people whose businesses we have registered. They have had to leave the country and we are left with a business that does not exist! Can you imagine the consequences?'

Again, I cudgelled my brains. The only answer I came up with was: 'Not really, other than to cross out the entry in your books.'

Judging by the lady's state, this could not possibly have been the right answer to a question which was anyway purely rhetorical and demanded so loudly that even the depressed crowd sitting behind me were perking up and looking interested.

'Go to the Préfecture, *monsieur*. Obtain your *carte de séjour* and then come back here and we will consider the registration of your business.' At that point she called out the next number.

I got out of the door with another fellow who had finished his dealings with one of the other harpies at about the same time. He winked at me, squared his shoulders and strode off like a man with a weight off his mind, while I got out my map and worked out how to get to the Préfecture.

We had applied for our *cartes de séjour* the moment we arrived. It was all done at the Mairie of Sauternes and we were both given a pink piece of paper, called a *récépissé*, with our photo on it. This meant we had made our application, and were, as we hoped the business would be, *en cours d'immatriculation*. That was six weeks before the expedition to the

Chambre de Commerce and we had heard nothing about our *cartes* in the meantime. We had, however, been told that it would take from three to six months, or even more, to get them, and that we should not worry if there was a prolonged silence. We had not worried, nor indeed thought about them again, until this moment.

After the appalling experience of the Greffe du Tribunal, I was wary of the Préfecture. The building is the modern equivalent of pomp and circumstance: all tinted glass, thick carpets and muted Tannoys. Policemen with dark glasses guard the entrance. It is a less grandiose place than the Chambre de Commerce, but then we have become less overt in our displays of power than people were a hundred or so years ago. I doubt whether the Bordeaux Préfecture will have quite the same effect a hundred years hence as the Chambre de Commerce does now! My money is on the latter to be still there, looking much as it does now, and the Préfecture to have been razed to the ground.

In the meantime it fairly seethes with activity. No beggar could possibly give directions to the stream of people entering it, but he would be redundant in any case; the place was purpose built and full of signposts.

By far the busiest part of the emporium was the section devoted to car registration. Every kiosk was in action and every one had a long queue in front of it, a good-natured, patient and orderly queue, what's more, not at all like the ill-disciplined scrum which we like to think characterises the French Queue! There isn't much choice. It is a legal obligation to re-register your car every time you move house to a different *département*. Many people prefer to deal with this personally, rather than to confide their precious *cartes grises* (log books) to the post and risk problems with the gendarmes while they are without them. The outcome of re-registration is a new set of number plates with a brand new number containing the code for the new *département* at the end—thirty-three for the Gironde. The result is that a re-registered banger has a number which is indistinguishable from that of a brand new car. I think this practice would cause great frustration if it were extended to the UK. We do like to know the age of our neighbours' cars.

The foreign section was easy to find with its large sign 'Titres de Séjour, Passeports', and here things were more like the Chambre de Commerce. The woman behind the counter, this time fully protected by glass, was haranguing three young North African men. She was using much the same tone of voice as the malignant midget in the Greffe du Tribunal had used on me. She had a lot to say and it was having a great effect on the young men, one of whom was more or less in tears while the other two hung back and looked sheepish. The woman finished, dismissed her customers with an abrupt shooing gesture and they left, with the man who had been in the firing line now weeping openly. Then she turned to me, smiled a dazzling welcome and enquired with great politeness if she could help Monsieur. So this one was not only a power-crazed functionary but apparently a racist, power-crazed functionary.

She must have been, so beastly had she been to the young man in front of me and so grovellingly polite was she to me—even obsequious when she learned that I 'owned' a château in Sauternes. For the second time that morning I was embarrassed and it was hard to decide which was the more disagreeable: being shouted at in public or being treated as a member of the master race in public, for there were other foreigners behind me and to the left and right, and most of them were not Caucasian! As usual, one was obliged to swallow the treatment in the interests of addressing the problem in hand.

The absence of open hostility at least meant that a chance was available to explain the situation. I was determined to box clever this time; I would not admit to having been slung out of the Chambre de Commerce (one good functionary might well support another); I would merely say that I was enquiring about the progress of our application for *cartes de séjour* as we had heard nothing and some time had elapsed etc., etc. This was accepted without the bat of an eyelid and the lady behind the glass went off to fetch a surprisingly fat file. We had not supplied all that paper; they had been checking up on us! She then started to tap on her computer keyboard: a knowing smile, a nod of the head, 'I'm finding my way round pretty well,' and then a shadow passed over her face. She looked up at me and frowned, '*Monsieur*, there is a problem.'

'*Ah oui?* What sort of a problem?'

'To be granted a *carte de séjour monsieur* must have a means of supporting himself and his family in France. It appears that you have none.' (Ah!)

'*Au contraire*, I have a hotel and restaurant at my château in Sauternes.' I did not bother to claim a vineyard as well. Not a single grape had yet been turned into wine.

'*Mais monsieur*, it is not registered at the Chambre de Commerce.'

Eh voila! The perfect circle, Catch 22. So much for boxing clever. I could have failed at the Préfecture without so much as showing my face in the Greffe du Tribunal! I made a feeble attempt to save the day, 'I have been to the Chambre de Commerce and was recommended to come to you first before registering the business.'

The reply was clear and the tone of voice was now tending towards the all too familiar contemptuous bullying: there was nothing she could do. The regulations were cut and dried.

I became indignant. I pointed out that I was perfectly respectable, that I had spent the whole day trying to fulfil my obligations vis-à-vis the administration, that I was likely to create employment, and that situations like this had surely occurred in the past and therefore there must be solutions to be found somewhere in the archives! All of which took a long time to express and caused fidgeting in the ranks behind me before it was finished.

The lady, while reverting to politeness, remained unmoved. There was nothing she could do, 'May I suggest, *monsieur*, that you return to the Greffe du Tribunal and explain that the Préfecture is quite clear on the regulations. The Greffe must register the business as a prerequisite for consideration of the application for a *carte de séjour*.'

This closing statement bore a depressing resemblance to that delivered so loudly by the bad-tempered Madame at the Chambre de Commerce. Apart from this it seemed most improbable that anyone there would be impressed by imperatives issuing from the Préfecture. But there was no alternative to going back there and delivering the message; unlike the lucky Notary's Clerk I had no one to pass the job on to. We had thought of all sorts of problems we might encounter in France but had never imagined this nonsensical wonderland of administrative blind-alleys.

I stepped through the tinted glass exit of the Préfecture into the dazzling light and heat of midday. The entrances were guarded; no one was allowed in. It was twelve o'clock and time for the two-hour close-down for lunch. There was no point in returning to the Chambre de Commerce before two o'clock. The bullies behind the desks would be refuelling themselves for another vigorous session thrashing Bordeaux's business community into administrative line.

I passed the time wandering through Bordeaux in the direction of the Chambre de Commerce, and then beyond into the old quarter. What a fine, grey city it is! Full of interesting nooks and corners, not too big, magnificence from the eighteenth century, open spaces, the river, some masterly twentieth-century developments, a city well worth exploring. I have not changed my opinion since, but we have never explored it. Trips to Bordeaux always seem to be for unpleasant errands like the one I was trying to run that day (I still cannot pass the Chambre de Commerce without a slight sinking feeling), or carried out in a tearing hurry as when shopping for the restaurant or delivering children to athletics meetings or swimming competitions on Sundays and worrying about getting back in time for the restaurant to open.

Back at the Greffe du Tribunal the full two-hour break was being taken. It was 2.05 pm before the clanging of bolts signalled the resumption of 'services'. Already a little knot of people had gathered at the door but I was head of the queue and I reckoned to have a four to one chance of missing the little monster I had seen in the morning. In fact I got the lady next door to her, who was altogether more pleasant but quite impotent in the face of the administrative conundrum which I represented. While she went off to consult a superior, out of sight in a neighbouring office, I could not help hearing what was happening to the client next door. Lunch had not improved the tyrant's temper. The man in front of her, it appeared, had blotted rather badly and had thus given her the chance not only to harangue him, but also to threaten him. She had seized the opportunity with both hands and the man looked very worried. I managed to grasp the gist of the conversation by eavesdropping attentively: the man's business was in difficulty and he had been unable to pay the old-age pension contributions due for his employees. The organisation that collects them had slapped on an *inscription de privilège*—a sort of minor mortgage which ensures priority over other creditors in the event of the business folding and has to be registered at the Greffe du Tribunal. Having paid off his debt, the man had come to remove the *inscription*, but had reckoned without the total lack of cooperation he was now receiving. Despite the fact that he had a receipt which authorised the lifting (*mainlevée*) of the *inscription*, the little brute behind the desk was refusing to do so because he was behind with another payment. Some deadline was involved and this is why the man was so worried. From what I have since gathered, the woman had no right to obstruct the *mainlevée* in this way. The function of the Greffe, I was told, is simply to register such a transaction: if the authorisation is there for a *mainlevée*, it should be carried out. It is not for the receptionist to decide otherwise. Perhaps the staff was overstepping the Greffe's powers and that is why the office had changed so dramatically when I revisited it a few years later.

My new lady was gone for some time, which is how I came to have such a detailed knowledge of what was happening at the next-door desk. When she came back she was accompanied by a smartly dressed woman, plainly from the higher administrative echelons, who was not introduced and was no more able to resolve the difficulty than the others had been. There would have to be, she said, discussions between her office and the

Section Etrangère at the Préfecture. She was cagey, 'We proceed according to the regulations and the Préfecture proceeds according to theirs. We are blocked by these two sets of regulations and I cannot see how progress can be made.'

Then came the inevitable disclaimer: '*Mais, bien sûr*, it is not for me to say.'

What I really wanted to say was, 'Find me someone who can say.' Had the conversation been in English I would also have expressed disbelief at the lack of precedents and made a formal complaint about little Hitler, who was still going at it hammer and tongs not two yards away. As it was I merely said 'thank you' and left, and that was the end of the day's wrestling.

When I got home, two friends from a village near Charlbury had dropped in, on the way to their dream farmhouse in the Dordogne where they spent happy weeks enjoying the sunshine and food, completely sheltered from the aggravations of the administrative dragon by their impermanence in France. How shocked they were by the saga of the day! I'm not sure we didn't put them off moving to France on a more long-term basis. That evening it took a greater than usual intake of Sauternes and a particularly glorious sunset to restore my spirits.

So did we ever get the business *immatriculated*? The answer is yes! What is more we did not have to lift another finger to achieve it. The day in Bordeaux had not been entirely wasted and it was the Préfecture that finally gave way; about six weeks later I had a phone call from the Section Etrangère: 'Monsieur Reay-Jones, we have decided to grant you the *carte de séjour*.'

I was so staggered, I hope she thought I was overwhelmed with gratitude; I could not resist asking, 'But the business is still not registered. What has made you ignore your own regulations?'

'*Monsieur*, you are the owner of a château in Sauternes. You must therefore be a man of means and able to support yourself and your family. For this reason we are granting you the *carte*.'

In the face of this awesome surrender of administrative rigour I could only murmur, '*Vive l'Etat Socialiste!*' There was silence from the other end of the phone.

The secretary in the Mairie of Sauternes told us later that it had been quite a saga. The matter had risen through the administrative ranks until it had reached the Heads of Department who had slugged it out until the boss at the Préfecture had come up with his spurious formula. Spurious it certainly was; we did not own the château. All we had done until then was to sign a *sous-seing* and put down a deposit of F200,000. The Préfecture could easily have verified this had they wanted to. We guess that they did not want to because they needed to resolve the situation. After all, we did have a right to be in France and the business had a right to be registered. I wonder how a matter like this would be sorted out in the UK? It would probably not arise in the first place; even our regulations tend to be slightly less daft than many French ones, but if it did I doubt whether we would be so willing to turn a blind eye to the realities of the situation in order to find the reasonable solution. In this respect the French system is often very practical!

5

La Rentrée Scolaire

The unpleasant experience of the administrative dragon happened during the first few days of September. Our minds were not on it for longer than the day in question, probably not even for the whole of the day in question. As usual we had a multitude of preoccupations, and difficulty with the allocation of time to each of them. There was still 'The Problem' of opening the restaurant, and there was also 'The Problem' of the approaching grape harvest and 'The Problem' of the declining pound, now declining so sharply that there was a fair chance of our working capital disappearing without trace in the conversion to francs. There was not much we could do about this last one at any rate, except worry about it. However, the hardest immediate nut to crack was the impending school term and confrontation between the children and the reality of living in France. So far they had been a merry little holiday band, ably assisted by the visitors in the gîtes they had not learned more than a dozen words of French between them in their six weeks in France.

The school had been carefully inspected, but only from the outside. What we could see was quite encouraging: two brand-new buildings in a large, gravel and grass playground, with trees, goal posts, swings and sand-pit, surrounded by a high fence separating it from the vines of Château Guiraud behind and those of Château Filhot to the right and across the road in front. At this season it was all shuttered up, the grass was long and the place had a dusty, permanently abandoned look to it. We had gathered from our source of all local knowledge, the secretary at the Mairie, that the headmistress, one Madame Guicheney, kept an orderly house. In fact she might even turn out to be a bit fierce, but we did not tell the children that. The secretary was going to telephone to tell her to get in touch with us, 'tell' her mark you, not ask her 'if she would be so kind as to...', thus speaks the functionary. No doubt she would also warn her that she was about to get landed with four non-French speakers of varying ages.

There was another teacher but he or she was new this coming year and here the secretary's lips were sealed, as the Parish Council had not yet made its choice. At this point she put on her official, forbidding face, which duly forbade further discussion.

Officious, nosy and occasionally sarcastic, we had not immediately taken to the secretary, an elderly lady with dyed-black hair and a most off-putting habit of wrinkling up her nose at new arrivals as though they were accompanied by a nasty smell. Some of them probably were but this mannerism had the totally innocent function of hitching up her glasses so that she see more easily. Unfortunately, it created the impression that her clients were unpleasant intrusions into her peaceful ordering of the affairs of Sauternes.

Her manner was in the best tradition of the French functionary, as exemplified by the personnel of the Chambre de Commerce and the Préfecture in Bordeaux. But it was only a manner—have I then wronged all those people in Bordeaux? Over the months she revealed herself to be thoroughly helpful, solicitous for our well-being and pleased when she could smooth away administrative difficulties. For example, we often required a thing called a Fiche d'Etat Civile—a piece of paper with passport-like details on it, date and place of birth, parents, etc., formally stamped by the Mairie and used for all sorts of administrative purposes to show that you are really you. We got through a lot of these when starting out here, frequently the worst sort, the Fiche Familiale d'Etat Civile, which lists the entire family and both sets of grandparents. To get one of these things from the Mairie you are obliged to produce all the relevant birth certificates and your marriage certificate. As all our documents are in English and we have, between the seven of us, no fewer than eighteen Christian names, also English, the production of a Fiche takes quite some time. Madame Secretary decided to keep a permanent, personal copy so that she could churn out Fiches, both Individuelle and Familiale, whenever we wanted them without the obligatory reference to birth and marriage certificates. This saved us hours of waiting in the Mairie and avoided queues of grumpy locals who, quite reasonably, did not take kindly to having the services of the secretary monopolised by us invaders.

She retired at the end of the following year and I am ashamed to say I never even knew her name. I used to see her afterwards wobbling about Langon on her bike, now with her nose permanently wrinkled in her effort to see where she was going. It was no use waving to her; it was all she could do to steer a line along the side of the road. Just as the Chambre de Commerce was re-equipped with casually dressed and friendly young ladies, so the formidable old secretary in Sauternes was replaced by a young, friendly and approachable one who can only be faulted for not being the same mine of information and gossip as her predecessor.

If the secretary would not tell us about the new teacher, she had plenty to say about the old one, none of it very good. This lady had been senile well before her retirement and had had, in any case, about as much imagination as a woodlouse. We were lucky to have missed her; an opinion shared by others. The politest comment we heard came from Madame Pouey, the wife of the baker in Léogeats, *'pas terrible,'* she said, which simply means, 'not great'. Naturally the new arrival was stimulating discussion, but no one knew anything definite. The Parish Council kept its secret well.

* * *

We had been baffled from the middle of August by the supermarket hoardings announcing La Rentrée, with things like Prix Bas (Low Price) Chez-Whatever-The-Name-Was. We had wondered what exactly this 'return' was to, or from. I dimly thought it might mean a return from holiday, the French being well known for closing everything down during August, with a consequent need to stock up on household goods, so providing the shops with a brief mini-boom. But as the advertisements proliferated with the advance of August it became clear that La Rentrée was La Rentrée Scolaire, the return to school, and that was big business. Entire new departments developed in the supermarkets, trademarkets and even the village shops. Quite unbelievable quantities and varieties of paper, exercise books, pens, school bags, not to mention displays of 'sensible' clothes for school wear, appeared on the shelves, and from the moment they did so, a good month before the date of the Rentrée, they were the focus of a spending spree which resembled nothing less than the Saturday before Christmas. For nothing is provided at secondary schools and little enough at primary schools. This explains why quite small French children can be seen on their way to school weighed down with great backpacks full of equipment. They have to carry not only their homework and the books that go with it, but everything they will use during the day. At least exercise books and most of the paper are provided at primary school, but there is still a remarkably long list of obligatory, multi-coloured pens and pencils to buy. At secondary school the situation is much worse. Every subject generates a list of *fournitures* sent out to parents with the year's signing-on papers. The list includes the type of paper preferred by each teacher, the kind of notebook (and they all like different ones) and even the required writing implement. In addition to all this many French parents like to start the school year with a total refit for their children and the school bag (*cartable*) trade is a major industry with all the big brand sports wear and fashion houses vying for backs across which to sling their logos. It is therefore not for nothing that the French government, mindful of forthcoming elections, provides a hand-out of F1,500 per child at the Rentrée for all who qualify for the full child allowance (not bad for us that!) But I have seen an expenditure of F3,000 on one child in the excellent but pricey stationers and booksellers 'Laguerie' at Langon. Of course, the state aid system does not envisage Chevignon files, Rip Curl sports bags and Creeks pencils and pens, but this example does illustrate how seriously the French take this drain on the domestic economy and what a boost the Rentrée is for the turnover of stationers and supermarkets.

* * *

Three days before the beginning of term, tipped off by the secretary at the Mairie, Madame Guicheney phoned to ask us to come and meet her at school and inscribe the children on her list. She sounded friendly and not a bit fierce.

The school no longer had its dusty abandoned look. It was a hive of activity: the grass was being cut, the fence painted and the gravel renewed. A large bread-bag hung on the front gate. All the shutters were open. Someone was singing loudly in the right-hand building which, we discovered, housed the *maternelle* (kindergarten) and the school *cantine*. Madame Guicheney was with the new teacher, Monsieur Desautel, and gave the children a warm welcome, turning them beetroot red with embarrassment when she kissed them all in turn on both cheeks. They retired behind us for the rest of the meeting in an awkward, shuffling line. Madame Guicheney remarked cheerfully that they would soon get used to this French habit. Actually, it took them about five years.

She was smartly dressed and carefully coiffured, looking more like the wife of a prosperous vineyard owner than the *directrice* of a village primary school. This is not altogether surprising, as her husband owns Château Trillon on the top plateau by Château Yquem. Mind you, he doesn't resemble a prosperous vineyard owner. The contrast between

Monsieur and Madame Guicheney is striking. He is small and scruffy, a tough, self-made son of the soil, not much given to self-display. I once came across him in the shop at Léogeats, a misleadingly tiny place where you can buy everything from a ton of fertiliser to a pair of boots, from good Roquefort to ancient, mouldy jam, apparently overcome with admiration for a pair of awful, bright felt carpet slippers, of the kind elderly country people wear almost everywhere, replacing them in wet weather by rubber things like sawn-off wellingtons, sometimes with the slippers still on inside them. He was trying them on amid exclamations of delight, surrounded by onlookers, and was so pleased with the result that he bought two pairs, at F40 each! Madame Guicheney would not be seen dead in anything less than patent leather high-heels, or at a pinch the most stylish of brogues. It is a matter for wonder that she is prepared to be seen dead with her husband, but there is perhaps more to him than his rural exterior suggests.

Monsieur Desautel, the new teacher, was a neat, fit-looking middle-aged man, also mindful of his appearance. Casually smart, expensive tinted glasses, dyed hair carefully permed (which is much more common in France than in England), open-necked shirt with gold chain, his manner was relaxed and confident. He admitted cheerfully that he had no idea what he would do with the children but, '*On verra bien!*'—We shall see!— and he would no doubt manage. The impression given was that in his thirty years of teaching he had never yet been stumped and did not think he was going to be now! In our innocence we had thought that some kind of assistant might be brought in for four non-French speakers, but we had reckoned without the chronic underfunding of education in France. The situation is at least as bad as it is in England and it was made clear that it would all be down to Madame Guicheney and Monsieur Desautel. We wondered how they were going to do it ... indeed '*On verra bien*'.

That morning it was decided into which classes the children would go. There are five years in French primary schools and the normal age of attendance is from 6 years to 10 years old. So Robert, aged 6, would be in the first class, the *cours préparatoire*, and would thus learn to read and write in French from scratch. He would be greatly hindered by not knowing any French, but helped by having already learned to read and write in English. Mind you, French handwriting is not the same as English handwriting and Robert's duly changed. Madame Guicheney taught the first year and the one above it, CE1, *cours élémentaire un*. The other three years, CE2, CM1 and CM2, the two *cours moyens*, were the domain of Monsieur Desautel. As he pointed out a little ruefully, our lot

would probably give him effectively a fourth year. The children would
at least start in the *cours* appropriate to their ages. That put the twins
in CE2 and Thomas in CM2, for he was scheduled to go to secondary
school the following year. It was understood that the suitability of these
arrangements would be kept under review—'*on verra bien*' once again.

* * *

When planning to move to France we had placed the children, so to
speak, in the balance and decided that to make them bilingual and
bicultural would be such a worthwhile thing to do that it would justify
the rashness of our scheme. To put it crudely we could say, 'well anyway
it will be wonderful for the children'. Well was it? They are all bilingual
in the generally accepted sense that when you hear them talking French
you can't really tell them apart from the natives. More to the point, the
natives can't either. This is not quite the same as being 'truly' bilingual. By
this I mean being able to speak, and write, equally well in two languages.
Edward, the youngest, did not write English nearly as well as French.
This is hardly surprising and it was possible to redress the balance later.
Thomas, the oldest, would have written English better than he does now
if he had continued his education in England. On the other hand, he has
an unfashionable knowledge of grammar. Unfashionable, that is, for an
Englishman.

There are many stories of English children becoming fluent in French
within a few weeks of moving to France. I must say it took ours longer
than that. Some of these stories are no doubt legendary and I suspect
others result from children progressing so much faster than their
parents that the latter are lost in admiration of their accomplishments
in comparison with their own lack of progress. Fluency is therefore
relative. It took six months for ours to start being ashamed of their
parents' English accents and ungrammatical constructions. Probably our
little anglophone world at Château de Commarque did not help their
initial process of assimilation. In the long run I am sure it has helped to
preserve the children's English. We did try speaking French when they
came home from school but it was so ridiculously artificial that we soon
gave it up.

After a couple of terms, when the early problems had been put behind
them, we often wondered just how good their French was. We had little
way of telling. We took them to school and brought them home again
in the evening. Occasionally there were a few words at the school gate

but they tended to be tongue-tied towards their friends when we were around. They were doing 'all right' in French at school and that was as far as it went.

One evening someone telephoned for Francis, always the most taciturn of the five children. He picked up the phone, listened for a moment, said quite clearly, '*Salut, toi*', and then launched into this rapid stream of apparently effortless, and to us incomprehensible, slangy school-boy French. We gaped at each other, we really did, and wondered how a small, quiet English boy, whom we reckoned to know quite well, could have enclosed this small, voluble French boy that we didn't know at all. After that we stopped worrying about the development of the children's French.

Certain details of the first day at school have stayed with all the children over the years, with the exception of Francis who maintains a resolute amnesia under cross-examination. Was it really too awful for him to want to remember? Apart from boredom in class on the part of the three older boys, the result of not knowing what was going on, the memories are, by and large, not unpleasant.

The moment the children entered the playground they were surrounded by a crowd, 'Gabbling and laughing,' as Thomas put it. 'But friendly, even if we were more of a curiosity than anything else.'

There was an incessant shouting of, 'You speak Eengleesh? You speak Eengleesh?'

When Madame Guicheney called everyone in Robert remembers someone pulling him by the hand and whispering urgently, '*Avec moi, avec moi.*'

Robert went with him and made his first friend, Marc-Antoine, within two minutes of entering the school.

The other three were just swept along by the press until they reached the classroom. Everything was done in lightning-fast French and no attempt was made to explain it to them. Monsieur Desautel, whose name they had absorbed deeply as Monsieur de Sauternes, thus adding richly to his mystique, was totally occupied by his three separate years. However, at the end of the day homework was given out—yes! Everyone does homework in Sauternes, and everywhere else we have come across, from the *cours préparatoire* upwards, although strictly speaking it is not legal. Thomas remembers quite clearly that he understood what had to be done but pretended not to and was careful not to write anything down. When he returned the next day having done nothing, he was promptly demoted to *cours élémentaire deux* along with the twins. This was exactly what he had been hoping for. He admits that he used this ploy on numerous occasions afterwards when faced with tasks he preferred to avoid. We are not wholly convinced that he has ever given it up.

Break time was the next hurdle to be surmounted. Francis and Thomas managed it quite easily, prodded a little by Monsieur Desautel, because they played football and all the other games usually enjoyed by small boys. Since the rest of the children were basically friendly and, we suspect, acting under orders from Madame Guicheney, they joined in without difficulty. William on the other hand does not like football and therefore does not play football. He does not like any ball games, but is a very good swimmer, so it is a measure of his isolation that morning that he spent the whole of that first 45-minute break, and many subsequent ones, bouncing a ball on his own in a corner of the playground! After a few days he made a couple of friends: Laurent (but he was always being kept in after class for misbehaviour) and Regis, 'Who never knew anything! Whenever he was asked a question his reply started, *euh! euh!* (French for er! er!) and the tears formed in his eyes.'

He was always being kept in for not having done his work, so William was often left to bounce his ball alone. One day, when in extreme difficulty, Regis said that his granny had died that morning. This had, as might be expected, an immediate effect on Monsieur Desautel's deteriorating temper and mounting sarcasm. So completely did Regis escape the opprobrium which was his daily lot that, as William put it, 'His Granny's death became a regular feature of school life. She must have died at least twenty times that year.'

The school canteen provided a first insight into French eating habits. Once again it was Thomas who has the clearest souvenir: 'The first course was tomato salad, swimming in vinaigrette, like a good little boy I ate it all up but I didn't know what to do with the vinaigrette so I just left it. Madame Guicheney was patrolling round the tables and when she came to me, she looked at my plate and cried out, '*Ooh! là! là! tout ce bon jus!*' Then she grabbed a piece of bread, mopped it round my plate and stuffed it into my mouth. I thought it was great!'

Just as well! It could have put him off French food for life.

From the second day onwards Monsieur Desautel spent three-quarters of an hour every afternoon trying to teach the boys French with the help of *Bruno et Caroline*, a book which, says William, 'makes Peter and Jane look like Shakespeare'.

The result was long lists of vocabulary to write out at home and learn. The children did it but it was not really helping them to learn French, with its rules of conjugation, agreement of adjectives and precise use of articles.

It wasn't Monsieur Desautel's fault. He simply did not have the time to teach a fourth year. So for the three older boys class-time passed slowly during the first few weeks and much of it was spent gazing at the walls.

This was not wholly unprofitable! The walls were quite well adorned and the boys' contemplation led to an abiding interest in maps for Thomas, whose bedroom was still covered in them from floor to ceiling for as long as he lived at home, and a complete knowledge of the *départements* of France, with their numbers and principal towns, for Francis. William passed his time less usefully, constructing paper fans that looked like people, and playing 'Jocks and Geordies' (characters from the comic *Dandy*), with different types of pencils. He too noticed the maps on the walls but did not bother to consider what they were, preferring to discover faces or animals in different countries and oceans: Russia was quite distinctly a rat. Later on, Monsieur Desautel was to become fond of praising his imagination—but could not resist lamenting his maths. It was up to us to break this pattern by finding help outside school hours and that is what we did, but it took half the first term to realise it was necessary.

Robert meanwhile was having less difficulty and far more to do in Madame Guicheney's class. He was in the thick of it, relearning reading and writing, helped along in maths too by having already done some of it in England. He also came home with lists to learn, lists of syllables, designed to allow recognition of every syllable in the French language and so read them accurately. Do I hear groans of horror from English teachers? We called this Blee, Bla, Blum, for reasons which will be obvious from the following extract of one of Robert's sheets:

Bla bli ble blé blè blê
Blo blu blau bloi blou
Bra bri bre bré brè brê
Bro bri brau broi brou ...

So, Robert would announce his homework as 'reading, two sums and a new Blee, Bla, Blum'. He was a meticulous little boy so BBB suited him quite well. The result was striking; by the age of 8 he could read Voltaire, Sartre or Balzac unhesitatingly, with perfect accuracy and without understanding a word! I don't think he has suffered any ill effects, but I suppose there is a danger that children might come to expect not to understand what they're reading and so become discouraged from reading in the future.

It would be wrong to think that Robert got through his first weeks without difficulty. Much of what he did was done without really knowing what was happening, and with help, in halting English, from Madame Guicheney, who was very kind to him. So for example, the first time Robert encountered a dictation Madame Guicheney said to him, 'Just do what your neighbour does.'

Adeline, the little girl sharing his desk, wrote '*Dictée*' at the top of her sheet of paper, so Robert wrote '*Dictée*' at the top of his. She then added the date beside it so Robert added the date as well. Then Adeline wrote 'Adeline Dunié' in the top right-hand corner of her page and Robert wrote 'Adeline Dunié' in the top right hand corner of his page ...

After a few days William asked, 'Why does Monsieur Desautel keep talking about Sooty?' Everyone looked blank.

'What do you mean, Sooty?' Thomas asked.

'Well I don't know what he's saying about him but he's definitely talking about Sooty.'

The mystery seemed to be impenetrable, then someone asked, 'What does it actually sound like?'

'It always seems to be "on Sooty" or something like that,' William replied. 'Then he waves his arms about or points...'

We got it! Monsieur Desautel was telling someone, or the whole class, to be quiet: '*On se tait.*'

The solution to problems like these lay in Maïte Bodis, an ace English teacher from one of the *collèges* (comprehensives) in Langon. She took a bit of finding though. We started the search in the private sector, in the mistaken belief that resources would be more plentiful there than in the underfunded public sector. But much of the private sector is run by the Church, in the interests of ensuring a good Catholic education, for the state system does not have the right to teach religion, and the Church does not charge very much for its services. The Catholic *collèges*, at least round here, are older and tattier than their state counterparts and the one we visited had a dispirited, and dispiriting, air which was only emphasised by the unenthusiastic, if not despondent, position adopted by the headmaster: it was all likely to be very difficult. He could not think of any member of staff who might be able to help us, nor could he suggest any other way of obtaining the kind of tuition we needed. We left wondering if he would have been more positive had we come in clutching our rosaries, or at least with an introduction from Monsieur le Curé of Sauternes.

Then came one of those *tuyaux*, like the one that led to Monsieur Saint-Martin, which really altered our life in Sauternes. This particular introduction had a more far-reaching effect even than that stout *vigneron* has had, for it governed, and still does govern, the education of all the children. We were told to contact Charles Lataste, the *directeur* (headmaster) of the Collège Toulouse-Lautrec in Langon. We were told that he headed a dynamic school with the best academic results of any *collège* in the Gironde and what is more, he was the sort of man who would be interested in our problem. The only disappointing note struck was that the children of Sauternes were unable to go to Toulouse-Lautrec because the village was outside its catchment area. They were obliged to go to 'The Other One', which was a much dimmer affair.

Charles Lataste had all the trimmings of the dream headmaster. He was young(ish), handsome, confident, had a beautiful voice and a phenomenal memory which allowed him to know all the 800–900 children in his school, and their parents as well. He had played rugby, in this land of rugby, at the highest level (Dax) and legend has it that he has even had a cap or so for France, or was it the B team?

It was he, in years to come, who was to wave at me and shout across the road and across the crowd of children coming out of school: 'The twins should go to the international section at Magendie in Bordeaux. I'll send you the papers.' Thus launching William on a career which will end with certificates that state he is truly and properly bilingual—but not Francis, who took fright at the famously shabby building and the loony headmaster!

Monsieur Lataste would always be there at the gate, apparently talking to ten people at once, arranging futures, moving on cars, joking with parents, surveying the road crossing and generally being a presence. In our experience he is an exception among Directeurs of Collèges and Proviseurs of Lycées (Sixth Form Colleges. They usually seem to be anonymous administrators, deeply interested in the management of their schools but not in contact with the individual pupils. We prefer the Lataste model.

He sounded exactly as he had been cracked up to be when I telephoned him, with all the optimistic bounce so lacking in the manner of the church-school headmaster. He had already heard about us and had been warned that we might approach him. How on earth does this kind of intelligence network operate? We had only heard of *him* twenty-four hours previously. He respired dynamic commitment: an appointment was made for that very afternoon, we should bring the children, he would like to meet them—no! of course they were all at school—he knew several people on his staff who would be interested in this kind of work, he would decide who would be best and talk to them etc, etc. At the end of the conversation Monsieur Lataste revealed a charming flaw in his talents with his farewell, delivered in English: 'See you later, my dear!'

Our interview lasted just four minutes. Monsieur Lataste had done everything he had said he would do and one of his staff (Madame Bodis) would telephone us that evening to make the necessary arrangements. I think he just wanted to see that we were what we claimed to be, and he used the excuse of writing down the children's names and ages to shoot keen glances at us from behind his desk. We had no sense of being hurried, yet there seemed to be no possibility of extending the interview, a classic headmasterly skill, essential in a region where the endless discussion of the obvious is such a highly prized social activity. Madame Bodis sounded, and is, as charming and efficient as Monsieur Lataste, but she wanted a lot of money for her skills. How, though, could we refuse when everything had been arranged for us so smoothly and efficiently?

Curiously, none of the children, not even Thomas, can remember exactly how she taught them French. They remember sitting at the kitchen table talking to her but that's about all. I recall this too: they sat in a row, hanging on her words with rapt attention. Had Madame Bodis told them at that moment to levitate six inches off the table top, such was their concentration, they would have done it. It was a study of a gifted teacher, as the French say, '*dans ses oeuvres*'.

They also remember her first arrival and the strange intonation with which she said, 'Hello': 'Halloww'. Not, 'Hallow'; the accent is on the second syllable and the 'ow' sounded like 'Ow! I've stubbed my toe', then there is an upward inflection at the end. It induced a dangerous attack of ill-suppressed giggling.

Whatever she did it worked. After only a few of her expensive hours she announced that she could do no more for the children, who should now be able to follow everything that was going on at school. I do not think this was pure magic. They were poised on the brink of fluency and just needed a nudge of confidence to set them going.

One more step was necessary, however, to get them out of the habit of not listening in class, of gazing at the walls, or of playing Jocks and Geordies. This was to suggest tactfully to Monsieur Desautel that it was time to abandon 'Bruno et Caroline' once and for all and to make the children do what everyone else was doing. Unable as we were to devise a formula, especially in French, which would avoid giving the impression that we were dissatisfied with his efforts, I took the direct approach.

'The children would like to participate more in class now.'

Monieur Desautel was visibly put out. '*Mais*, Monsieur Reay-Jones, nothing is preventing them from participating!'

This was accompanied by a dramatic step backwards, a hunching of the shoulders and an expansive upward and outwards movement of the arms, fingers apart, palms at 45 degrees, as if to imply that all imaginable circumstances were conspiring to beckon the children to a full participation. How precise and expressive these gestures are and what a wealth of inadequate words they serve to avoid. We northerners don't make much use of them. I suspect that a form of communication which can neither be recorded nor used in evidence does not appeal to us! I understood from it Monsieur Desautel's (polite) indignation at the idea of my dissatisfaction, his willingness to react positively to my request and the absence of practical impediments to this. I persisted in my coarse, literal, British way.

'But they don't understand this. They have got into the habit of not participating because they don't always follow what is going on and they give up and look at the walls.'

The effect was dramatic. The following morning Monsieur Desautel marched into the classroom and barked: '*Bien!* Your father has been to see me and everything has got to change.') '*tout doit changer.*'

He pitched them right in it and it worked. Slowly, with occasional hiccups, Thomas, William and Francis rose to the tops of their respective classes and once arrived they stayed there, to our immense satisfaction and relief, plus some mild surprise. We did wonder how they managed it, especially the rapid development of their imaginative writing in French, an aspect of their work at which Monsieur Desautel never ceased to marvel. We decided it was not all due to their native brilliance but also to the lasting benefit of their education in England, with its emphasis on self-expression, a quality less highly esteemed in France than accuracy of spelling and grammar. There is obviously something to be said for each camp but as our lot had the chance to dabble in both, they were perhaps at an advantage. One other factor which may have helped was the immense wealth of children's books available in English which does not exist in French. As all the boys were keen readers it is possible that they had simply encountered more imaginative writing in their short lives than their fellow pupils and so developed their own abilities. Perhaps *Messieurs et Mesdames les Professeurs de Français* would do well to keep the grammar exercises for school hours and set reading and more reading for homework!

6

A Cook, a Waitress—the Restaurant Opens

A breakthrough had been achieved on the restaurant front, at about the same time as the Rentrée Scolaire. Like so many solutions to so many problems here, this one came from a totally unexpected source (England) and had little to do with us.

We were just thinking about restarting our advertising for a cook when a friend in Charlbury told us to phone a restaurant owner he knew, in Chipping Norton of all places, who had successfully used a small agency in Nice to find himself real, French cooks. I phoned him and he told us all about the Association des Hôteliers et Restaurateurs Réunis, whose sole function was the provision of personnel for hotels and restaurants. It was presided over by an elderly lady of autocratic outlook who was said to be 'A bit odd but quite efficient'.

Madame Bercovici's manner was odd, but I didn't notice at the time. I was quite used to being spoken to as if I was a small child or mentally deficient so I simply assumed that her slow delivery and exemplary clarity, her simple vocabulary and insistently reassuring manner were tailored to her perception of my needs: constant morale boosting for a sub-normal 10-year-old. In fact she talked to everyone like this.

'*Ecoutez*-Monsieur-Reay-Jones-don't-you-worry-I-know-just-what-you-want-and-I-shall-find-you-your-cook-soon-so-don't-you-worry-about-it-I-shall-look-in-my-files-and-choose-the-best-one-then-I-shall-ask-him-to-phone-you-do-you-understand …?' Etc.

We were therefore mildly surprised when, a week later, our young cook, 'aged between 20 and 25, with a couple of years' experience in good restaurants, reliable, capable of working on his own and with enough initiative to help relaunch an abandoned restaurant', materialised in the form of a thin, saturnine 39-year-old ex-alcoholic who had just graduated from cookery school ... '*Mais, Ne-vous-inquietez-pas-Monsieur-Reay-Jones.*'

That is unfair to Marc Etchegaray, as Basque as his name suggests, but he had a difficult start.

Marc was as much under the thrall of Madame Bercovici as we were. From our point of view he was bound to be what we wanted if she, in her wisdom, had sent him to us. So we were just waiting for him to accept the post and he, in turn, was plainly going to like it at Commarque if Madame B. had made him come here. However, the kitchen, or lack of it, was as big a surprise to him as he had been to us; but he had years of cooking in the Douanes (Customs) before going to proper cookery school and had been in some peculiar places. So, after the initial shock, he was able to look at it with a practical eye and merely said, '*Il faut faire avec—* but you will have to spend some money before we can start.'

The matter was a foregone conclusion, but Marc had to go all the way back to Istres, near Marseilles, where his cookery school was located, to collect his things before he could start work. We were to take him to Langon station to catch his train but we thought it polite to offer him supper first. This he accepted readily and said he would like to make something for it. We looked round the empty and implement-free kitchen and wondered what on earth he could do, but he announced dramatically, 'All I need is some oil, an onion and a tea-towel and I will prepare you a dish.'

Consumed with curiosity, hoping for something miraculous but with just a faint doubt, we found him what he wanted and left him to it.

It should be explained that our partners, plus their three children, were staying with us—their first visit—to see what exactly they had let themselves in for. There were, therefore, eight children in the house, the eldest aged 10. We briefed them carefully: the new cook was making something for supper. No matter what it was like, even if they hated it, they must eat it up without making a fuss and say thank you afterwards. If we had said instead, 'Try to express revulsion, disgust and horror in as many different ways as you can,' we could not have hoped for a finer display than the children gave us and Marc.

He arrived bearing a large, earthenware tureen he had found somewhere in the restaurant and set it down reverently on the table. All eyes were on him and his tureen as he whisked off the lid with a grand flourish to reveal a brilliant green liquid within. A strong smell of cooked weeds filled the kitchen. The children cringed visibly. Someone said, 'Mummy, do I have to ...?' and was immediately suppressed.

Francis's eyes started to fill with tears; he always was a fussy eater. The liquid was ladled out and handed round. The stench of elderly weeds became all but overpowering. There was a profound silence, broken by a scuffling under the table, as the adults tried to remind the children, with a variety of squeezes and nudges, of the solemn promises they had made.

It was no use. *La Soupe aux Orties*, for it was Nettle Soup, passed the lips of just four of the children and instantly passed them again in the reverse direction. A chorus of spluttering and coughing followed and the four who had actually tasted the concoction could be seen clutching their throats with their tongues out.

Marc was astonishingly unperturbed, while we adults started prolonged apologies along the lines of, 'Fussy English children, never tasted anything like that before,' (no more had we) 'bound not to like it and he shouldn't worry, we thought it was … quite nice!'

A tame finish but there are limits to the perjury one is prepared to commit in the name of politeness and we did not want Marc thinking he could produce absolutely anything and still keep us happy. We need not have worried. Marc was strong in the knowledge of his own excellence as a cook. He was to remind us often, just as Madame Bercovici had told us several times, that he had passed out top of his class at Istres. His age and experience must have given him certain advantages over his fellow students, most of whom would have been teenagers, but nevertheless it cannot have been an outstanding class.

We drained the soup to the bitter end, and bitter it was from start to finish. When I think of the soups Georgea has produced: Le Velouté de Moules Bordelais, La Soupe aux Oignons et au Fromage de Chèvre, Le Potage d'Automne aux Cèpes, La Crème de Poisson, and she has never been top of a cookery class. She has never been anywhere near a cookery class.

Of course, Marc was improvising and, of course, it takes more than an onion and elderly nettles to make edible soup, but we were not reassured by his willingness to try it. I suspect he would not have done so if his audience had been French.

By the way, if you want to try making nettle soup, which you may not having read the above, use only very young, tender, spring nettles. It is the only chance you have of making it edible, let alone pleasant.

* * *

We put Marc on the train to Marseilles and went home to await his return in two days' time. Four days later we decided he had gone the way of previous cooks and were just summoning up the courage to complain to Madame Bercovici when the phone rang and I heard Marc's unmistakable voice, a voice at once husky and Basque, but polite and correct. Marc was proud of his command of the French language and not without cause. Thomas was to profit from numerous grammar lessons given simultaneously with instruction in the making of *brioche* and pastry, but that day the voice also sounded feeble and trembly. It explained that its owner had had a 'slight' accident getting off the train in Marseilles and had been confined to bed for the previous two days with a cut on the head—*'une blessure à la crane'*. The clear reference to a *cranial* injury made it sound much more serious. He was on his way, however, and would arrive that afternoon.

When the train came in Marc was visible from afar by virtue of the great turban of bandage in which his head was swathed. He walked slowly, with more than his usual stoop and a hangdog expression on his face, which went with the gravity of his injury and his days of suffering. However, he leapt into the van (the one that had brought the furniture from England) with surprising agility and his voice gained in strength and vigour as he recounted in detail the story of his accident. It was banal enough: he had missed the step getting out of the carriage because he was waving to his friends from the cookery school, who had come to pick him up, and he had cracked his head on the corner of someone's suitcase as he fell forward onto the platform. Two days later, when the yards of bandage had been unwound, a tiny cut, almost completely healed, was presented for our sympathetic examination while Marc inspected the lint that had covered it for residual bleeding. There was none. Marc was both accident-prone and hypochondriac, and I suppose we should be grateful that nothing serious befell him during his time with us. If a spark of hot fat from a sizzling pan happened to alight on his hand he would fall back against the wall with a cry and search minutely for signs of a burn. With Marc we leaned the significance of the Accident de Travail and the subsequent dreaded Arrêt de Travail (Work Stoppage) paid for at least, by a generous social security system, at the rate of half the normal salary but lasting long enough to allow complete recovery from a double amputation, let alone the half-inch cut on the index finger for which it was given. His most spectacular effort came one morning the following spring when he failed to appear in the kitchen at the usual time. Martine, the then waitress—of whom more later—went up to his apartment to see what had become of him. Her panic-stricken cry and the running of feet overhead told us there was a real problem.

'Come quickly, come quickly,' cried Martine. 'Marc is seriously ill.'

He was lying flat on his back with his head tilted up so that his beard stuck in the air, gasping for breath and clutching his chest.

'What is it, Marc? Where does it hurt?' I asked urgently.

'*J'ai un bar*'—a searing pain—'*ici.*' And he pointed to the top of his chest, moving his head from side to side pathetically and panting ever more rapidly.

'Look how he's suffering,' wailed Martine. 'Call the doctor quickly.'

We appeared to have grounds for serious concern, and ten minutes later Dr Daubech's car slewed to a halt in a shower of gravel and Dr Daubech jumped out with an animation stimulated by Martine's colourful telephone description of Marc's condition.

'Stay here until I call,' he ordered us and went up the stairs to Marc's apartment two at a time. He did not call, however, and descended much more calmly five minutes later with a slight grin on his face.

'He'll be all right now,' was all he said, 'and he won't need an *Arrêt de Travail.*'

'But what on earth's the matter with him?' I asked.

'He has a slight sore throat,' replied Dr Daubech, and left, still grinning.

Half an hour later Marc was at work, looking—did I imagine it?—slightly shamefaced, but with never another word to say on the subject. He was full of gory tales about young cooks impaling themselves on great knives, slicing off their toes because they weren't wearing regulation shoes, and numerous other dangers inherent in this most dangerous of all *métiers*, but after that incident I'm not sure we would have taken him seriously even if he had shown us his severed hand sitting on the kitchen table.

So he was accident-prone and hypochondriac, but he was also thrifty. '*Avec moi, pas de gaspillag* [no wastage]', and he had a clear grasp of what was required in order to open the restaurant. In this respect Madame Berçovici had understood exactly what was good for us. Moreover, his train accident had not prevented Marc, as he was at pains to point out, from working on the list of items necessary to make a workable kitchen. We would find all of them at the great trade market Metro in Bordeaux.

For those in the trade such empires are old hat, but for us Metro was both a revelation and a temptation. The temptation was to cast aside Marc's moderate and carefully considered list crying, 'We'll have one of those!—What's that for? Shouldn't we have one?—Don't you need that for making sauces?—That for cooking fish and a complete set of those for whatever it is they do?'

I am exaggerating, but it is easy to understand why so many new restaurants do not survive more than a year or two. Our professorial, omnicompetent builder-electrician-plumber, the charming Gerard Arlic, known, inevitably, as Mister Garlic from the sign on his van, has constructed over a hundred professional kitchens in Bordeaux of which, he thinks, two are still in existence. Everyone insists, he says, on buying everything brand new and equipping their kitchens like five-star hotels. With places like Metro to contend with, it is not surprising.

We started in what I would call the heavy machinery section, which sells cookers, fridges, washing-up machines and the like. We bought a plate-warmer for F3,000 and that was all. We passed by the immense, stainless-steel ovens with 6-inch gas rings on top (F18,000, plus VAT), we passed by the steam ovens (F30,000) and the ovens à *air pulse* (F40,000). We also gave the special vegetable fridges a miss, even though they were only F8,000, and the cold chambers (from F20,000). We decided not to buy a glass washer with a two-minute cycle (F11,000), nor a 6,000-watt washing machine for the laundry at F22,000, and we even ignored something so basic as a *bain-marie* mounted on a cupboard (modestly priced at F5,500). The grills, slicers and mixers big enough to mix the foundations of a small housing development we never even looked at, but lots of people do—and buy them, with attractive credit terms provided by Metro. With all this kit it is surprising that so many restaurants manage to produce such undistinguished food!

Marc was, to his credit, a resolute minimalist, even though he was spending someone else's money. His policy, which we endorsed wholeheartedly, was to improve the equipment in line with the hoped-for increase in customers. For the moment, as there were no customers, we should make-do with as little equipment as possible. So we stuck to the two, small, four-ring domestic gas cookers that sat in the corner of the kitchen and the three elderly fridges against the opposite wall. We bought things like wooden spoons, ladles, spatulas, whisks, sieves, stainless steel bowls, frying pans big enough to cover all four rings of one of our cookers, saucepans, a few knives and one luxury: a stainless-steel lined copper pan (F360). We moved on and bought white tablecloths, white napkins, white plates (cheap), glasses (not so cheap, my weakness) and carafes. Marc, by the way, had done some waiting in his time and was just as able to equip the dining room as the kitchen, another plus provided by the perspicacious Madame Bercovici. We bought fish knives and forks, but the restaurant was otherwise well stocked with cutlery, menus, candle-holders and ashtrays. All of things, and many more, Marc had carefully listed, with the necessary quantities, in his notebook. By the end of the morning, we had gathered the lot and we spent the afternoon unloading it at Commarque and then making a new set of lists, this time of all the food items we needed, for the second trip to Metro the following day.

Metro's food section is even more impressive than the equipment side. Children under 14 are not allowed in, although this rule is not enforced as strictly as it should be considering the danger from high-speed fork-lift loaders. These have a habit of springing out at you from behind the stacks, their drivers oblivious of anything at ground level, having their eyes fixed firmly upwards, on the loads teetering 20 feet above their heads at the level of the top shelves. They stop for neither trolley, customer nor colleague, but as I have never seen even the slightest accident, I suppose it is less dangerous than it looks. In this massive, inelegant temple dedicated to the satisfaction of the needs, or more accurately the desires, of the stomach, it is possible to buy boxes of live lobsters, whole lambs (dead), tins of cooking oil big enough to pass muster in an army petrol dump, and containers of olives or gherkins not much smaller, 10 kilo boxes of chicken legs at eight francs a kilo and *foie gras* prepared like Granny used to do it, wrapped in a checked cloth, for a thousand francs a kilo, truffles, *cèpes*, *girolles*, fillet of venison, English pheasants, Polish wild boar, tropical fruit and vegetables in season, turbot, salmon and any other fish you might fancy, every herb and spice in the world; tons of yummy ice-creams of a quality and price only available to restaurants, and all those cheat powders that allow restaurant cooks to prepare sauces which make you think they are better cooks than you are! It is a testimony to the power of the catering trade that these powders are not generally available in shops, although they are beginning to creep into supermarkets in an attenuated and overpriced form. Sweet shops can equip themselves at Metro, so can greengrocers, *alimentations générales* and delicatessens. The only disappointing part, to me, was the wine section, but I learned later that there are special wine displays at various times of the year which are as mouth-watering as the rest of it.

So we took this second load home, Marc started to cook in his more-or-less equipped kitchen and Maïté (pronounced My-eater), a local girl we had found through the *Sud-Ouest* newspaper, which had so signally failed to find us a cook in July and August, took up the post of waitress and started to wash and polish the dining room and to lay the tables with all the newly purchased crockery and cutlery. But all of this had taken time and it was already the beginning of October. Not only had we missed the summer season but we had missed the fine autumn as well and I recall only too well the 'grand' opening of the restaurant on a wind-swept October night, the château lashed by rain and the leaves from the plane trees swirling into squelchy heaps around the courtyard. Inside the restaurant, however, there was a blazing fire, Maïté was dressed in the snappiest black and white affair and Marc had a brand-new jacket and apron for the occasion. It did look lovely but there was no one to see it except us, and so there we all stood, glumly watching the rain beating against the windows.

At about eight o'clock a couple scuttled out of the rain into the foyer but all they wanted was a room for the night and they had already eaten elsewhere. They managed to cheer us up by saying how beautiful the restaurant was and announced that they would come in and drink some Sauternes. So we sold them an expensive half-bottle of 1971 Château Filhot, and that was the sole receipt for the restaurant opening over which we had agonised for so long.

Meanwhile, we had failed to collect the grapes and it was Papy Dartigues who was to transform them into what he dignified, quite unjustifiably, with the name of Sauternes.

7

The Countryside in Autumn

At the start of September, a week or so before Marc's first visit, we were looking to the future and the enticing possibility, one of the great attractions of Commarque, of enlarging the vineyard. We still had those *droits de plantation*, not as many as Mr Jenkin-Lee had claimed, but enough to extend the restaurant patch of vines to the hedge at the top of the slope down to Mahourat, where Bernard and Papy Dartigues live. We planned to plant this the following spring, despite the gently sliding pound. In the event this plan had to be abandoned permanently when the slide turned into an avalanche leading to the sin, abominable in an area like Sauternes, of loss of *droits*, which occurs irreversibly ten years after the last declared crop.

The preparation of ground for planting vines has to be started well in advance of the actual planting. The first operation, after clearing your patch, is to plough it deeply—and by deeply I mean a good 60 centimetres. This demands a hefty plough not normally found in the repertoire of tools of a small vineyard. Monsieur Saint-Martin did not have one but he had a friend, '*Mon Gros Ami*' (My Fat Friend) the only name by which I have known him, who had a forest plough big enough for the purpose and in fact what many vine growers use in this area surrounded by the pine forests of the Landes. But… '*Attention*. My Fat Friend is expensive.'

The implication was that he was *too* expensive, although he would do the job properly, especially as Monsieur Saint-Martin would be around to check up on him. As he got into his car to leave, Monsieur Saint-Martin let drop the interesting information that his Fat Friend was 78 years old and had got married a few weeks previously, adding, 'I'm sure he's lost weight since!'

Twenty-four hours later the Fat Friend arrived on a huge, ancient tractor quite devoid of any modern safety devices, such as a flashing light or anti-roll bar, which are legal requirements for driving on the highway, and with a single immense ploughshare on the back, a contraption big enough to act as a rudder on an ocean liner. Seen from ground level looking up at the high seat over which he was spread, the bulk of Monsieur Saint-Martin's friend was impressive. If marriage had slimmed him down, then he must have been unimaginably *gros* before. He approached the château at a stately four miles an hour, and when he had descended from his seat, a lengthy process accompanied by much grunting and wheezing, his progress on foot did not achieve the half of this. He was much shorter than he had appeared stuck up on the tractor, although just as fat, and was clad in grubby dungarees that looked as though they had been made for a man 18 inches taller but of comparable girth. The legs had simply been sliced off at more or less the right distance from the ends to leave the baggy and frayed bottoms flapping round his bare ankles, above feet clad in carpet slippers. A holey felt hat completed a picture of decrepitude belied by the appraising gleam in his little eyes and the vigour of his handshake. Monsieur Saint-Martin gestured at the small field in front of us and a machine-gun conversation ensued of which I barely grasped a word but listened to nonetheless, marvelling at the density of the Fat Friend's accent and the rat-a-tat roll of his gutteral Rs.

Monsieur Fat Friend finally turned to me and said, '*Cinq cent frrrancs, m'sieur*. I cannot do it for less than *cinq cent frrrancs.*'

I concealed my relief. From the tones of the conversation I had inferred a discussion of high finance, in danger of putting the whole exercise out of my reach. I think Monsieur Saint-Martin had been beating him down, which was kind of him considering he was *his* Fat Friend, not mine. The latter wasted no more time but started to climb laboriously back up onto his tractor. Monsieur Saint-Martin helped him unceremoniously on his way by putting a hand under the ample seat of the dungarees and shoving hard with a cry of, '*Eh 'op, Papy!*' His friend wheezed into position and his face twinkled with a youthful grin as he remarked that he would be needing a crane to get to work (*une grrrue*) if he did not retire in the near future. As the tractor moved away the wheeze of breath mingled with the leisurely chug of the big motor and was then drowned as Monsieur Fat Friend lowered his plough and revved the tractor to a dominating roar.

Monsieur Saint-Martin went home and I stayed to watch for a few minutes. The plough sliced effortlessly through the light soil and left a small sand dune in the wake of the advancing tractor. After two hours the field had been turned into neat rows of dunes, which from ground level resembled line after line of wind-swept sand hills in a great desert. It was a dramatic transformation and it looked like a significant start to our ground preparations. Unfortunately, it never went any further than that.

Monsieur Fat Friend stopped his tractor and went through the complex sequence of slow movements, a suitable subject for time-lapse cinematography, needed to get him off the machine and onto the ground. He shuffled towards me, removing his hat and wiping the sweat from his face and bald head with an enormous handkerchief. Apart from this inevitable sign of exertion, he gave no indication of adverse effects from his two hours of work in the full sunshine. He was a tough old bird then, who might well install a crane to lift himself on to his tractor, rather than give up work!

As he approached he pointed up and over my head at the tower of the restaurant behind me and said, '*M'sieur*, I think you have *un prrrobleme* up there.' I asked him what sort of problem, fearing he was going to tell me that some major repair was necessary, but it was not that at all.

'You have a hornet's nest in the tower.'

He had watched the great insects coming and going all the time he had been ploughing. He went so slowly that he had had plenty of time to study what was going on around him, but I did feel a bit foolish for not having noticed them before he did. On the other hand we had, at that time, little reason to be in the restaurant and less still to be behind it where the entrance to the nest appeared to be located. Monsieur Fat Friend gave me a solemn warning about hornets:

'You have children, *n'est-ce pas, m'sieur*? You should know that two or three hornet stings can be mortal for a small child. You must call the fire brigade and have the nest destroyed.'

I thanked him for his advice, paid him for his work and waited impatiently for him to complete the ascent of the north face of his tractor and make his leisurely exit from the property before rushing into the restaurant to locate the hornet's nest.

The moment I set foot inside I could hear the deep, steady hum coming from the tower. I climbed the steps as quietly as possible and gently, very gently, opened the door. The hum was transformed into a profound, throbbing resonance with which the room seemed to vibrate; a sound both powerful and menacing. The air was thick with beating wings and I glimpsed briefly a brownish, seething mass of movement in the spider's web of the rafters before banging the door shut and bolting it firmly. Outside the restaurant the disturbance I had caused was clearly visible around the roof of the tower: a swishing cloud of hornets rose above it, in defence of their realm. Gone was the steady purposeful flight Monsieur Fat Friend had pointed out; now the movement was jagged, urgent, a violent casting round for enemies to drive off. I did not wait to be driven. I scarpered. I told everyone to stay well away from the restaurant and the children to stay indoors for an hour while the hornets calmed down. Then I telephoned the fire brigade.

Monsieur Fat Friend was right about the effects of a hornet sting and if you examine the beast itself it is easy to understand why: it is three times the size of a wasp, striped in brown and yellow and the sting itself is a good quarter of an inch long. But hornets are not attracted to food and people in the same annoying way wasps are attracted to them. They tend to remain aloof and to continue their sonorous passage without paying the least attention to the jumpy humans ducking and swiping beneath them. When they come into the house, which happens occasionally, Commarque being well known for the richness of its fauna, they tend to fly steadily close to the ceiling, giving the impression that they are calmly seeking a way out rather than looking for the jam pot. It seems rather unfair to climb on the table in order to swat them, but one must bear in mind that long, venom-pumping lance borne at the end of the abdomen. Disturbing the nest, of course, is quite another matter and guaranteed to sour the temper of even the most serene and patient hornet.

The firemen, two of them, turned up the following morning in a 3-ton truck filled with equipment. They unpacked long boots, protective suits, masks, breathing equipment, heavy gauntlets, helmets and large cylinders of insecticide to which they attached pipes and atomisers. I read the labels on the boxes containing the cylinders and decided to keep well out of the way while they sprayed. The two men climbed into their protective gear, picked up the assembled spraying equipment, strapped the cylinders onto harnesses and strode towards the restaurant. But they had not bothered with the masks and breathing equipment and they both laughed when I asked if they had forgotten them.

'Don't you worry about us,' said the older one. 'Once we start spraying those hornets won't be able to get near us. This is powerful stuff.'

I could not really point out that this was precisely what was bothering me. It was not the effect on the hornets but the effect on the men that I felt was being underrated, but it would be insulting their professional competence to say so. I contented myself with a murmured, '*Ah! d'accord,*' but the muttered conversation and prolonged fumbling with the cylinders that preceded the attack on the tower only reinforced my misgivings. One had the strongest impression that these men, for all their training, had never actually assaulted a hornet's nest before that day.

On the other hand, the way they went through the doors of the tower was terrific! No screen baddie has been more forcefully broken in on than those hornets were. Sprayguns at the hips, one large boot for each side of the double door, they drew themselves up, the older one whispered, '*un, deux, trois*', and they kicked the door open and rushed inside, firing as they went. The doors banged shut behind them and for a moment the only noises were the hissing of the spray guns and a rising hum from the afflicted hornets. Then the coughing began. Fifteen seconds (or so) later the doors were flung open and out of the mist inside the two firemen staggered, choking and spluttering, eyes streaming, spray guns dragging along the ground. The older one still had the presence of mind to bang the doors shut while the younger one retched over the bannisters.

Five minutes later they were making light of it and I went along with their obvious desire to play down an incident which might have caused a great deal of mirth at their expense back at the fire station. It seemed superfluous to say, 'told you so'. I am sure they will have used all that expensive breathing equipment next time they had to get rid of a hornet's nest.

The effect on the hornets was more dramatic still. Within ten minutes of the assault it was possible to enter the tower, holding one's breath, and open the window. The floor was thick with dead bodies and there was the nest, a hanging Chinese lantern of translucent papery material, bereft of inhabitants, suspended among the rafters. The firemen brought a ladder and cut it down. It was surprisingly fragile and had collapsed into several pieces, losing its elegant drop-like form, before I could show it to the children. Nevertheless, William kept a large piece on a shelf in his room for several years.

* * *

The following Sunday morning found us, for the first time since the middle of July, quite devoid of hotel guests and therefore able to enjoy what we told ourselves was a well-earned lie in. We had just treated ourselves to coffee in bed when war broke out at Château de Commarque. The rattle of gunfire came from all round the walls, much of it seemingly just outside the courtyard, but we had the impression that the whole area was up in arms, especially across the plain of vines to the north and east. The intensity of firing suggested a strenuously disputed battle and, as the children shot into our room in panic, we were for the moment unable to reassure them, having no idea what could have provoked this violent outbreak of fighting in our peaceful neighbourhood. Then it dawned on us: it was nothing more than the opening of the hunting season!

Within an hour the firing had diminished to what sounded like little more than sporadic encounters between enemy patrols and, by mid-morning, we felt able to venture outside the courtyard. In the meantime, we had had two showers of pellets on the kitchen windows and many others rattling on the roofs and gravel and falling through the plane trees in the courtyard with a noise like heavy rain. The lawns around the walls were littered with hundreds and hundreds of cartridge cases in all colours of the rainbow.

Was it like this round all the houses? Were we to be subjected to this every day from now on? Had Mr Jenkin-Lee put up with this without protest? These questions became more urgent when we found a comprehensively perforated cat lying in the first row of vines behind the restaurant. This was too much! Where cats had been, small children might follow and anyway, what on earth would hotel guests make of a disturbance on such scale?

The landscape was free of soldiery by now, although firing could still be heard distantly from several directions. However, in the course of the morning khaki-clad figures could be seen moving singly and in groups between the parcels of vines and down the rows, not to mention others who came up the track from the field between the vines and the Ruisseau de Commarque and then stood, guns on shoulders, in search of prey among our vines in front of the château. We did not venture out to remonstrate with them because we did not know our rights, nor theirs. We decided to consult the Secretary at the Mairie who would be bound to know all about it.

The transformation of mild family men into heavily armed desperadoes, which the opening of the hunting season seems to provoke, is a widespread curiosity in France. The process is identical in Provence, Sauternes, the Dordogne, the Ardennes and even the cabbage fields of Brittany. We are not anti-hunting, but its wilder manifestations do not sit well in the immediate vicinity of a supposedly peaceful country hotel, especially one occupied by several small children. The situation did not improve as the children got bigger. Why should a keen athlete be prevented from training on his own land because some gun-toting moron is incapable of distinguishing him from a rabbit? Not to mention incapable of controlling the dog that bites his bum as he runs past on the public highway if you please!

At the Mairie the Secretary was full of indignation on our behalf: we did not have to have the hunters on our land if we did not want them. Apart from anything else, she said, they included, '*Les gens les plus bêtes de la commune*' (the most stupid people in the parish). But had we put up Chasse Interdite signs? No? A big mistake! We must put them all round the entrances to the property, but in any case the hunters had no right to shoot towards the house and the *histoire* of the cat was an absolute disgrace. She would 'send us' the Gardien de Chasse, the gentleman responsible for policing the hunters in his commune.

The Gardien was very polite and exceedingly condescending: of course, he understood that we were not conversant with country ways, nor could we possibly know how knowledgeable all the local hunters were and how carefully they followed the regulations, which he personally saw to that they all knew more or less by heart. He read us a lecture about how natural hunting was and how it contributed to the harmony of the natural fauna etc, etc; a view, incidentally, not shared by the government, judging by the strict legislation introduced a year or so later! Georgea could see steam beginning to issue from my ears, so she trod on my toe and muttered, 'Show him the cat.' Then asked innocently: 'Do the regulations allow the shooting of cats?'

The Gardien threw her a look of withering contempt and replied that no hunter would ever shoot a cat and that Madame's question only showed that she understood nothing of the subject. So I threw him the cat. Well, I threw it at his feet. It was so plainly riddled with buckshot that there was not a lot he could say and he contented himself with muttering that he supposed a mistake could happen but it was very rare. Georgea then asked: 'Are the hunters allowed to shoot at houses?'

After the cat question the Gardien reacted cautiously to this one and threw a sideways glance at the house as if he half expected to see the walls as riddled with shot as the cat was.

'*Non, Madame,*' he replied.

'Do the regulations have anything to say about how far from houses hunters must stay when shooting?'

'*Oui, Madame.* They must remain at least one hundred and fifty metres from a house when shooting.'

She led him outside the courtyard and showed him the litter of cartridge cases on the lawn, a litter that started a thin 10 centimetres from the wall and extended, more or less unbroken, to the vines perhaps twenty metres away. Fury lent wings to her French.

'*Monsieur*, we did not put all these things here,' gesturing at the cartridges. 'Your hunters are plainly suffering from *trous de mémoire* [amnesia]. You had better remind them of the regulations and soon.'

After that he did not stay for long and made no further attempt to convince us of the desirability of hunting. He seemed genuinely surprised that his flock was less angelic than he had supposed and promised that the matter would be fully discussed at the next meeting and that he would instruct everyone to stay away from Commarque. In the meantime, would we please put up Chasse Interdite signs as soon as possible. This I did, and while making the tour to ensure that I had marked all possible access routes, I came across an old sign nailed to a tree down the back hill toward Bernard's. house. It was shot full of holes!

The result was not perfect but it did improve things, although our stock went down several notches with a section of the locals and we were dubbed '*Eco-cons*', the local slang for the ecologists who were at that time campaigning for the preservation of a number of song-birds, to the intense annoyance of the hunting lobby. Never forget that the French have fought long and bloodily for personal liberty and that includes the liberty to shoot whatever they like. Any action perceived to threaten a piece of personal liberty is likely to provoke a surprisingly violent response; surprising, that is, to outsiders. The '*cons*' part of '*eco-cons*', by the way, is not an abbreviation of 'conservationist' but a straightforward example of the use of the word *con* as an insult.

The following autumn Henri de Vaucelles telephoned out of the blue to ask if we had been bothered by hunters and in answer to my emphatic 'yes' he said, 'Right, I will put all my woods beside Commarque *sous réserve*. *Comme ça* the hunters will not be able to pass through them without my permission and I will not give it.'

We still had a few neighbours who resented the restriction of their hunting ground by us outsiders. They pushed these restrictions to the limit and would patrol the alleys between our vines and those of our neighbours with their dogs and guns and make a point of crossing our land, which they have a perfect right to do, and just occasionally of shooting across it and sending a dog to retrieve the kill well inside the Zone Interdite. On one occasion a year later we were talking in the courtyard with a group of hotel guests before their departure when a double shower of pellets rattled round us and bounced off the roofs of their two Renault Espaces. The guests were astounded and the men ran to the front gate to see if they could make out where the shots had come from. Georgea knew without looking and jumped on her bike to remonstrate with the offenders before they could disappear into the woods. There were two of them, from the house on the corner at the end of the lane where we turn left to go to Sauternes.

Georgea addressed herself to the older man, a retired vineyard worker at Château Filhot, until now exceedingly polite, in the habit of doffing his cap to us in an old-fashioned gesture and of exchanging cheerful greetings with the children.

'You've just showered us with shot,' she said to him. 'You have no right to shoot in the direction of the house.'

'Spent shot won't hurt you,' he replied, then laughed nastily, raised his gun to his shoulder and pointed it straight at her. 'On the other hand, if I shot at you from here it would hurt, badly.'

'Are you threatening me?' Georgea asked.

'No, just stating a fact.' They held each other's eyes.

'Well now I'm threatening you,' said Georgea. Oh! How Magnificent! 'If ever I find you, or even your dog, on my property, or if ever you fire in the direction of the house, I shall report you to the Gendarmes. I shan't bother with your mate the Gardien de Chasse and I shall do my best to get your licence withdrawn.'

Georgea and her bike were left holding the field alone and victorious while the hunters withdrew amid insults about the English and Ecologists. I have to say that we have not been so friendly with this gentleman since that episode, which is one of very few that have made us feel less than welcome in our adopted country.

There is another kind of hunting that occurs here, of a more peaceful nature, though keenly contested nonetheless. That is hunting for *cèpes*.

These lovely mushrooms are the quintessence of autumn: plump, rounded, richly brown, their form when freshly picked is that of the perfect, toy-town toadstool. If left alone, which doesn't often happen round here, they lift themselves higher out of the leaf mould and flatten, expanding into dry, firm dishes, as much as eight or nine inches across and weighing up to half a kilo. They are delicious, not unlike ordinary mushrooms in flavour, but supercharged, rich, fragrant and filling. They are wonderful in omelettes, they perfume soups beautifully, with garlic and parsley they are a dish all on their own (Cèpes à la Bordelaise) and they make a royal accompaniment to a Magret de Canard. Their other great attribute is that in good years there are plenty of them!

On the other hand, the season is short, a month, or six weeks at the most, and the growth of *cèpes* is capricious. They are found on the edge of woodlands, beneath oaks and chestnut trees, and occur in ones and twos, not in clumps and not necessarily where you feel they ought to be.

Many people round here are out every day picking for the whole year and their harvest is bottled in oil or, less traditionally, frozen. Others are out for profit because even in the most abundant years the price rarely drops below fifty francs a kilo and twice that figure is not uncommon. Unemployment is high in the countryside and *cèpes* gathering, along with grape picking, offers everyone the chance to make a little money during this season when mists are more or less certain and mellow fruitfulness is ardently hoped for. Everyone has their favourite spots and everyone keeps them a closely guarded secret, although I suspect that the real experts in Sauternes know everyone else's secrets off by heart. The keen hunters are in the woods at first light, or even before with the aid of flashlights. The casual picker who fancies a late morning stroll will find only what has been overlooked or, on a lucky day, when the owner of the woods, or the guardian of the secret, has decided not to do the tour, what has been scheduled for dawn the following day.

Sadly, nothing is exempt from greed and violence and la Chasse aux Cèpes is no exception. We have been a good deal more cautious about where we go since Georgea overheard two elderly ladies discussing the latest *cèpes* scandal while waiting in Monsieur Boisseau's pharmacy in Sauternes for their voluminous prescriptions to be prepared.

One of the ladies had a neighbour who was in the habit of doing the tour of her property every day at dawn in search of *cèpes*, an enjoyable, harmless activity in which she had indulged for many years without it ever crossing her mind that anything more dangerous would ever befall her than tripping over a bramble. Two days previously she had found herself face to face in the half-light with two strangers armed with knives who forced her to give up her basket of *cèpes*, knocked her to the ground and then disappeared into the undergrowth. The poor woman was so shaken she had sworn she would never go out in her woods again.

Many interesting snippets may be gleaned at Monsieur Boisseau's, mainly because the French enthusiasm for medicines and the complex administration that accompanies dispensing of prescriptions means that it takes a long, long time to get what you want there. With this in mind, and because he has many customers who are no longer in the first flush of youth, Monsieur Boisseau has installed a handy and comfortable bench seat inside the door of the pharmacy so that they can be seated while awaiting the completion of the lengthy formalities behind the counter. Conversation can be lively and very frustrating if you are in a hurry!

One day Georgea went in for some headache pills or cough mixture or some such—by the way, the chemists have a monopoly of medicines in France—and found herself behind a stout lady for whom Monsieur Boisseau and his assistant were piling mountains of packets and bottles on the counter. The lady was worried about one of the potions that had been prescribed, an antiseptic containing iodine to which she was allergic. She therefore needed, she said, to be very careful about what seafoods she ate in case they too contained iodine. This was a crying shame because she did like a nice bit of fish.

At this point she leaned forward and settled herself comfortably on the counter. What she liked best, she said, was to roll the fish in flour and cook it in piping hot oil to give it a lovely crispy skin—so much better on her wood-burning stove than on a modern electric one. Monsieur Boisseau and the lady chemist had stopped assembling medicines and were poised, pencils motionless above the forms waiting to be completed, listening attentively and nodding wisely. Someone chipped in, 'But you must add a little shallot and pepper to bring out the flavour', and the conversation was launched.

Twenty minutes later, after a brief sequel to the fish saga, delivered sotto voce, that is audible to the eight or ten people in the shop and not to anyone outside, about the time she had had her lower torso examined by scanner, the stout lady picked up her four carrier-bags of medicine and turned to go, revealing for the first time her face, covered in large pink blotches!

* * *

The vineyard had not been forgotten during this eventful period. We had watched the grapes swell and ripen, as grapes do in fine weather, but with everything else to contend with I had failed to equip a *chai* (winery) for the now imminent *vendange*. This may seem rather extraordinary considering that we had come to France primarily to pick grapes and make wine, but it was a question of priorities and other things seemed to have become more pressing since our arrival, like the presence of customers or, more likely to produce revenue—which we certainly needed—like getting the restaurant opened. There was also the never-ending need to mend and maintain, as well as improve, our new empire: there are, for example, nearly 2 acres of lawn to mow, the courtyard to keep weeded and to re-gravel, 300 yards of track with potholes that needed to be filled, and broken roof tiles, which gave rise to tap-like leaks when it rained, to seek out and replace.

My ignorance concluded the matter. I had got fixed in my mind that the complete works had to be installed before one could consider winemaking: concrete floor with drainage, stainless steel vats, a means to cool them, a well-insulated roof and so on. Also, I had no means of estimating how much juice would be involved. The answer, of course, was not much.

I now know how I could, and should, have done it. We needed to install the 380-volt agricultural electrical system, which could easily have been done in the grubby shell of the would-be *chai*, a small wine press, instantly available from the ever-obliging supplier Duluc across the valley in Budos, and a wine pump. Apart from that, a hole in the ground and two plastic *garde-vins* (small vats), one to catch the juice from the press and one to settle it overnight, were the only pieces of equipment we needed. A few barrels would suffice to ferment the juice and, incidentally, add an extra dimension of flavour to the resulting wine.

The only solution seemed to be to ask around and see if anyone else could provide me with a corner for my grapes. I went to see the Comte de Vaucelles but it was more than his life was worth to have Commarque's grapes in Château Filhot's cellar.

'As a *Cru Classé* Château Filhot is forbidden to have the grapes or wine of any other vineyard in the same cellar. If I was caught with your *vendange* here the whole of my crop would be declassified and I could only sell it as *vin de table*.'

Looking out across the park to the extensive plains that make up the vineyard of Filhot I could see it was totally unreasonable to expect anyone to take such a risk. Monsieur Perromat at Château d'Arche had a second *chai* but, '*Je regrette*. It is too late now to prepare it. Contact Monsieur Ricaud at Château Saint-Amand. He knows everyone and he might have some ideas.'

But he did not. He thought, and promised to continue thinking, but he never called me back with a solution to the problem. So it was that I asked Papy Dartigues if he would like to pick the grapes, rather than leaving them to go bad, rather than committing the ultimate agricultural crime of failing to collect the harvest.

Papy came and did what was being done all over the Sauternais that autumn season, but generally with a better sense of timing. It was not altogether his fault. By the time I offered him the *vendange* a fair bit of it had already gone bad, the grapes an orangey-brown colour, smelling of vinegar and surrounded by hordes of tiny fruit flies, a disorder known locally as *Bouyroc*, pronounced more or less, 'Boo-ee-rock'. The flies lay eggs and the maggots burrow in the sugary grapes, introducing the bacteria which convert sugar to acetic acid—in other words, vinegar. Eventually, the ruined grapes shrivel and dry up and can no longer harm the crop but it is fatal to allow the milky, vinegary juice into your fermenting mixture. If you do, the juice is doomed before it is even made. But Papy was making wine for home consumption so he was not bothered about the legal limits of acetic acid in it, nor did his family and friends, who came to help him with the *vendange*, want to spend days picking out and throwing away all the grapes that were *piqués* (pricked). They threw out the worst, leaving the bunches along the middle of the alleys between the rows of vines and carted away the rest in a score or so of plastic bins loaded on a homemade trailer and pulled by one of Bernard's enormous tractors.

The following spring I was invited to taste the wine. Papy led me into a small dark shed in which crouched half a dozen blackened old barrels and several hundred empty bottles in grubby piles. He picked up two glasses from somewhere in the gloom and a short length of hosepipe, one end of which he lowered into the nearest barrel. Then, stooping painfully (he is one of Monsieur Boisseau's better customers), to ensure that the siphon worked, he sucked, clamped his thumb over the end of the pipe and spat abundantly onto the earth floor. He gestured for my glass, removed his thumb from the pipe and filled the glass to the brim with, I have to admit it, wine of a glorious, deep golden colour. Its colour was its only glory. The overriding flavour was of honey; honey and bad wine. For that is what it was. Picked too late and made without the benefit of laboratory supervision, it never had a chance, but Papy was quite happy with it, while admitting freely that it was *piqué*. He claimed the honey was, '*Une astuce des vieux*. The only way to cover up the vinegar in the grapes.'

I reckon there are other things which would cover it up just as well, for example marmite or hot mango chutney, and I doubt if the result would be any more disagreeable. I learned later that the use of honey *is* occasionally recommended for Sauternes that is thin and 'green', that is made from grapes which are not ripe enough, but the dose is 1 kilogram per 10 hectolitres (1,000 litres) and the objective is just to round out the wine slightly and smooth away the hardness. There is no question of being able to taste honey. Papy used, I guess, at least 10 kilograms of honey per barrel, or nearly fifty times the recommended maximum dose.

I asked the Great Master, my Oenologue-Conseil, the omniscient Henri Ducourneau, if the practice of adding honey was legal. After a split-second hesitation the reply came back, 'Put it like this: it is not a matter that figures in the text of the regulations.'

I know that it works because I have tried it under his directions. Papy Dartigues promised me a couple of bottles of his preparation when it had passed through another winter and was ready for the *mise en bouteille*. I got them, complete with fruit fly cocoons *inside* the bottles, a fitting testimony, we thought, to the origin and history of this wine. The year that had elapsed between tasting it from the barrel and tasting it from the bottle had done nothing to improve it and I am afraid we poured it down the sink. I had sworn a great oath after the first tasting that I would do better than that in 1987.

8

The State of Play

We were beginning to get used to our new surroundings by now and there were fewer surprises to be encountered each day. The children were more or less integrated at school, with their fellows at least, if not entirely with the schoolwork. The restaurant was open and running, although 'sauntering' would be a more accurate description of its level of activity. We had several months in which to consider the proper treatment of the vineyard and we had found Alex, an energetic English girl who lived near Barsac. She helped with the hotel rooms, the ironing, decorating—there was a lot of this—and she brought her 6-foot-6-inch boyfriend, together with his 6-foot-5-inch brother to build and repair things for us. Pirrin and Wally had worked for Mr Jenkin-Lee and were another example of the useful contacts he had given us. Other left-overs of his presence were less welcome, like the stream of creditors who came searching for him throughout the summer, now happily dwindling to a trickle, and the reputation of Commarque that he had left behind. The first time Pirrin went to buy building materials the reaction of the builders' merchants was all too clear: 'We're not having anything to do with Commarque. They're all crooks over there.'

They took some persuading, too, that I was not Mr Jenkin-Lee and that not all the British behaved like him!

We were then less preoccupied by novelties, had organised something like a routine, and, as autumn merged gently into a winter that seemed to us more like an average English September, we had a chance to consider the question: 'Do we like it here?'

It was a premature question. Given the enormous number of problems still to be overcome no one could have exactly liked our situation, so we rephrased it, 'Are we *going* to like it here?'

The answer was equivocal but the chances of weighting it in favour of 'yes' seemed, well, not bad even if the list of reservations we could write was long. Georgea, sounding a bit like an estate agent, put the plus side of it like this: 'I recommend Château de Commarque to any woman who would like a magnificent, rural château, with no visible neighbours, and wonderful views over pine forests and the rolling vineyards of the Sauternais, an isolated existence, during which you may see no one you know for days on end and have little to do with those invisible neighbours, a spacious house with infinite possibilities for trying out your decorating skills, as much gardening—lawns, flowers, shrubs, vegetables, vines and more vines—as you want and the pleasing twin status of *patronne* and château owner.'

Many would say, 'I'll take it.' But estate agents paint the best picture they can and we all know there is always more to it than they have let on!

The overriding memory of that first summer is of harassment, heat and optimism, in descending order of importance. Among the things we had not expected and not enjoyed was mopping up the house and hotel after the violent thunderstorms that blew in from the west, bent the Wellingtonia into a creaking, groaning bow shooting small branches and pine needles over a hundred metre radius, and then burst in a deluge of rain that would turn the courtyard into a lake within minutes and pass straight through the back windows of the house. To cap it all, the electricity usually failed.

Storms are more frequent in some years than others and I have the abiding impression that we were particularly badly hit during our first two years here. This could just be because of their shock value to us novices and the unreadiness not only of ourselves, but also of our somewhat dilapidated roofs to withstand them. I have to admit that 'somewhere in Sauternes' there stands an abandoned building, the roof of which has sacrificed itself unselfishly over the years in the interests of protecting us, our customers and our wine barrels. The strength and destructive force of the wind is impressive, not to say frightening. We have had all five children in bed with us when a storm has struck at night and the house has shaken with the force of it. Once we thought the roof would lift off and that night it must actually have risen and then settled again on the gatehouse gîte because the elderly English couple staying in it were subjected to a dense flurry of leaves blowing through the room as a particularly violent gust caused the building to shudder. That night they clearly heard the crack of the breaking pine tree, the one outside the courtyard that snapped off cleanly at roof height and was removed from the vines in the morning by Bernard and his men.

After storms like this a whole day can be spent drying floors, retrieving garden furniture and scraping up fallen leaves and branches, just to return to where we were twenty-four hours previously. There have been cheering occasions when hotel guests have turned out to help and I can remember sheltering under the front arch and seeing, with every lightning flash, the row of hotel rooms opposite vividly lit up, the occupants seated comfortably in their open doorways, east facing of course, so sheltered from the rain, admiring the firework display. There was even a ragged cheer, feebly audible between the rolls of thunder, for a particularly close strike.

Some years later Sauternes' all-time record storm left us surprisingly dry, and undamaged if you do not count the odd tree blown over and the swimming pool filled with leaves and branches. It caught us napping by coming from the wrong direction, driving out of the east one early evening. For two hours it raged, returning again and again just as the colour of the sky, changing each time from purplish blue to a dirty yellow grey, appeared to be announcing its departure to the northwest. In those two hours 112 millimetres of rain fell, double the average for the entire month of August and equivalent to 560 tons of water falling on a football pitch. The commune of Sauternes itself, a little over 2,500 acres, soaked up 1.3 million tons of water that evening, or if you prefer it—a cube of water 100 metres long, 100 metres wide and 113 metres high! Deep ravines appeared in the soil, the roads were blocked with mud and water, trees were down all over the place—but luckily for the vines there was no hail.

At Commarque the rain swept under the front door of the house at such speed that three people only just managed to keep it from spreading through the entire ground floor. Georgea's sister Wendy and her husband were having a rude introduction to their summer holiday in sunny France.

The roofs, on the other hand, withstood the battering surprisingly well, showing that the 'Other Roof' had not been pillaged in vain. The hotel was full and on a visit to the restaurant, where dinner was in full swing despite the violence outside, I learned that one customer, newly arrived, was making an awful fuss. He was complaining about huge puddles in his room and was very upset. Before going to his rescue I glanced into the restaurant which seemed well filled with people dining tranquilly in the candle-lit gloom—there was no electricity of course—while Georgea and Gilles the cook rushed round the equally gloomy kitchen and peered into the dark interiors of the ovens, trying to ensure that the right ingredients ended up in the right recipients. Fortunately, the cookers are gas not electric. I squelched out into the storm with Wendy to see to our disgruntled customer and we found him in the middle of his room with a rolled umbrella held in front of him for some reason, pointing at a puddle not 15 inches across, spreading from the doormat across the tiled floor. Was the bedroom soaked? Did he need new bedding or a change of mattress? Were his things ruined? Where was the major problem? It was there before us, none other than the small puddle. While Sauternes suffered the greatest deluge in its history, Monsieur Brenzi, who presumably lived safely sheltered from the elements in the middle of a giant block of flats, was saved from the carnage of his room by Wendy, armed with a couple of small towels.

Most customers are not like him, but the constant presence of people one did not know was another thing that took some getting used to. They were to be found in some odd places. One morning I returned from the baker's to find Francis, still in his pyjamas, playing snooker with a total stranger, similarly clad. Another day Georgea came into the kitchen to find a lady helping herself to the remains of our breakfast. She had emerged from her room, gone the wrong way, wandered into the house and found what looked like an open invitation to a self-service breakfast, a pretty scruffy one at that! Then there was the German lady dressed in a swimming costume I found sunbathing in the middle of the flower bed at the end of the house, not to mention the middle-aged English couple who sat in the vines, in the burning afternoon sun, reading poetry to one another.

The worst encounter was with the laundry. At that time we had just five hotel rooms; there were also the two gîtes but they didn't count because the people who stayed in them had to provide their own sheets and towels. If all five rooms are booked and the guests stay only one night, that means ten large towels, ten small towels, six double sheets, eight single sheets, twenty pillowcases, five shower curtains and five bath mats, all of which have to be crammed into one domestic washing machine the next day, then hung out to dry on the 150 metres of clothes line I had constructed. They are easily filled. If there is a thunderstorm, by the way, all this washing has to be retrieved from the prickly acacias, the brambles and even the vineyard. This operation may have to be repeated the following day and the day after that. It frequently was, because most of our guests at that time had not reserved in advance, not knowing of our existence, and were only stopping here en route to somewhere else. This can mean up to 300 items to iron each week! The enormity of this task, especially when mixed up with many others, and its relentless repetitiveness, induced in Georgea, she now admits, a profound sinking feeling.

It took a year or so to develop a clientele of visitors who came because they actually wanted to stay at Commarque and so remained here for several nights, to the relief of the laundry system.

What we had most enjoyed since arriving was the continuous stream of family and friends anxious to see where the Reay-Jones had landed themselves, often making astonishing diversions for the sake of visiting us. Thus Cesco and Bridgie, our almost-partners in a vineyard, who have strong family ties with Cesco's parents' native village in northern Italy, redesigned the route from Colchester to Bardi to include Sauternes and have taken this immense loop nearly every year since. Georgea's parents had never crossed the channel together and her father had only ever done it the once, on a certain memorable June day in 1944, but holiday journeys to Scotland quickly turned through 180 degrees and ended in Sauternes. There were friends from Charlbury and colleagues from work, together with my 'assistant' Stephen, and Georgea's 'assistant' Helen, who had come to help with the children and learn some French. What enormous meals we had! There were usually at least twelve of us, hard work to feed, but maintaining an irresistible holiday feel, even on the hardest of hard-working days. There were enough people here for a hotel without even counting the real hotel! But they came and they returned to Britain while we stayed. By the beginning of October they had all gone. Even Helen and Stephen had left to start their careers and it dawned on us that we had not really met anyone yet except in the course of business. What was missing was a bit of social life. We began to listen enviously to Alex's accounts, over the ironing, of weekend trips to stay with friends in the Dordogne, parties in the Pyrenees or even nights spent in the bar at Villandraut, when Wally would drink quietly and steadily until he rolled off his stool, was bundled into the car and taken home by the back roads to avoid the *flics* (cops). It never seemed to diminish the energy he devoted to shovelling cement the next day!

We had quite literally no time now to go out and meet people and, so far, people had not come to us. It is true that the people of Sauternes are not of the type to embrace outsiders with open arms—but come to that, why should they? Monsieur Boisseau the Chemist remarked that it took him and his wife years to be accepted, despite having a job that places him squarely at the heart of the community. He reckons this is because Madame Boisseau was born 50 kilometres away. What chance then did we have, members of the ancient enemy race?

Not surprisingly, our first social contacts came via the children who had made friends, visited their houses and met their parents while we had done no more than say *bonjour* and *bonsoir* at the school gate. People were kind to the children who had quite definitely caused more of a ripple in the community than we had!

There was a good cross-section at the school, despite a memorable remark made by the president of the Sauternes Wine Syndicate when Madame Guicheney had asked for financial help to send the children on a week's Classe de Neige in the Pyrenees. His reply was that he 'could not see the use of paying for vineyard workers' brats to learn to ski'!

It would appear that not all French men and women have digested the lessons of the Revolution. The president of the syndicate is obviously not strong on either *égalité* or *fraternité*, but is quite happy to exploit the existence of enough *liberté* to get away with such feudal utterances. It is wrong, then, to think that everyone like him lost their heads in 1789. If Madame Daubech, the doctor's wife, had had her way Monsieur Lamothe would have been guillotined outside the Mairie that very evening, immediately after the meeting about the Classe de Neige which had echoed with her loud disapproval. Madame Guicheney had not wanted to pass on the remark, saying that it was *trop bête* to be repeated, but she was pressed hard to do so and I thought she sounded glad to unburden herself. In the end she got the required finance from the Mairie. Monsieur le Maire, the Marquis de Lur Saluces, whose family presumably had had a few *ennuis* during the Reign of Terror, thus proved himself to be more fully imbued with Revolutionary spirit than that miserable commoner the president of the syndicate! So the children of Sauternes got their Classe de Neige and ours had their very first skiing lessons.

Among the parents at the school was a bilingual, globe-trotting couple who, by virtue of their fluent English and a generous spirit, had become sort of liaison officers between us and the school. Through them we learned how to get lunch tickets, when school meetings were taking place, how to participate in the canteen supervision rota and so on, and they also helped our halting conversations with Monsieur Desautel and Madame Guicheney. Then they invited us to a musical soirée, our first invitation into a French household since arriving. Delight, however, was tempered by apprehension. They had 'heard' that we played the classical guitar. We would, of course, bring our instruments and play for the company. Everyone would be doing a 'turn'. Georgea and I had first met playing duets on the guitar, but while Georgea had been a peripatetic music teacher up until leaving England, I had hardly played since the children started to appear in numbers, and we had certainly not had time to play together for years. But the soirée was weeks away so we had time to prepare for it.

Wait though!

Could we really leave the children and the château for a whole evening?

The organisational feat needed seemed insurmountable, even though we were only slipping over to Bommes, 3 or 4 kilometres away, and only for three or four hours. But the château is large and isolated, the children are small and, above all, we have not done it before.

When Marc heard about it he was adamant! Of course, we must go! It was a great opportunity and, 'I will look after everything for you. Alex can baby-sit, *bien sûr*, and why not try out your guitar pieces on me? I have an excellent ear.'

Helpful and ever modest Marc!

So we accepted the invitation and set to work to coax stiffened fingers into at least temporary mobility. Some progress was made but Marc said, trying to be kind, that we sounded like good players who were out of practice. With our confidence duly undermined by this muted endorsement of our skills, we turned up for the soirée and were quickly reduced to abject terror!

The place was packed with people, all of whom knew each other well and all of whom were deeply engrossed in conversation. The resulting hubbub, in French, made it doubly difficult to understand what any of the couples to whom we were introduced actually said to us. We had just spotted the Daubechs (oh the relief of a familiar face!) across the room when a tall black man, holding a flute, stood up and beckoned to a fellow wearing a boater adorned with a brightly coloured ribbon. Together they picked their way through the company in the direction of a piano in one corner of the room, at which the man in the boater sat himself down. Without further ado they started to play the 'One Note Samba'. They were brilliant! They had that ability to combine precise, infectious rhythm with a sense of lazy drift that gives so much more to the music than mere accuracy and is usually the preserve of professionals—and we were going to have to follow them!

The One Note Samba came to an end, there was applause and the pianist played again, with equal panache, and then gave up his place to someone else. We were introduced to him, Jean-Bernard Bravo, of the family that owns the Grand Cru Barsac vineyard Château Caillou. He spoke English to us and was very friendly. We learned that, despite the quality of his piano playing, he was unable to read a note of music but had what he called a 'reasonable ear' which, we found out later in the evening, meant that he could play anything perfectly almost before he had heard it all, embellish it, play variations on it, turn it upside down–and all without the slightest apparent effort. He also let on that he played the guitar. Oh dear! And it was our turn soon.

We played! We played quite badly, but were politely applauded and told we must play again later. We managed to avoid this, which was just as well for we had exhausted our little repertoire of rehearsed pieces the first time round. One small pointer that we may have made some sort of impression was that Jean-Bernard's guitar remained firmly in its case for the evening!

None of this has to do with what was, for us, the most riveting aspect of that soirée: we were learning what it meant to spend an evening partying with vineyard owners! While the buffet dinner was splendid, although neither of us remember much about it, the wine-tasting which preceded, accompanied and followed it, was mind blowing.

Shortly after we arrived bottles had started to pass through the house and they had kept on coming, dozens and dozens of them. Their destination was a table, or rather two, joined together to make a 3-metre-long surface, now rapidly filling from end to end. Some of the bottles were empty, which was mystifying, until carefully packed boxes of stoppered carafes were placed beside them. Each carafe bore a label round its neck with a date, and each was placed beside an empty bottle. Georgea got a brief look at one before being borne away to meet someone. It said Château Caillou 1949. We thought we could fancy a bit of that before we had to play, but these were surprisingly self-disciplined people, music first, booze afterwards—and what booze! Two vineyards were represented that night, both Barsacs, apart from Caillou there was Château Mont-Joye, the owners of which were relatives of our hosts.

This was 1986 so we started with the most recently bottled decent year: 1983, delicious; slipped rapidly through the indifferent seventies, stopping only for a 1976, voluptuous, and got into something a little more mature: 1967, splendid, and 1962, the Mont-Joye showing signs of fatigue here! The fifties were represented by 1959 and 1953, magnificent. Then we stopped to eat, being offered 'only' 1949 and 1947 with the meal, plus several red wines of which I have not the slightest recollection. The pre-war vintages were reserved for after dinner and at this point words fail me. I seem to think we got as far back as 1928 but I cannot be sure, and Georgea says things had become pretty hazy long before that.

We left as Jean-Bernard started to play the piano again and two distinct, but both quite heated, discussions on the relative merits of different vintages were developing at opposite ends of the room. It was now 1.30 am. We were incapable of drinking another drop, let alone finding the strings on our guitars. There was Alex to relieve in the house and work the following morning, Sunday being the busiest day of the week if you have a hotel and restaurant. The rest of the guests looked fit to go on until daybreak and I gather they did.

Two weeks later we invited the de Pinoses to dinner but the invitation was refused, 'Eric travels so much that when he is here at weekends we make a point of never leaving the house.'

Nothing else followed from that extraordinary musico-vinous soirée and the hoped for *décollage* of our social life did not materialise that winter.

* * *

The answer to that question, posed at the beginning of this chapter: 'Are we going to like it here?' was in reality more equivocal than I have let on. I have not told the whole truth. I have joked my way round storms, odd people in odd places, and the laundry, not to mention relative social isolation. But if you like the place, the environment, the *gist*, none of this is more than incidental, the mere periphery of a life which could still be full, satisfying and enjoyable—if we had been the right sort of people to make it so. There were, however, disturbing signs that we might not be, although neither of us would have put it clearly yet, especially me. Georgea had already had a premonition, three weeks after arriving, being naturally more perceptive than I am, and more homesick than I was: 'This place is not right. We shouldn't be here. I don't like it.'

Surely you can't get much clearer than that? Some premonition! But perhaps it was just a reaction to leaving England, I reasoned with her. She admitted to homesickness, to culture shock, to disliking the house, so much tattier and more crumbly looking now that Mr Jenkin-Lee's handsome and suitable furniture had been removed.

'I know it sounds silly but I had this picture of being absorbed into French life and it isn't happening,' she said.

'It *will* happen,' I replied. 'Give it a chance. We've got masses of problems to iron out. When the place is up and running properly then we'll get into French life!'

Georgea agreed with her brain, but not with the rest of her. 'I suppose you're right,' she said. Meaning: *I cannot think of any convincing argument to contradict you, but I think you are wrong.*

I would have worried about this more if I hadn't been working so hard to get 'up and running', and even Georgea was swept along. Swept along is, I suppose, what has mainly happened to us!

She has since said: 'I think I realised that it wasn't going to be fun and all along I had imagined it would be. Everything was so complicated. I remember the bath blocking up and it wasn't like in England when you called the plumber if you couldn't fix it in ten minutes and *he* fixed it in ten minutes. It required a digger, new drains, tons of gravel and several days' work. Everything was so gonky. Everything had been so badly done that it was permanently teetering on the edge of collapse.'

Once again, we are circling the problem by alighting on a relatively trivial incident. Of course, one could ride this. We are not as drippy as all that! The real problem was that *everything* was a problem that had to be ridden. We became experts at teetering on the edge. The place needed doing up from top to bottom but we hadn't the money to do it, so we teetered. Hard work, which we didn't mind at all, was accompanied by a permanent condition of anxiety, which we did mind a great deal.

There was an incident towards the end of August which caused an argument between us. An enormous silver Mercedes with Austrian number plates drove into the courtyard and two enormous men got out of it. The smaller and less imposing one walked towards the house while the other lit a cigar and looked round the courtyard with an air of calculating condescension. I went out through the front door to meet the man.

'I am the legal adviser of Herr Gunther Müller of the Austrian wine house Müller. Herr Müller,' and he nodded in the direction of the other man, 'is deeply interested in this property and would like to buy it.'

'But I've only just come here,' I replied. 'The property is not for sale.'

The enormous Austrian was taken aback. He had mistaken me for Mr Jenkin-Lee and had not heard that Commarque had finally been signed for by us. Herr Müller strolled over and leaned over me in a cigary and ever-so-slightly menacing greeting. This was plainly a man of substance, the sort of person Nick Ryman had had in mind when I spoke to him for the very first time, the sort of person who *should* have bought Château de Commarque. The situation was explained to him.

'Wouldn't you like to change your mind and go back to England? I've had my eye on this place for some time. I'll buy it from you for whatever you paid for it.'

The tone of voice demanded the addition of 'little man' to the sentence; his manner was, to say the least, ill-chosen if he was opening negotiations and I bristled. Of course I wasn't going to sell out to this condescending mountain who appeared to assume so naturally that I would do his bidding. Anyway, if he had wanted Commarque for some time why hadn't he been here sooner? The place had been on the market for long enough, even after we had become involved in it. I concluded he was after a bargain. He had expected to find a desperate Mr Jenkin-Lee still in residence and had not had the presence of mind to shift his bargaining position when he had found me instead; or perhaps he was just trying his luck.

Had he suggested: 'I will pay half a million francs more than you paid for it', then he *might* have got a foot in the door. He definitely would have if he had been talking to Georgea. She said I had thrown away our chance to get out before it was too late. I pointed out that if Herr Müller bought Commarque *we* wouldn't get the money, Mr Jenkin-Lee would. There would be no job to go back to in England and not enough money to buy a house without the mortgage we would not now be able to get. We had properly burned our boats! Anyway things would get better here ... we couldn't throw in the towel already; we must pursue our new life. I kept quiet about the abysmal loss of face that would follow such a lightning capitulation. Georgea responded with impeccable logic that if we were going to get out it would be easier now than later. She preferred to go back to utter penury in England. She was upset. We were both upset. It was obvious I was keener on the whole affair than she was and our difference remained unresolved. I kept the card proffered by Herr Müller's lawyer and Georgea kept her point of view, while throwing herself heart and soul into the effort to make Commarque work. She was to say later, even years later, when things were particularly bad, 'I told you we should have got out at the start.'

But she accepts also that we were bound to do this foolhardy thing, that it is, has been, not all bad, that staying in England might have been an even worse option—but it's not even worth speculating on that—and Herr Müller never came back with a better proposition.

Georgea has never been too keen on spare time, the time to sit and think about where she is and what she is doing. Fortunately she doesn't get much. We are driven by exhaustion to relax for an hour or two in the afternoon during the summer season. We sit behind the Wellingtonia in our 'decliners', reclining chairs in which we will pass our declining years. This is enjoyable, but we always have to keep an eye on arrivals, to listen for the ringing of the bell in the restaurant. None of this is exactly part of the original scheme, but one gets used to things.

You certainly find out about yourself, doing something like this. To be a hotelier you need to like having people around; lots of people. You need to want to go out to them, to be interested in them. We didn't. We discovered we were rather private people and not very warm and outgoing. I don't mean we didn't care what happened to our customers. On the contrary! We worried over them excessively, minded that they were comfortable, liked it here, liked the food and wanted to stay. We worried over them, and then resented worrying. Georgea accused me, with justice, of being more concerned with *them* and *their* comfort than with us and ours. I suspect lots of hoteliers don't much like their guests and I have some sympathy with sour-faced, miserable hotel staff. They're in the wrong job! Mind you, most of our customers were, and are, very nice and one sees them at their best: relaxed, enjoying themselves. Commarque is a place for a holiday, not a businessman's stopover hotel. There are people whose annual visits we positively look forward to, but occasionally, inevitably, someone disagreeable turns up and they are right there in your home ... there's no question of locking the door of your office and turning your back on them, shutting them out of your life until tomorrow. They'll be there this evening and tonight and first thing in the morning.

But *we* chose to do this and aren't we lucky to live in such a place? Lucky, indeed, to have a roof over our heads when many don't?

9

The Final Purchase

Marc had not been unduly disturbed by customers during our big night out and they had been dwindling from the third week of October onwards, as the temperature began to fall together with the leaves on the plane trees in the courtyard. We were learning the lesson that people do not come to you just because you are there! An effort would have to be made to entice customers down the bumpy track, especially local ones who would continue to have grave doubts about Commarque unless given good reasons not to do so. Mr Jenkin-Lee's reputation lived on, and there is always the more general suspicion, among the French, regarding the ability of the British to run a restaurant.

We had taken steps to try and attract people's attention by advertising in local papers. At first we had followed Mr Jenkin-Lee's advice to stress 'reopening', so as to be sure of getting back all those old customers of his who were just panting for a chance to eat at Commarque again. When that had failed to produce the hoped-for deluge of people, we changed the format. But we stopped that too when it became obvious that we were just flinging money into the wintry grey, and should be concentrating our attention on next spring instead. With this in mind we took out costly advertisements in a variety of publications, all of which were abandoned a year later when their lack of effect had become apparent.

There were periodicals sent to, or bought by, just the kind of couple (we were always assured) who would be bound to want to come to Commarque. So there were magazines for doctors, lawyers, businessmen and the electricity board; there were others that would be found in every office in Bordeaux, or targeted the organisers of company outings, went to bus tour operators throughout Southwest France, or even reached every rich old lady with nothing to do.

Then there were those publications which took the form of guides, not to be confused with 'real' guides like the Michelin, Gault et Millau or

Champérard. Some of them are produced under the aegis of the Tourist Office of the Gironde or other reputable and respected bodies. Others are just bits of private enterprise. So there is everything from 'the Restaurants of our Region' to the Guide Motard, produced for motorcyclists from Bordeaux to have nice days out in the countryside.

The trouble with the magazines is that many are little more than waiting room bin-fodder, and in any case the advertisements are often totally incidental to the main subject matter. They are, therefore, even less likely to be read than the articles. It is one thing to advertise wine in a wine magazine, quite another to advertise a hotel-restaurant in the '*Poodle Fancier's Monthly Gazette*'.

The trouble with the 'guide' type of publication is that there are just too many of them. The respectable examples, the officially backed ones, usually have free entries, sometimes with the option of an advertising slot, for which you pay. They are often distributed free. Others are not and one needs to ask how many are being printed, how are they going to be distributed and are they likely to be read? I have decided, after years of rueful and expensive study, that the answers are not enough, badly and no. But you have to try something and anyway, hadn't we better be in this one? Look, everyone else is! So you place your advert, for F3,000, and at the end of the year you have no clear evidence that *anyone* has come your way because of this expenditure—despite all the assurances of the sales rep about how long people keep their rotten rag, how long they will remember the impact of your wonderful advert, and how many of their friends they are going to tell about it. Things reached such a point of disillusion that we developed a technique of repelling the more persistent reps by asking them to work out how many extra customers were needed to pay for an advert of, say, F3,000 (they can be much more!), all eating a menu at F125. Taking into account the fixed costs, the answer is surprising and unlikely ever to be realised. Even the officially backed guides, produced in enormous numbers, suffer from the drawback that many are picked up by passing tourists one day and dropped in the bin the next, when they leave the region. Even if they have read the thing from cover to cover, how many of the fifteen restaurants listed in the Sauternes/Langon area can they visit in twenty-four hours, or even a week? Disillusion was complete when the wonderfully smart, confidentially flattering and permanently ego-boosting lady who flogged advertising space in none other than 'the Restaurants of Our Region', published in five languages, which was costing us F4,500 a year, turned up in August with her car boot stuffed with copies. They are normally sold for F20 each, but she was offering me a hundred, or two hundred if I liked, to give away in the restaurant. We didn't bother to point out that if someone had turned up because of her guide, they were hardly likely to want another one; and if they hadn't, we weren't interested in promoting our competitors. The guides went in the bin. I fear this is where most of them belong. Then there are the 'real' guides. I wrote to some of them but these are cautious people. They test discretely, they store letters of recommendation, they move in mysterious ways and they take time. Not so if you are a 'Well Known Chef', or have run a 'Beautiful Mountain Retreat' in the Rockies; open your resto in Paris or country hotel in Sauternes and they are on to you in a flash. But a pair of greenhorns fresh out of England, unknown and untrained are, justifiably, treated with suspicion and either rejected out of hand (Bottin Gourmand) or scrutinised at length (Michelin). So for 1987 we did not figure in any real guides.

It may be concluded that in establishing a clientele, as in many other aspects of life and business at Commarque, we were novices. The wisdom of hindsight suggests that incompetence in this area has cost us dear. The essence of bad business is tapped when the fundamentally important is permanently obscured by the immediately essential. The former, in our case, was marketing, which should have occupied much of my time—although at that stage I barely knew what it was I was trying to market! I am not naturally suited to this and realised later that I didn't much like doing it. By embracing the immediate essential there was ample opportunity to avoid the marketing, without even noticing I was doing so. In 1986 and 1987, that meant the scramble to get started. Later, it meant serving breakfast, followed by shopping, writing up the accounts books, seeing to Monsieur Saint-Martin, receiving guests, writing letters, receiving more guests, repairing the shower in room three, washing up in the restaurant etc.

What about the winter? Well there was making the wine, treating the wine, dealing with the vineyard, doing the accounts, writing letters, the need for permanent readiness in case someone turned up…. There really wasn't enough of Georgea and me to go round and not enough money to pay for extra hands and brains. This suited my weakness, excused that fatal business flaw! How could I go off for a whole day to visit all the bus companies in Bordeaux when there was so much to do at Commarque? This wasn't Georgea's patch either; looking after five children is enough of a job for most people. She came to have, in addition, a full-time job as a cook, a part-time job as a vineyard worker, and occasional jobs as receptionist, *femme de chambres*, accounting clerk and gardener ... anyway, she didn't much fancy marketing either.

* * *

We said a reluctant good-bye to Maïté at the end of October. There were not enough customers now to justify paying two people to look after them and her original contract had been for just one month, a sort of 'wait-and-see-what happens' contract. She had something lined up for the expected non-renewal and her departure meant one less mouth for Georgea to feed. How, one may well ask, does Georgea come to be feeding the waitress? The answer is by another *bêtise* that we managed to commit during that first 'season'.

In an effort to be sociable, we had invited Marc and Maïté to eat with us once or twice before the evening service. Once or twice had become several times a week and then slipped unnoticed into a daily habit. So Georgea's ingenuity was exercised in devising dishes that would please on the one hand five small English boys, whose preferred food was sausage and chips, tinned spaghetti and roasts, and on the other hand two French adults, both professionals in the catering trade. Quite a feat it was! But she managed it, at the cost of more deadlines to meet—the restaurant opens at 7.30 pm, therefore supper must always be on the table at 6.30. It eventually dawned on Georgea that she was cooking for more people than Marc and Maïté were paid to look after. At this point she asked herself, then me, the reasonable question: 'Why am I cooking for the cook? Shouldn't he be cooking for me?'

Well he did, occasionally, but from the children's point of view he started with the severe handicap of having that nettle soup to his account, so his offerings were automatically regarded with deep suspicion, especially by Francis who often preferred to stick to bread and yoghurt, rather than risk another nettle soup catastrophe. Marc's only success was his deliciously unhealthy *Pommes Forestières*: potatoes fried in duck fat with bacon, mushrooms and herbs, but Francis would carefully pick out all the pieces of mushroom before eating the other ingredients, so, on the whole, it was better to leave Georgea to keep the culinary peace.

The last straw was laid on her shoulders when Marc strolled across the courtyard at 6.30 one evening, got his feet comfortably under the table as usual, and then told us all about his restful holidays with his daughter and her husband and how the thing he liked best was, 'Just being able to put my feet under the table and be served my meals, without having to lift a finger.'

He never knew how close he came to getting a full bowl of good Scotch Broth on his head that evening! Shortly after that the practice of cooking for the cook came to an end but, it has to be admitted, those Gauloise-scented meals were good for our French and that of the children. Marc took our education in this area quite seriously and was never so happy as when correcting our numerous faults. The only exchange I remember, however, was in English, between Maïté and William, always a sociable little boy. Maïté looked at William one evening as he tucked hungrily into his meal and said: 'Weelyam, beeg peeg!'

William glanced at Maïte's ample plateful and replied unhesitatingly, 'My-Eater, big eater!'

The puzzled looks which accompanied our howls of laughter cleared slowly and without conviction as we tried to explain what was so funny. With the departure of Maïté, Marc took over the waiting in the restaurant as well as doing the cooking. At least that was the idea; his idea. He had explained at great length how straightforward it was to cook and serve up to five or six tables and that, as he had great experience as a waiter, it would be especially easy for *him*. At this point legends of Wagnerian dimensions were forthcoming about what Marc could deal with alone on the waiting front. We were given to understand that if we had had a queue from the door of the restaurant to the end of the vines, Marc would have had everyone seated and served before you could say *Foie Gras*. In the event he burnt things when talking to the customers, at which he had real talent, and failed to serve the wine, or forgot the bread, when cooking. So for those uncommon occasions, such as Sunday lunchtime, when we had more than one or two tables, I was taught by Marc the rudiments of waiting and took my place, where I should have been from the start, in the *salle*, as *le patron*. It was to be a year before Georgea took *her* place before the ovens as *la patronne*, thus leaving, as may be easily calculated, no place for Marc.

He was perhaps best at teaching grammar and was very helpful to Thomas, who needed to polish his French more rapidly than the others because of his scheduled ascendance into *collège* (secondary school). Marc had him down in the restaurant kitchen during school holidays and at weekends and as he did his work he gave Thomas a complete course in the conjugation of verbs, the use of pronouns and articles and those other fundamentals of French which seem so complicated and rigid to us with our hazy ideas and dim memories of the structure of our own language.

One day Thomas told Monsieur Desautel that he knew the subjunctive off by heart, to which Monsieur Desautel replied rather sniffily, '*C'est très bien*, but you need to learn when to use it as well.'

Thomas retorted, probably rather cheekily if the truth were known, that he had learnt when to use it, upon which Monsieur Desautel, put out that someone other than himself was acting as *meneur du jeu*, proceeded to cross-examine him. Thomas got it all right, he says, and Monsieur Desautel, now thoroughly out of countenance, muttered that 'he thought he wouldn't bother so much from now on as there was so much private teaching to be found in Sauternes'.

* * *

Over the other side of the Entre-Deux-Mers the Notary's clerk was putting the final touches to the *actes* of purchase of the château. At the same time, the company that was to do the purchasing, the Société Civile Immobilière Château de Commarque, was emerging from a dimly understood (by me anyway) nebulosity of papers and legal publications. A second company, a S.A.R.L. ('Société à Responsabilité Limité'), was also being set up to run the hotel, restaurant and vineyard. These two companies have always remained, to me, somewhat nebulous and cumbersome, especially given the modest scale of our operations. It cost good money to set them up and it costs too much to keep them running, both in time and money, and the detailed accounting required puts a serious strain on our organisational resources. It was not our idea to create companies. We were obliged to do so by the *Conseils Juridiques* (sort of inferior notaries) who advised the English lenders. They had not worried about it until these advisers brought it up and all *they* wanted were the fees for doing the work. As soon as the paperwork was finalised and the statutes were published, the tax authorities announced they could not countenance a S.A.R.L. running the vineyard as well as the hotel and restaurant. So the vineyard had to be set up again in my own name, and a complete second set of papers was generated to ensure this new registration. Not to mention a second set of contributions for medical insurance, pension fund and so on, payable to the agricultural social security department—but paid with difficulty as there was no agricultural income with which to do it.

The main payments for the château came over from England, to be locked in the Notary's bank account until the signing of the *actes* was completed. At this point the full loss resulting from the slide in the pound was revealed. Our calculations had been based on getting 10.7 francs to the pound. We actually got 9.1 francs, and there went the new vine planting, extra hotel rooms, interest on the loans during the first winter and more or less everything else that might have ensured a smooth start to our activities. The prearranged number of pounds did not translate into enough francs even to buy the place, so I had to write a cheque on the French bank account to finish the deal. The bank was surprisingly generous in those early days!

The signing of the *actes* was scheduled the 23 December 1986 and I was to be accompanied by a representative of those Conseils Juridiques who looked after the interests of the English lenders. He was a fat lot of good. A slip of a boy who might just have completed his law degree, he announced, in answer to my question about what he was supposed to do, that he would have hard questions for the other party and would ensure that nothing was signed unless he was satisfied that my interests and those of his firm's clients were fully protected.

What baloney!

He was mainly interested in getting the thing finished in time to catch his flight back to Nice and was in a frightful twitch when the traffic round Bordeaux did what it usually does in the early evening, let alone during the week before Christmas, and ground to a halt a few miles the wrong side of the Pont d'Aquitaine, the bridge over the Garonne. We reached the airport eventually and my last view of him was as he pushed and struggled to get through the crowd at the entrance, about as effectively as he had struggled with Mr Jenkin-Lee's friend the Notary's Clerk that afternoon.

The hard questioning that had been promised lasted a full two minutes and was answered in a tone of amused tolerance, which should have infuriated my brave champion by its condescension had he not been more preoccupied with glancing at his watch. The conversation was conducted at breakneck speed and employed many unfamiliar words so I was unable to follow it, despite the progress in French which had been made since the summer. As for Mr Jenkin-Lee, he didn't even bother to listen. So the interminable reading of the *actes* continued until everyone in the room was yawning their head off and it was not only my Conseil Juridique who had his eye on the time.

I am not sure of the purpose of this ceremony. If it is to make certain that everyone has understood what they are about to initial on every page and sign here and there to boot, then speaking for myself, it was a dismal failure. It took some years to realise what useful, information-packed documents these *actes* are! It also took some years to realise how badly they had been drawn up and how much of the work which should have accompanied the signing had been left undone. So much for my legal defence. I should have taken Maître Allain with me, even if it had cost half the price of the château! It turned out that while enough money had passed through the Notary's bank balance to pay off Mr Jenkin-Lee's major debts, the Etude had not bothered to ensure the lifting (*la mainlevée*) of all the accompanying mortgages and *inscriptions de privilège* on the property.

I only discovered the truth from a friendly banker who had wanted to lend me some money to make new hotel rooms and now found himself, fidgeting with embarrassment, obliged to backpedal furiously on what he had more or less promised because of Château de Commarque's lavishly garnished extract from the Register of the Conservateur des Hypothèques (the Keeper of the Mortgages) in Bordeaux. I did not get my money and the unfortunate successor to the struck-off Notary across the Entre-deux-Mers, whose sole responsibility it was to sort out the mess, had a terrible time finding all those ex-creditors of Mr Jenkin-Lee and asking them if they would be so kind as to sign an *acte* de Mainlevée concerning a debt which they had long since forgotten and for which, in some cases, they could find no trace! One of the companies had even ceased to exist and their inscription still encumbers the château; fortunately it is only for the sum of F7,689.

On 23 December 1986 we were not worried about this sort of thing and I got home with my copy of the *actes*, all initialled and signed, and a detailed map of the property, an extract of the Plan Cadastral, which showed every nook and corner of ground that the S.C.I., of which I was proud manager, now owned. The following afternoon we set out to walk the boundary, first to check up on what we had got, and second because it was Christmas Eve, the children were as overexcited about Christmas as they had every right to be, and this seemed like an excellent way of filling their afternoon and of tiring them out before bedtime, so making Father Christmas's job a lot easier! Coats and boots were donned, Edward was perched on a shoulder and Thomas, as the eldest, took charge of the map.

William and Francis insisted that if the boundaries had to be walked then the boundaries must be followed exactly, brambles permitting, even those bits that we already knew off by heart, such as the vines to the right and left of the bumpy track and beyond the restaurant. The swimming pool vines do not touch any boundaries and therefore would not figure on our walk. So we began over by the woods at the corner of the restaurant vines because it was easy and would get us into the spirit of the thing. Then we started down the track towards the back gate, an ancient wrought iron affair with tall, rotted stone pillars, opening onto the bottom road to Bommes, beside the flat meadows of the Ciron valley. But instead of descending all the way to the gate, we turned right at the top of the steep slope and skirted the edge of Château Filhot's woods. There we found the tatty fence in the scrub and undergrowth which marks the boundary with our great neighbour and discovered that we had more land on the flat at the top of the slope than we had thought. A pause for contemplation followed as we stood and imagined this plateau and all the sloping ground down to the field, which Bernard had planted with winter barley, covered in vines, for this land is all in the Sauternes planting area. From this high vantage point, the view across the valley of the Ciron is immense. How vast this country is! On the opposite valley side Budos sits, a tall spire, the huge, ruined château, an ugly water tower, then wave upon wave of rolling pine forest to a far blue horizon in the north west, beyond which lies the city of Bordeaux. We saw clear across the Garonne valley to the high ground of the Entre-deux-Mers, visible only on a clear, clear day like Christmas Eve 1986.

At the end of our plateau-with-slope we turned down, following the fence and the line of tyres Bernard had put there for some purpose in the distant past, to the woods between the field and the road which proved to be impenetrable. This looked like *cèpes* country, but we would have to wait now until the following autumn to hunt for them. Along the bottom edge of the field then, with Edward—now happily self-propelled at ground level—and Robert balancing on the ridge of soil at the edge of the ploughed area of field, falling off regularly and squashing Bernard's little plants. The field comes to an end at the track down to the back gate and, to be thorough in our pursuit of the boundaries, we passed round the gate, easier than going through it, and along the road, carefully checking how far our land went. It ends just beyond the sandpit where we and half the commune of Sauternes take sand out of the bank for building. The hole has become enormous over the years, and I have had to refuse requests for several trailer loads from certain of the larger châteaux because the bank will certainly collapse and cause trees to fall if this hole continues to enlarge away from the road. A pause was taken here to allow the children a few minutes jumping into the hole, then a few minutes emptying their boots and brushing the sand off their socks.

We retraced our steps to the gate and started to skirt Bernard's boundary fence. This meant passing uphill towards the oak park behind the hotel and then turning right along a track which Mr Jenkin-Lee had intended as a back entrance for cars. Rally drivers would enjoy it, but not the rest of us. Eventually this track peters out by the bottom meadow, the one full of butterflies in early summer. So we had passed the house on our left, the swimming pool and the swimming pool vines, all on higher ground with that enticing plantable land between them and the track we had been following.

The meadow gave rise to lofty imaginings. I suggested, 'Two or three short golf holes here with tennis courts at the far end.'

William had a far more ambitious and comprehensive plan. 'What you should do here,' he declared, 'is cut all the grass and brambles and make a park like you find in England with benches and paths and big trees.'

I could almost see the bandstand in the middle. He went on: 'You can still have the tennis courts at the far end, a bigger swimming pool and mini-golf—and this end, why not fruit trees, so the people in the hotel can come and pick their own fruit?'

Why not indeed? It spread out in the mind's eye as easily as the vines had done half an hour earlier, but possibly without the mini-golf!

The southern edge of the meadow is marked by a continuous line of tall trees beneath which flows the little stream, the Ruisseau de Commarque, that makes our boundary. The children made a point of walking along the middle of this, as the true position of the boundary, all the way down to the lake which is more or less in line with the track which had led us to the meadow, but hidden behind trees in which the fascinating remains of an ancient mill lie damply hidden. They should really have crossed the lake as well, because the boundary does so, but it is far too deep and anyway there was more than one bootful of water by the time they had negotiated the swampy 'delta' of the Ruisseau and stood on the lake's edge. At this point, inevitably, Edward got stuck in the mud. He came out much more easily than his boots did, so while I carried him to solid ground, Thomas was delegated to rescue the red wellies peeping out of the weeds at the end of the Ruisseau. He approached them confidently, grasped one in each hand and pulled incautiously as hard as he could. The boots came free simultaneously with a sucking plop and Thomas sat down firmly in the mud, to the immense enjoyment of the rest of us. But when you are 11 years old and it is Christmas Eve, who cares about a muddy bottom?

The Ruisseau had now to be walked upstream, passing beyond the point where we had gained access to it, roughly in the middle of the meadow, to the far end where the tennis courts and mini-golf were scheduled for construction. There we landed on the far side and climbed the slope to Labouray, where our last half hectare of vines, plus a field and woods, are situated. We followed the fence to the road, turned left and left again to come into the vines at the far end, down to the bottom part of the field of lucerne rented by Papy Dartigues from the owner of the cottage beside our land. At the very bottom on the right we found a little parcel of land, shown on the map as ours, perhaps 20 metres square, surrounded by a hedge of brambles, which we did not even know existed; the perfect spot for a small house, with a view back across the valley, where the Ruisseau flows, to the main parcels of vines and the château!

We were coming to the end of the boundaries now as we descended once again to the Ruisseau, 'did' the end of the bottom meadow and came up the slope to the vines on the right of the track as you leave the château. For the sake of form we followed the boundary round them, crossed the track to take in the vines on the other side, thus bringing us back to where we had started, at the corner of the restaurant patch, over two hours previously. We had all thoroughly enjoyed ourselves and Edward was nearly asleep already as Thomas went off to change out of his mud-caked pants and trousers.

We had closed for Christmas several days earlier, having seen no one for a good week—and then wondered if we were doing the right thing when the telephone rang several times and people asked whether we were open on Christmas Day and if we had a special menu. But we had decided to be shut, and shut we have always been for Christmas. It was to be for the children. Throughout the rest of the year they have often taken second place to the restaurant and hotel. Many is the time Edward has been left sitting alone on his bed with his bedtime story open in front of him but no one to read it because we have been summoned by someone arriving, too many tables in the restaurant or whatever. His brothers were taught to replace us, but it is not the same.

So everything still shuts for Christmas and we always do the boundary walk on Christmas eve.

The scenery that presents itself has barely changed since that first circuit: the plantable slopes remain clothed in scrub, the butterfly meadow is still devoid of fruit trees, tennis courts or mini-golf but is perhaps richer than ever in butterflies because Papy Dartigues no longer cuts it for hay. None of the dreamed of changes have been made and one attraction has definitely gone downhill: the lake is heavily silted up, partly through development of a new water source by order of the local authority, which sent cascades of yellow, sand-laden and chlorine-stinking water racing down the Ruisseau de Commarque a few years ago, partly because a huge tree has fallen across the middle of it. We have been forced to concentrate on improving those assets we already had, rather than creating new ones as originally intended. In the new year of 1987, when winter struck with undreamt of intensity—we did not leave England for this!— we even came close to losing some of the assets we had.

10

The First Winter

Marc had gone to Saint-Jean-de-Luz to pass a feet-under-the-table Christmas with his daughter, but he came back in time for the New Year which, although taken very seriously by the French as a holiday, did not lead to an overwhelming deluge of customers. However, he had taken telephone calls, discussed menus earnestly, shown people the restaurant and generally dealt with a mild awakening of interest and some promises to return with the *beau temps* in the spring. So we were not discouraged, feeling that our publicity would bear fruit later in the year as people digested the name of Commarque and word of mouth began to spread that it was 'not too bad'. We banked the proceeds of the dozen covers we had served on New Year's Day and turned our attention, now that January was here, the truly dead, dead season, to the vineyard. Marc went off on holiday again as there was no point in keeping the restaurant open. Anyway, he'd had precious few days off—his idea not ours—and had already suggested that if he absented himself for the period of *plein hiver* (mid-winter) he would work non-stop when he was really needed later in the Year. None of us could have foreseen how long he was to be away and therefore how many days off he would owe us when he finally returned; enough, we calculated, to see him clear through the summer working seven days a week. Once again, this was his idea, not ours—and as it turned out, a very bad one.

There were two kinds of work in the vineyard that first winter: there was the kind that happens every year, which consists of pruning the vines, untangling and pulling out the cut wood, removing it from the vineyard and burning it, then attaching what is left of the vine to the lowest wire, or to personal little posts, known locally as *carrassons*, in the case of young vines like ours. Each winter the vineyard must also be fertilised, broken wires and damaged posts replaced and any special treatments carried out, like putting chalk on acid soil. The other kind of work was to set the vineyard up properly with its wires and posts, identify all the dead and missing vines and order their replacements for the spring.

Work of both kinds had started before Christmas. Monsieur Saint-Martin and his brother were busy pruning, as they have done every winter. This is the one manual task we have never tried, simply because it takes too long if you are not expert. I would have to pause and reflect in front of each plant and it takes hands of steel to keep going at this task for more than an hour or so. The Saint-Martins had started at the age 15 and pruned several hundred thousand plants a year, travelling as far as the Medoc, north of Bordeaux, to exercise their pruning skills. I have never understood quite why they felt the need to do this (although obviously the money is good) when they have their own hectares of Graves to sustain them, but we have been grateful for their intervention in our vines. So they would arrive in the early morning, often unseen when it was foggy but clearly audible in the still air. Their rapid-fire conversations echoing across the vines to the château, punctuated by current affairs programmes on a radio that Monsieur Saint-Martin carries strapped to his belt. They worked unbelievably fast, two hunched figures, rarely straightening up, dressed for winter but, as we were soon to discover, it is impossible to keep warm in the vines on a cold winter's day, whatever you wear, unless you are pulling down the cut wood or carrying it out of the vines to burn it. All the rest is squatting and fiddling, and with this goes freezing! At the ends of the rows the Saint-Martin brothers would finally stand up, stamp their feet and massage their right hands, the ones that did the cutting. Monsieur Saint-Martin told me once he had calculated that he did 20,000 clips a day when he was pruning flat out. Even his steely tendons suffered under such a brutal regime.

Once cut the vines were our domain. The branches have to be pulled off the wires—although that first winter there were precious few wires for them to be attached to and the branches themselves were pretty feeble—gathered into bundles and carried out of the vines to be burned in enormous bonfires, hard to start with the sappy green wood but alarmingly violent once properly alight. Many vineyards use contraptions like giant high-sided wheelbarrows, the sides pierced with holes to draw in air, which act as furnaces and burn the wood at a phenomenal rate. They are pushed along the rows, or towed by tractors in the case of the real monsters, to avoid the time-consuming and tiring need to carry all those spikey bundles out of the vines. The spirit of most of these engines is emphatically home-made. I have seen them put together from old pram or bike wheels, with the frame of an ancient wheelbarrow or small cart clad in thin sheets of metal several feet high. Some of them look set to fall apart at any moment but they reappear year after year and on a still winter's day every few hundred metres for miles around, the plumes of smoke announce the burning of last year's growth in the vineyards. Some people leave the branches spread along the middle of each row and then drive over them with a special *broyeur*, a machine which reduces each stem to dust and small pieces of twig, but this can leave diseased wood in the vineyard and in these days of Eutypiose, Esca and other ghastly vine illnesses it is better to burn the lot!

Daniel had started on the big posts which had never been installed in the swimming pool patch or Labouray. It is astonishing how many hundreds of these heavy acacia *piquets* are needed even for this area of less than a hectare. They have to be installed right along each row, 1.7 metres sticking out of the ground, 30 centimetres underground and six vines in between each one. Between the last two vines at each end of every row a *piquet* is put in sloping back over the very last vine. It is to this one that all the wires running the length of the row are tied and it is held sloping by a wire attached to a post driven deep into the ground beyond the last vine. Bernard had delivered the posts at the beginning of December, 6 francs each, strictly cash, and had distributed them along the ends of the rows to minimise the carrying. I gave Daniel my dad's old 14-pound sledgehammer and he could be seen and heard, sweating and cursing, standing on a box and whacking in the *piquets* in slightly imperfect lines. It was all too much for him and he returned the next day with a piffling little 6-pound hammer and a couple of friends. Between the three of them they laid out, held and whacked the *piquets* into position much more cheerfully than Daniel had done on his own—and he never asked me to pay his friends. I think that he didn't want to acknowledge openly that an English sledgehammer had been too much for him.

Daniel had done the posts but it was up to us to deal with the wires. The whole vineyard was to be involved in the wire installation and we were wondering how on earth we were going to do it. Even those parcels which already possessed their posts had never been set up with their double middle wires. These lie slackly on the ground, attached only to the end posts, until the new season's growth has advanced enough to lift them up onto hooks driven in half way up the *piquets*, so holding all the shoots upright and supported until they can wrap their tendrils firmly round the wire running from top to top of each post. A brief calculation showed that just to put in these two required 19 kilometres of wire.

Most vineyards are equipped with an apparatus fitted to a tractor which holds the great rolls of wire in position and allows them to unravel as the tractor moves slowly along the rows. There is even apparatus that will roll up old wires for you as well. We, of course, did not have this apparatus. What we did have were children: these small, active bipeds are highly manoeuvrable, can travel almost as fast as a tractor over short distances and are controllable, more or less, from a distance. On the other hand, they tend to seize up after relatively short periods of operation and are subject to severe overheating in the summer. Frequent lubrication with ice-cream and fizzy drinks prolongs their working life.

Unrolling wire was the ideal job for them. It did not require great strength, had a reasonably amusing play element, and a lot could be done in a short time with several fast-scuttling boys! So I bought two unwinders, I know of no better word in English, which consisted of a metal spike to be driven into the soil with a frame that rotated freely on it upon which the rolled-up wire could be fitted. Once the wrapping was removed the wire unrolled smoothly with a gentle pull. Well, usually it did.

Our system went like this: I transplanted the unwinders from row to row, Francis and William, then Robert and Thomas, took it in turns to run the wires up the rows to Georgea at the far end, who wrapped them loosely round the end posts as they arrived. That left Edward to drive his matchbox cars in the sand anywhere but in the row currently being run. As this changed regularly he tended to get confused and was several times up-ended by wires passing rapidly on either side of him. The system worked extremely well—when it worked at all—but Robert, who was only 6¾, complained that Thomas was always shouting at him. This was, to some extent, true, but then Robert was infuriatingly indecisive when faced with a question like, 'Which wire shall I take this time?' William fell flat on his face half way up a row, trying to keep up with the fleet-footed Francis and went off in a huff when everyone laughed. But it all got done and a great deal quicker than we had expected. We were pleased with our progress.

The matter of the missing vines had been organised well before Christmas. A careful count up made before the leaves had fallen revealed the awful truth that in our vineyard of some 14,000 plants, no fewer than 3,580 vines were missing, asphyxiated by weeds, the worst being couch grass, or starved on poor, ill-prepared soil, the case near the woods at Labouray. What a truly abysmal performance in plantations only two and three years old! The plan was to replace every one of them the following spring but I needed to be quite clear what had to be done to prepare for this so that the new plants 'got away' better than the old ones had done.

Surprisingly little was the answer. I had been recommended the previous autumn to the nurserymen 'Bougès' (*très sérieux*) and they were. The Monsieur Bougès who came to see me insisted on walking every part of the vineyard, studying the ground intently as he went. After lamenting the use of just one type of *porte-greffe* throughout, that is the Phylloxera-resistant American root stock on which the 'noble' French grape variety is grafted, he drew up a plan with different *porte-greffes* to suit all the different soil varieties he had found. Particular attention was paid to the very dry, sandy soil at Labouray where he wanted a double dose of organic fertiliser to be provided. For sheer professionalism and concern for the customer the Bougès nursery takes some beating. In later years Monsieur Bougès even offered me a thousand plants and said 'just pay me when you can', to avoid losing our precious planting rights. Unfortunately, the ground preparation and fertiliser were more expensive than the vines and the rights were duly lost for ever.

It was explained to me that there was no soil preparation to be done in advance but, and here Monsieur Bougès became magisterially solemn, the planting sites must be weed free, 'I mean, weed *free!*'

No wonder Mr Jenkin-Lee's planting efforts had not been 100 per cent successful! As a preliminary he suggested the unorthodox remedy of spraying a weed-killer, '*un coup de Roundup*', immediately. This was early November and Roundup is usually applied to weeds at the period of their most active growth, in summer. The faster they are growing, the quicker they die and in the case of 'difficult' weeds like couch grass, the less likely they are to reappear. But Monsieur Bougès was unhappy about our rich and varied weed flora: 'I have rarely seen such a wide range of species in one vineyard.'

And anything that would limit their growth before our delicate replacement operation was worth trying. Monsieur Bougès, the advisor, took advice and was told: 'it might work'. It would also be safer than a mid-summer spray because our vines had lost their leaves and were more or less asleep for the winter, with the result that they would themselves be less affected by the chemical if touched by it than they would be if actively growing. So Monsieur Saint-Martin 'passed', as they say, '*un bon coup de Roundup*' and three weeks later Monsieur Bouges inspected the results with satisfaction. Yellowed and shrivelling weeds were everywhere but, and it was a severely delivered but, in no way should we be fooled into thinking this was enough. Every planting site would have to be hand-weeded in the spring. Delivery of the baby vines was scheduled for the end of April, to be accompanied by detailed planting instructions.

I also managed to solve the other major problem for the winter: that of fertilising the vineyard. Organic fertiliser it was to be because analysis showed that our soil was very poor in organic matter, Mr Jenkin-Lee having predictably failed to provide adequately for his baby vines. This would be followed by a *coup d'azote*, an application of nitrogen, in the spring to give our undernourished vines a fast getaway. Later we would avoid nitrogen, for while it gives you nice green leaves, it tends to make the flowers fall off, the dreaded *coulure*.

The organic material was to be applied in the middle of winter and lightly worked into the soil. How though were we going to distribute what turned out to be 25 cubic metres, an enormous blackish-brown pile, of crumbly, peaty stuff that steamed gently in the cold air? The 'lightly-working-in' I could manage with a toothed implement called a *griffe*, one of the few tools we possessed to go on the tractor. *Mais, pas de problème!* The agricultural cooperative in Langon which had advised me on the stuff would organise both its delivery and its spreading and we would not have to lift a finger except to sign the cheque, fortunately not due until May, for the hefty bill that came with it! It was, however, a necessary expense, so it was ordered and the date for spreading it was fixed, when winter, which had just been trifling with us up until now, struck with a rude and icy hand.

This was far beyond our imaginings and much more severe than anything I had had to put up with on my very first visit here, when the absence of heating had been so painfully obvious. There was still no heating, but it *was* planned. Wally and Pirrin had been building a boiler house behind the hotel under the direction of our plumber Christian Jeantet, another Jenkin-Lee *tuyau*, but he was only now due to start work on a heating system which was to do for both the house and the hotel. So far all he had done was to disconnect the wood-burning stove in the kitchen from Mr Jenkin-Lee's useless and incidentally illegal radiators dotted about the house, with a view to linking up the new installation at least with the existing pipework. So we had a nice warm kitchen and there was the fire in the sitting room, but the rest of the house remained what one usually calls 'freezing cold'. Now in every day speech this generally means just uncomfortably cold, not literally freezing. At Château de Commarque, as the temperature plummeted and went on falling that January, the expression took on its correct and literal meaning. The first victims were the geraniums, supposedly overwintering safely downstairs in the end room. They perished one and all in a single night as the temperature outside dropped to minus 20°C. We did what we could with electric fires and bottle-gas heaters but it did not amount to much and we quickly got into the habit of getting dressed to go to bed: jumpers, two pairs of socks, tracksuit bottoms, gloves. Then it snowed heavily and we could not even get out of the place. The children were missed that morning at school and Dr Daubech came down the track to see if we were still alive! He had chains on his car, not so much because he was a country doctor who needed them for his rounds, but because he was a keen skier and they helped him up the mountains. In answer to the question, 'Where can we get some of those?' he laughed and answered, 'You won't find a single one now between Bordeaux and the Pyrenees.'

It was nice to feel that someone had noticed our absence, but after that the isolation was complete until the weekend when the de Pinoses, breaking their weekend rule about not leaving the house, walked over from Bommes, dressed like Eskimoes, to see how we were getting on.

In the meantime we had made a point of getting the children to school. It meant going on foot but it was only a matter of 2 kilometres. Once there they were much warmer than they would have been at Commarque! All work had come to a halt, so we were quite free to accompany them on their hike. The Saint-Martins would have frozen in their boots if they had continued pruning and I had been knocking in the hooks which would hold up our newly installed middle wires but had been forced to give up when my *pointes charentaises* just bent feebly against the posts or bounced off the rock-hard wood and vanished in the snow.

There had been a great store of old vine stocks in the shed opposite the house, a mountain that had reached the roof and looked to us as though it would last for years, but by Christmas it had all gone and now Georgea and I found ourselves out in the woods beyond the restaurant vines, equipped with 'his' and 'hers' rip saws, providing the household with the means to keep warm! Truly, we had not left England for this! At the weekend the children were out there too. They found the wood, we cut it up. But before the next winter I bought a large chain-saw and took instruction from Bernard on how to use it. We did at least discover the wisdom of that old adage about cutting the wood for the fire being more warming than the fire itself!

So we coped with the cold, as if there was any choice in the matter, but we were wondering anxiously if the vines were going to do the same. The memory of 1956 is still fresh in this neighbourhood, inured though it is to natural catastrophe: '*on est tous tributaire du temps*'—we are all slaves to the weather—they will intone mournfully to you and it is true. That year the temperature had descended to minus 24°C and even lower. Many vines had been killed outright. As rumours went round that Léogeats, just down the road and admittedly a little lower than us, had hit minus 22°C, we began to think that our count up of dead vines had been premature and that our vineyard was in danger of being killed off before it had yielded us a single grape. For might not our small, weak vines resist this bitter cold less robustly than their older, better nourished brethren? There was no way of telling. All we could do was wait for spring and hope.

* * *

The temperature climbed reluctantly after a week or so but remained firmly below zero. At least we could be outside now and not risk frost-bite! The children started to enjoy themselves. I seem to think they had not had their fair share of snow over recent years so this was something of a novelty for them. Just the other side of the Ruisseau de Commarque there is a very steep, grassy slope, part of Bernard's land, flattening before the Ruisseau and the lake and cropped smooth by Papy Dartigue's sheep. Here they went tobogganing on fertiliser bags. It worked marvellously well and an ice-smooth track was developed down which they would hurtle, clutching the front corners of their sacks, skidding to a halt just short of the lake. We have photos of this that should win prizes: a brilliant sun, half seen between the trees at the top of the hill, bobble-hatted figures in shadow on the slope and Edward standing short and stout beside the ice-track looking behind a plunging fertiliser sack, so quickly had it passed him.

At half-term we gave up the struggle briefly for a respite in England, warming ourselves in other people's centrally heated houses, while at Commarque Monsieur Jeantet, the plumber, set up his workbench outside the hotel and worked patiently in the cold on our oh-so-keenly-anticipated central heating system. The snow melted while we were away. The temperature rose and every pipe in the place poured water. But Monsieur Jeantet was there. He put down his tools, left his work bench and patiently put all the pipes together again. We had been taken so unawares by this sudden and bitter winter that I had not even considered trying to find all the stop cocks which might have prevented this sort of thing happening. I learned them after that, with some help from Christian Jeantet, and these days the pipes do not burst any more.

Well warmed and extremely overfed in England, we broke down on the return journey with a failed petrol pump, coming to a halt at the end of the slip road of a motorway service station. As I trudged back to the cafe and petrol pumps to summon the breakdown service it felt, after our carefree and comfortable holiday, like a gentle reminder that life in France had been and would continue to be less than straightforward. We were 180 kilometres from Commarque; it was Sunday afternoon and the van, a new one—or rather a new old minibus with Château de Commarque tastefully painted on the side—was full of silverware, china and paintings which my mother had decided would be better off at the château than in her cupboards and had kindly given to us, as well as all of us and our luggage.

Three-quarters of an hour later the breakdown lorry hurtled down the slip road, we were winched up on the back of it in a trice with all of us still on board, and driven without explanation to Saint-Jean d'Angely, some 20 kilometres away. Our high vantage point gave us an unusual and interesting view of the countryside and the boys enjoyed the passage through gates and along access roads that are usually firmly closed to the general public.

The garageman who had rescued us was a good-humoured and helpful man, despite the breakup of his Sunday afternoon, and undertook to keep the van and its contents under lock and key, to order the new petrol pump first thing in the morning and to telephone us as soon as the van was ready. Did he know an on-duty and not-too-greedy taxi driver? By all means! He telephoned him at once, telling him to hurry up. Mind you, for what it cost us to get home I suppose he would hurry up, but he had a 360 kilometre round trip on a Sunday afternoon and it was a big taxi. It had to be to fit all seven of us and the essential elements of our luggage.

Even though we both had at least one child sitting on us, more or less blotting out the view, we were able to take in the clear and dramatic end to winter which had been happening while we were in England. Apart from a general feeling of clemency that had filtered into the van as we travelled south from the Loire, there is a subtle climatic change 50 to 75 kilometres north of Bordeaux which we perceived for the first time in that early March of 1987. Where the plants of the motorway verges and banks and the woods round the fields of the north Charente were still bare and leafless, there was now visible a faint mist of pale green, of yellowish brown obscuring the sharp outlines of winter branch and twig, and cloudbursts of tiny white blossom appeared in the hedgerows. Spring was arriving a week or two earlier in Aquitaine than in the neighbouring region of Poitou-Charente and so it always does. It has to do with the influence of the Gironde estuary and is perhaps one of the factors, many and complex though these are, that add up to make Bordeaux the greatest fine wine area in the world. To us the sight of all these stirring plants was a great reassurance. In moving south towards what we had hoped would be, among other things, a better climate, we might not have moved far enough to avoid severe winters but they would at least be short! In Bordeaux winter finishes at the beginning of March!

At Château de Commarque everything starts in March. The vines, if still alive, will start their new season's growth, the restaurant reopens, the children go back to school with bags of hotly fancied English sweets for their friends, summer bookings start trickling in (at last!). Monsieur Jeantet will soon be ready to install his sister's central heating boiler but needs my help and that of any able-bodied man he can lay his hands on, to move this giant which is far too big for the house it currently occupies, and Marc? Where is Marc? Still in Saint-Jean-de-Luz, restfully on holiday, presumably with his feet still comfortably placed under his daughter's dining table. There is the van to recover, the bank balance to sort out, a waitress to find, reality to face!

We got the children to school next morning, plus those bits of their homework which were not buried in the van at Saint-Jean d'Angely, and a few minutes after getting back to Commarque the fertiliser spreader arrived. More accurately a Land Rover, a lorry bearing a JCB, a gigantic three-wheeled straddle tractor, tall enough to walk under and towing a huge trailer, made a majestic procession down the track. While these great engines proceeded to churn up the lawns in front of the château into a muddy waste ground under the fascinated gaze of Edward, who was still much too young to go to school, I was consulted by Monsieur Jeantet, Georgea was consulted by Alex, we were both consulted by the rep from the paint company which was supplying paint for the house, hotel and swimming pool, and Wally and Pirrin turned up to loaf comfortably in a sunny corner of the courtyard awaiting their turn in the consultation queue. That familiar hassled feeling came over us both and by lunchtime any residual effect of our trip to England had long since vanished.

That evening, I telephoned Marc.

'Ah, Monsieur Reay-Jones,' he exclaimed in well feigned tones of surprised delight. '*Vous allez bien? Et Madame? Et les enfants?*'

'*Tres bien merci, Marc!* And yourself?'

'*Tres bien merci!* What can I do for you Monsieur Reay-Jones?'

'Um, a bit of work?' No, I didn't really say that, but we wondered afterwards what he thought was the purpose of my call other than to ask him to resume his duties, assuming he could still remember what they were. Instead I replied: 'It's time to open the restaurant for the season, Marc.'

'Oh, you would like me to come back then, Monsieur Reay-Jones?'

This deserved a highly sarcastic reply such as: 'No, no, we'll send you the orders. I'm sure the Pommes Forestières will travel very well,' considering that he had been paid for doing nothing for nearly two months—admittedly through no fault of his own. But I was unable to manage this adequately in French and contented myself with saying: 'Yes please, as quickly as possible!' and hung up.

He arrived the following afternoon and that evening the tempting aroma of Pommes Forestières was once again wafting out of the restaurant kitchen.

The faraway garage telephoned on the Tuesday to announce the repair of the van. The problem was how to get it! In the rush of events over the past few months, Georgea's accident which wrote off our Peugeot estate car and nearly wrote off Georgea, Edward, Marc, his daughter and her husband, has escaped attention. What eventful lives we did lead. She had come round a sharp, narrow corner in that maze of little roads leading to the Bordeaux motorway and found herself face to face with a large lorry occupying all but a bicycle's width of the road. Luckily she hit the front wheels and bounced off, so avoiding going straight underneath it. The result was that for the moment the van was our only vehicle and there it was at Saint-Jean d'Angely! The solution to the problem was Daniel, over the moon at being able to help us in a matter involving motor cars, as it were, able to patronise the patron, and to show me the paces of *his* new car, an elderly Peugeot 304.

The trip was hair-raising. Daniel is talkative and had not lost that habit, so useful in the early stages of our acquaintance, of never addressing me without the aid of gestures and mime. So for measurable periods of time the steering wheel of his car rotated freely and unattended while Daniel used both hands to embroider and emphasise his conversation. In between these illustrated speeches and at any opportunity when a smart acceleration was possible, he would grasp the wheel tightly at ten to two, lean back in his seat so that his arms were straight out in best racing-driver manner, and put his foot down to the floor with repeated yells of, '*A bomber, a bomber!*', a misuse of French that caused Marc, when I recounted the story to him, much derision and head shaking at Daniel's debasement of the language. The word '*bomber*' usually means 'to make convex', and a surface that is '*bombé*' is like the camber on a road, but Daniel certainly did not mean that. He meant, 'let's go like a bomb!' He did, and the poor old car shuddered and shook with the strain of it!

Daniel avoided all the toll-paying sections of the motorways out of consideration, so I thought, for my pocket, but he was helping me to save money only so that I could spend it on his lunch! I had not thought of this. Insofar as I had considered lunch at all, I suppose a sandwich at a service station was what I had in mind, but Daniel is a large Frenchman and had not become one by eating sandwiches for lunch. So at quarter to twelve he announced that he thought we ought to stop soon. In answer to my question, 'Why?', he cried in astonished tones: '*Parce qu'il faut manger, manger!*'—We must eat, eat!—accompanying this with a repeated flexure of his hand in front of his mouth, fingers lined up together as though holding a piece of bread, gulping and swallowing like a fish. Then he performed a very fair charade of cutting into a big, juicy steak on a plate situated 3 inches above the steering wheel. I got the message and we stopped at the next roadside restaurant, thus ensuring that we walked into the dining room as opposed to driving into it, a real possibility if Daniel continued to emphasise the need for lunch with any more of his mimes. I watched him consume the entire menu while I tinkered with a dried trout sprinkled with burnt almonds and chafed at the passing of time. After that though the journey went off more calmly and without incident. The garageman had been as good as his word; the van went perfectly; the contents were safe and both Daniel and I got home safely.

* * *

Surreptitiously scratching a few vine shoots I was encouraged to find them green and fresh inside. Were they all going to have survived the winter? If they had, then we were well behind with tying them up. This meant attaching the main stock of each plant to its private post, the *carrasson*, and if the wood destined to provide the new season's shoots was tall enough, tying that to the bottom wire as well. Alex, Georgea and I worked away at this day after day; every single plant had to be tied because the job had never been done properly before. It was a back-breaking task. The girls were quicker and more dextrous than I was, and I must say I found it easier to crawl from vine to vine, rather than standing up and bending, standing up and bending! My technique is not one you see very much in the surrounding vineyards. We finished during the last week of March, and lo and behold! The buds on the vines were starting to bulge and even to break. The vineyard was alive and well, 3,580 replacement vines would be enough. It was time to start weeding the planting sites and confirm the order with Monsieur Bougès.

Above left: Midwinter at Commarque.

Above right: Nigel with a bottle of Château de Commarque.

The steps from the courtyard to the pool area.

Nigel in front of the hotel suites.

View of the vines in front of Commarque.

Above left: The main gates into the courtyard.

Above right: All five boys looking through a château window.

Cutting the grass outside the château walls.

The château's rustic kitchen.

An aerial view of the château before the vineyard was replanted.

Above: A bottle of Château de
Commarque 1990.

Right: Georgea showing
Edward how to drive a tractor.

The first grape harvest.

View from the château's furthest patch of vines at Labourey (frequently eaten by deer).

and Georgea in
Pyrenees.

Right: *Pourriture
noble*, or noble rot,
on bunches of grapes
ready to harvest.

Below: The *vendange*
in full swing.

Above: The swimming pool in summertime.

Left: Thomas, Francis and Edward playing in the château courtyard.

Nigel raising a glass of Sauternes.

11

Progress and a Party

In April it rained. Not torrentially, but in a fine, dense drizzle, blowing sideways from the south-west. It would last for hours, die away briefly and then start again. For days at a time it would continue like this, making a misery of our weeding operation.

The vineyard continued to claim a great deal of our attention. Therein, we felt, lay both the seeds of our future prosperity and the greatest scope for improvement now. The hotel was, despite obvious deficiencies, in a fit state to operate and there was time to complete the works we had planned before the summer season began, when we knew from the previous year that there would be customers. The restaurant was the unknown quantity; Marc did not hesitate to tell us how good it all was and at that time we did not argue. We had certainly not thought out exactly how we wanted it to be. We hoped, I think, that a good professional would automatically put us on the right lines and we didn't have enough of our attention on it to check whether Marc had perceived the right lines or was capable of putting us on them.

He was an excellent front man. He knew when to joke with customers, when to advise them and how to make them feel important. In short, he did not hesitate to use his devious skills to charm them. With hindsight it is clear that he was better at this than he was at cooking. So what exactly was he cooking? Did he rise above the Nettle Soup level?

To be fair to Marc the answer is definitely yes. He did some good things. Anyone who ate a meal of Pâté Piquant du Chef, Magret de Canard au Poivre Vert accompanied by those Pommes Forestières and a Tarte à la Bourdaloue for the prices we charged at that time, could not fail to leave feeling they had eaten an honest and well-cooked meal at a reasonable cost and there were some who praised it and came back! He dealt with squid, a Basque favourite, very well; Squid in Ink (Chipirons dans leur Encre), Stuffed Squid, Squid en Persillade, but it is not everyone who can eat squid. His best offering was a delicious dish of mussels, the one thing he showed us that we still do. I do not know if he invented it, but it seems to us to be original, in so far as anything so simple can be, and it is always appreciated. Marc called it Moules du Chef. He loved adding du Chef to everything but I suspect it's a name more often than not reserved for dishes where the contents are best left undisclosed! Now we call it Moules au Chorizo, the essential ingredients being spicy Chorizo sausage, red and green peppers and parsley, all finely chopped and cooked with the mussels in white wine, Château de Commarque naturally. The flavours combine with surprising subtlety without masking the essential character of the mussels.

There were some things in those early menus that make us cringe when we look at them now. There were those which were dead ordinary like Salade Basquaise (tuna, egg, peppers and always, always *dried* parsley) a sort of downmarket Salade Niçoise, Bavette aux Echalotes (cheap, chewy steak topped with shallots) and a Mousse au Chocolat made with that cooking chocolate which should be avoided at all costs!

There were those that were pleasant but *trop commun*, real workers' food, like Côte de Porc charcutière, with a brown stock-based sauce containing chopped gherkins—popular with the boys this one, and still is. Finally, there were one or two things that were frankly awful. I would single out Rognons d'Agneau (lamb's kidneys) Flambés Lyonnaise, a lovely name which disguises the true nature of this culinary faux pas. Marc would tell us, with a confidence and certainty which defied argument, that there were two ways to cook kidneys. (He was always telling us things in this way, assuming that ignorance, now steadily diminishing, would allow him to get away with any story he liked.) The first way was to just 'show' the kidneys the pan, so that they were served pink in the middle and meltingly tender. The second was to cook them for a long time, hours in fact, as anything in between left them tough and leathery. This is all true, but what we would add now is that if you cannot cook kidneys the first way you should not cook them at all! But Marc did. Those unappetising little brown bullets, swamped in thick brown sauce, would go out in a little (yes!) *brown* dish, accompanied—as I live and breathe—by a boiled potato! Compare this with Gilles' dish of kidneys that found its way on to the Carte just over a year later: Eminçé de Rognons de Veau Commarque (his name not ours), and subject to the same criticism as du Chef, consists of finely sliced veal's kidneys 'shown' the pan and set aside while sliced mushrooms, baby white onions and small cubes of bacon are cooked in it. The pan is deglazed with Madeira and Sauternes and the mixture is accompanied by a fragrant rice pilaff.

Marc's Soupe de Poisson au Fumet de Crabe was good, he made excellent omelettes, Basquaises of course, with tomatoes and peppers, and a decent Crème Caramel. But those things that were not Basque were conventional, not interesting enough to drag people down our bumpy track, and the Basque dishes were out of place. The notion of Cuisine du Terroir, with the use of local products, has greatly strengthened in recent years and we needed to cook with Sauternes and to use ingredients that characterise our region, not that of the Pays Basque. Realisation was slow in coming, but a turning point was reached at the beginning of August, with Black Sunday, after which Georgea put a strong hand on the reins of culinary power. But how one's early errors live on! Three years after the departure of Marc the restaurant was still being described as Basque by ill-informed and idle travel writers—such people really do exist—who had never tried it, and in some cases had never even been near Commarque.

Back in April 1987 Marc prepared his season as best he knew how, and not just on the strictly culinary front. He announced one day that he had found a waitress for the season.

'A local girl?' I asked, for we had no accommodation to offer her.

'From Biarritz,' Marc replied.

'Does she have somewhere to stay round here?'

'With me,' he responded, with a self-satisfied smirk.

Faint alarm bells sounded but were switched off. That could make two of *them* against *us*. In the event of anything going wrong they would have the power to stop the restaurant dead in its tracks, even more so than Marc could have done on his own, but this seemed a very improbable scenario. A more likely one was that if Marc imported his girlfriend all would be well for a time, then they would fall out and *we* would lose our waitress, possibly in the middle of the season, Marc would be in a foul temper or broken-hearted or both—but whatever the case, we would suffer more than if we had a cook and waitress whose relationship was strictly professional.

But we were looking over our shoulders at all that weeding to be done in the vineyard, at the swimming pool to prepare for the season and the gîte at the end of the hotel which was about to be converted into hotel rooms. The prospect of being able to solve one more problem without actually having to do anything about it was overwhelmingly attractive. So, we let Marc have his way and in due course Martine arrived.

* * *

The weeding of the planting sites for the replacement vines expanded to include the ridges of couch grass that ran along many of the rows, most developed here because it was inaccessible to the ripping out and drying in the sun effected not only by Monsieur Saint-Martin and his rotavator, but also by me and my *griffe*. The work was not properly finished until the end of the following winter and it took until 1989 to achieve a truly weed-free vineyard. The use of herbicides had to be limited because of our 3,580 baby vines—not to mention quite a few others not yet in a fit state to withstand the chemicals. The whole operation was clearly too much for us alone and Daniel seemed more prone to wilt after a few hours than he had been the previous summer. Fortunately, we had been asked for work by our chimney sweeps, a pair of cheerful young men with a van of chronic antiquity which was shortly to be restored to perfection, resprayed à *neuf* and is still going strong at thirty years old. They brought their brothers and sisters and set to work at Labouray, where their animated chatter and the clack, clack, of the hoes on the stony ground would carry clean across the valley of the Ruisseau, all the way to the château.

Monsieur Saint-Martin, interrupting their work briefly with the first *sulfatage* of the new season, referred to their enthusiastic labours approvingly, '*Ils font de tres bon boulot là-bas.*'

After a couple of days the workforce had dwindled to the two sweeps as the rest went off on some other temporary job, wheedled and pushed for by their father. That is how the Schmidt family gets by. They never continue anything for very long—apart from the chimney sweeping, which I suspect is the basis of their economy, but what they do they do with a refreshing gusto and gaiety, and one wonders if their whole life is infected with this spirit. Probably not, nothing is ever so simple!

By the last week of April we were as ready for the replanting as we were ever going to be. John and Celia, our partners, came out to help with this significant, if not symbolic, act of regeneration upon which, we felt, our mutual fortunes—both actual and figurative—might rest. They brought with them two robust friends, Jill and Alan, who could be guaranteed to plant vines with the best.

There was a practical aspect to this importation of personnel. Daniel and Jacqueline, the chimney sweeps and the chimney sweeps' brothers and sisters, not to mention Monsieur Saint-Martin, and his brother during the winter, did not work for nothing and although they all worked hard and gave good value for money, the money they received in exchange was capital, and it was diminishing fast. The flow of cash through the vineyard was decisively one way and would continue to be so for another whole year, at which point, in the absence of total disaster, we should have bottles of dry white wine to sell—and possibly even barrels of Sauternes. The hotel and restaurant were unable to contribute anything as early in the year as April, so six slaves (us), plus Daniel and Jacqueline, seemed the best way to deal with the planting exercise.

The slaves arrived two days before the delivery of the vines, giving themselves time to prepare mentally and physically for the task ahead. The mental preparation consisted of rigorous testing of samples of Roquefort and Sauternes, of Fromage de Brebis (sheep's cheese from the Pyrenees) and red Graves, and keeping Marc busy in the restaurant. After a day and a half everyone pronounced themselves to be in a satisfactory state of readiness, Georgea and I had hangovers and our visitors looked outside for the first time. They noticed that it was raining. This observation led naturally into the physical preparation phase: everyone bought 'Granny macs' at the Coopérative Agricole in Langon. The French name for these garments is something like *survêtement vigneron*, but they are worn impartially by *vignerons* (gentlemen vineyard workers) and *vigneronnes* (lady vineyard workers) and we call them Granny macs because of all the elderly ladies clad in these things to be seen in the neighbouring vineyards during wet weather. A Granny mac is an all-enveloping, all-in-one hood and long coat, made of thick, greenish-khaki, rubber-coated material, buttoning tightly up to the neck, with elasticated sleeves under the rubber sheath at the wrists, and reaching down to the ankles. It is impossible in one of these for water to trickle down your neck, up your arms or even into your boots, and they are sufficiently voluminous for a lady to retain her privacy even when relieving herself. Furthermore, they only cost about 80 francs. On the other hand they are stiff, uncomfortable things to wear and limit movement by their inflexibility. One develops a set of gestures of small radius to accommodate them and also to keep the pockets of warm air that develop inside them from escaping into the rainswept landscape outside! Daniel had an interesting additional adaptation; at least I speculate that's what it was for: he farted into his Granny mac.

I made this interesting discovery when he came to ask me a question during the replanting. We talked for several minutes during which time he putt-putted away without a break and apparently unconsciously, for he never acknowledged what was certainly a phenomenal feat of sphincter control and, much less importantly, is sometimes considered to be a lapse of good manners. I was so fascinated by his, well, breath control, that I did not listen properly and found myself having to ask him to repeat what he had just said. Inevitably, this led to an enrichment of his habitual gesture and mime, concentration on which, one would think, should have brought the farting exhibition to an abrupt halt. Not at all. It continued ripely and effortlessly to the very end of our conversation when he turned away and stumped off into the vines, switching off the gas outlet at the same moment.

He was certainly in a funny mood that day. We had left him and Jacqueline to put in the posts beside the little vines we had planted on the sandy soil to the left of the track, while we slithered around on the clay side. He spent more time shouting at Jacqueline than working. While she bashed away at the stakes with all her might, using a lump hammer held in both hands, Daniel strode up and down, gesticulating and shouting, probably farting as well, but we were too far away to hear. The next day he was more productive but I had to ask him twice to put his posts a bit nearer the vines and properly in line with the rest of the row. Some of them were so far away that we could never have tied the vines to them. The raffia is too short. Finally, I had to say again: 'Daniel, that's too far away from the vine.'

Upon which he shouted: '*J'en ai marre!*'—I've had enough!—threw down his hammer and marched off, leaving Jacqueline working doggedly along her row without even looking up. I asked her what had got into Daniel and she replied: '*Il n'a plus envie de travailler*'—He doesn't want to work—and that was all she said.

Daniel never worked at Commarque again, although Jacqueline came back and finished her job the day after. In answer to the question 'Where is Daniel?', she repeated only: '*Il n'a plus envie de travailler.*' I suspect there is nothing more to say. Daniel can manage just so much work and no more. He has never had a job of any permanence in all the time we have been here; a season of vines here, some grape picking there. He gets by and does not ask for more, or if he does it is Jacqueline who gets it for him! We quickly got back on friendly terms and on one occasion when I asked him if he could work for us, he was too busy doing *effeuillage* at a Graves vineyard in Arbanats towards Bordeaux.

So it was that we, the six 'free' workers, did the bulk of the planting, thus saving wages at the expense of aching backs and blistered hands. Softies and amateurs should really keep out of vineyards, but we did the job well; the vines grew.

The plants had arrived in a tall van with dozens of shelves in the back, containing row after row of polystyrene and plastic trays. The baby vines, each bearing two leaves, were planted in little peaty pots set in holes in the trays. There were twenty plants per tray; that makes 179 trays for us and *that* makes a grand array of little plants. One is forced to admire what they did at Château Myrat a few years later. The vineyard of this Barsac Cru Classé, with its huge rambling château, had been abandoned for years when the owners woke up to the fact that they were about to lose the *droits de plantation* for the whole thing. They reacted with commendable speed. Twenty-five hectares were prepared and planted in one year. At 5,000 plants to the hectare, that means 125,000 plants, not forgetting 125,000 *carrassons* and nearly 21,000 *piquets*, quite a tonnage of wood—enough to make Daniel fart with fright! Looking at the results a few years later one cannot say that it was a wonderfully well done but, like Dr Johnson, you are surprised to find it done at all.

Monsieur Bougès gave us three days to do the job, 'After that the plants will suffer in their pots.'

Suffer they must not! They shall not! The challenge was accepted and work began. Just carrying all the trays into position was quite a task. After that a hole was made with a planter, a thing with two handles at one end, two long, thin semicircular 'spades' at the other, hinged in the middle. It works very well but requires considerable strength and weight on clay soil. Alan was delegated; he weighed about 15 stone. Into the bottom of the hole goes a fistful of organic fertiliser, a little soil, the vine—10 centimetres of stock from the level of the graft above ground—more soil, firm up, a good watering of ammonium sulphate, then the post (if not put in by Daniel or still there from the old vine), tie up with raffia and on to the next one. John used the crawling technique, on a fertiliser bag because of the mud. Jill gave up for the last half day, volunteering to cook supper instead. The sun came out and the boys helped with the last few hundred plants. It was Wednesday and there was no school. That afternoon, by popular request, I 'passed' the *griffe* everywhere, to the satisfaction of all: there was the bare earth, broken into fine, clean lines by the teeth of the *griffe*, sprouting vines, rows of neat posts and wires. For the first time the whole thing looked like a vineyard, like other people's vineyards. We returned to the Roquefort and Brebis, the Graves and Sauternes and talked about kitting out the *chai* and grape-picking. Some fell asleep at the table.

* * *

A couple of weeks later Mr Jenkin-Lee turned up unexpectedly, together with his grown-up children, to show them the site of his former triumphs. He looked rather opulent and was driving a Volvo estate car that he certainly did not have before.

He looked round with an irritatingly proprietorial air and said: 'You've got it looking nice anyway,' as though he found this surprising.

Foolishly, I was unable to resist having a go at him about all the dead vines he had left behind.

'Ah,' he said, 'you should have earthed them up for the winter!' And was instantly pointing something out to one of the children and serenely ignoring my protests about the vines being well and truly dead the previous year. No doubt he went home and announced that we had already managed to kill off half the vineyard. Although he was only here for ten minutes he managed to leave us ruffled for the rest of the day! We hoped the visit would not be repeated.

The other arrival during May was, of course, the waitress Martine. She was one of those girls who gets on better with men than with women. That is not to say that she flirted with the customers, but her *accueil*, which was invariably warm, was even more lit up than usual for a table with young men in the company. She wore a lot of make-up but dressed smartly in black and white, was hard-working, honest and plainly keen on Marc, who was to be less than honest with her.

A few days after her arrival Martine announced nervously that she had a 4-year-old daughter and could she come for the weekend? She-was-very-well-behaved-and-would-be-no-problem-during-the-service-she-would-just-sit-quietly-and-play-etc—all in a rush! Of course we said 'yes', and Zelya, the bane of Edward's life, turned up that Saturday. To her, Edward, now 2½, was a large mobile toy who she pursued relentlessly with cries of, 'Where is *le petit Edouard*?' And Edward learned craft and subterfuge at an improperly early age in order to escape this harpy!

The situation was doubly difficult because he liked Martine and was quite happy to play with her in the absence of Zelya. That was fine in the week but not during the weekends when Zelya came to stay. The crunch arrived during the summer holidays when Martine very kindly invited Edward to the seaside on her day off, in company with Zelya. After prolonged discussions with Georgea on the safety aspects of such a trip and a certain amount of havering on the part of Edward, who could probably see what was in store for him, they departed—and returned safely. Any suspicions that Martine had taken Edward so that he could occupy Zelya's attention and give her mother some peace and quiet were allayed by the amount of entertainment that had been lavished on the children. But Edward had not enjoyed his day and complained that Zelya was a 'real pain', an expression that he must have learned from Thomas! After that he refused ever to play with her again and fled upstairs to hide in his bedroom whenever she came looking for him. By tacit agreement the subject was never discussed with Martine but it was all mildly embarrassing and it is to be hoped that Edward has not been marked for life by Zelya's unwelcome attentions!

The little girl was really no bother at all, except to Edward, but was clearly left on occasions without adequate supervision. She could not very well stay in the restaurant kitchen the whole day long and on one alarming occasion she was brought to the house, thus pinning responsibility firmly on us, dripping wet and howling, having been hauled out of the swimming pool by a hotel guest who happened to be there. Zelya would have drowned but for this gentleman. She could not swim a stroke and had been riding round and round the pool on one of Edward's plastic vehicles, had failed to negotiate a corner and plunged straight into the deep end. Martine was upset by the episode, but less so than her ex-husband, a pleasant, serious-looking man, older than Martine, who had delivered and collected Zelya and was obviously the parent most involved in her upbringing. After that incident he came for her as usual but never returned.

Apart from Edward's relief, and it must be admitted our own, Zelya was definitely better off out of it; Marc had been adopting a seriously paternal attitude towards her, admirable on the face of it, announcing that he and Martine would be getting married and having a child themselves shortly. By September certainly, if not sooner, he had another lady with a Spanish name, who actually came to Commarque with him and was introduced as his cousin! I don't think Martine was fooled.

Edward's life was becoming quite eventful. Apart from his precocious woman problem, he went to school in the summer term. This may seem rather shocking at the age of just over 2½, but it is quite standard practice in France. The *maternelle* (kindergarten) section at Sauternes school is fully geared up for children of this age. The only requirement for entry is that they must be potty-trained. Even so, many come to school with spare pants and trousers in their schoolbags. The hours are flexible for the little ones and Madame Poupot who ran it (and still does) is a kindly and patient lady who prepares the children very well for 'real' school in the years ahead. Her assistant, Madame Cailleau, known universally as Tatie (Auntie) Cailleau, of the huge booming voice and impeccably coiffed grey hair, makes a fine maternal figure, although I have heard, mainly from Edward observing his former stamping ground from the heights of the top class, that she has become a bit of a dragon recently. Mind you, some of the infants are beastly! Anyway, Edward went to the *maternelle* at first for an hour, and then for two, just in the morning and no question of staying for a meal. He took to this as easily as, or more accurately with no more difficulty than, his older brothers had done in England at a riper age and Georgea had a little time on her own to complete her ever increasing pile of tasks and so have more time for all the children when they came home.

Thus Edward started to learn French at a tender age and his speech, hitherto 100 per cent English, became larded with French words and expressions, uttered in tones of the purest Sauternais. This is roughly equivalent to finding a small French boy living in England who speaks English with a rich Devon accent. In the *maternelle* most of the children were of that breed so despised by the president of the Wine Syndicate and they spoke with the *bon accent du coin*, so naturally Edward did to.

The twin's ninth birthday party in happened in May, a party *à l'anglaise* which is a much more organised affair than a French one, where the participants tend to be left to their own devices and where the birthday tea is often a modest *goûter* with no more than a cake, sweets and fizzy drinks. That is not to say that French parties are not fun, but the children amuse themselves and will split up into groups to play different games—the boys football, the girls hide and seek, and so on. None of that at Commarque. Games from beginning to end: pass the parcel, musical chairs and bumps, egg and spoon races, obstacle course races, treasure hunts—here I must admit that the best ever was arranged at Adeline's birthday party, the little girl from whom Robert so carefully copied his first *dictée*. This event went on for the whole afternoon, involved cycling over the entire neighbourhood and was altogether a tour-de-force that must have taken weeks to prepare. Our own tour-de-force has always been a water-pistol fight to finish the afternoon, wonderfully popular with the guests, occasionally less so with the parents. Dripping party frocks and squelching shoes do come as a surprise to the uninitiated, for in our experience the girls are just as keen as the boys. The only problem with organising a water-pistol fight in France is the high cost of the weaponry! Water-pistols are five times more expensive than in England, and do not work as well. No matter! Our boys expect water-pistol fights at their parties and they get them.

Between them, William and Francis had invited the whole class but nothing ever works out quite as you plan it. The first problem was the French vagueness over time. The invitations said three o'clock. The first children arrived at twenty-five to, and some were still not here at quarter past; never mind! We had better start before the ones who *are* here disappear down to the lake or fall in the swimming pool. So we called them together, a rabble of jumping, pushing, shouting children who have not the faintest idea why we have called them, nor why they should not continue to run about all afternoon. Then it dawned on us that they were, for the most part, unable to understand a word we said to them! This galling truth presents a bigger problem: how are we to launch games that none of our guests know, and the instructions for which they are unable to understand? The answer is Thomas as Major-Domo. He, of course, knows all the games inside out and he also has a certain authority at school for some reason, where he is often asked to arbitrate in disputes! So, he rattles away in 'proper' French and gets everyone sitting in a big circle, waves the parcel for pass the parcel in the air and rattles a bit more, pointing at the record player, then he looks at Georgea and says: 'Right! They've got it!' And we start.

There is nothing quite like novelty. Deprived of such pleasures until this moment, the French children went at the parcels with a fervour and concentration, in a spirit of greedy delight, that instantly banished all fears as to whether this party would work or not. When the game was finished they shouted to do it again, but we had only made two parcels and even they had taken an hour and a half to stick together. So we moved on, with Thomas's help, to the musical chairs and other games. When the obstacle course was finished, and they insisted on doing it twice, so giving a victory to both William's team and Francis's team, we announced tea but had to promise to do the obstacle course all over again afterwards, and then there were the water-pistols, loaded, hidden round the courtyard, each marked with a name, and dustbins full of water standing by...

Those parties, Robert's and Edward's included, produced by far the most successful social contacts we have ever made here and make us popular with the local children, even if they confirm a few adult prejudices about the eccentric English!

12

Wind and Worms, Coaches and *Cuves*

The vines were clearly beating the weeds this year and it was high time to do the *levage*: that is lift all those new wires onto the *pointes charentaises*, fixed half-way up the posts—with which I'd had so much trouble in the cold. The result would be to hold up the nicely growing shoots, helping them to reach and then grab the top wire with their tendrils and so ensure their resistance to wind and rain for the rest of the growing season. Just as we were about to start, a storm of savage violence blew the vines flat, the same storm that had lifted the roof of the gatehouse gîte and snapped the pine tree outside the courtyard.

We could not believe the mess it made. There were broken shoots everywhere, many bearing flower clusters. Other branches were lying sideways across the rows; some of Daniel's *carrassons*, not deeply enough banged into the sand, had pulled clear out with the force of the wind against the plants attached to them, and the whole lot now lay more or less horizontally on the ground. Georgea and I, with some help from Alex, worked for three days to put everything straight. When we had finished, Madame Guicheney cheered us up by describing the storm as a *vraie tornade,* and assuring us that such ferocious winds occurred just once every five years or so. The next day the vines were knocked flat again by a second storm, as violent as the first. We made the depressing and exhausting round of the vineyard once more and this time we raised the wires against the third storm which never came, even though many of the shoots were still too short to stay in place between them. We learned our lesson for the future: get the wires up as early as possible and go round again, *deuxième levage*, and again if necessary (*troisième levage*), to tuck in all the unruly shoots that would not reach the first time. It is much less damaging and takes up far less time than letting a storm beat you to the *première levage*!

Another little problem became apparent in the vineyard at this time. When you have a problem, you ask advice. We were to discover that in the vineyard game, sound advice can be hard to come by, though heaven knows we needed it!

The cultivation of vines is carried out in the face of a barrage of diseases forbidding enough to make the toughest amateur gardener take up something less perilous—like solo rock climbing. If you are trying to make a living out of it, however, this is not an option. Apart from the usual selection of mildew, black spot, oidium, grey rot, mites (red and yellow), pyramid moths, vinegar flies, frog hoppers and withering of the stalks, new disorders have a habit of creeping up on us that you cannot even see until the vine is moribund. What about Esca? 'Apoplexy of the Vine': in midsummer a large, healthy-looking vine suddenly shrivels, the branches go black, the grapes lie withered on the exposed stalks, the vine has died in three to four days. Inside, the wood is a spongy mess, its structure destroyed by the unseen invading fungus. The worst is Eutypiose and there is no cure. It is the AIDS of the vineyard world, and like AIDS it gained ground every year. The latest one is *La Flavescence Dorée*, and I hear Bacterial Necrosis has reappeared in Cognac. What is more, the man who did all the work on it has retired, his group has been disbanded and all the files have been lost! Now there is practically no one left who can recognise the disease in its early stages!

As if all that were not enough the Phylloxera is still there, the disease that wiped out much of the French vineyard in the second half of the nineteenth century and cost France more than the Franco-Prussian War. The only sites safe from the aphid that spreads it are the low-lying *palus*, which are prone to flooding, but these fields do not produce really good wines. The solution was to graft the 'noble' French grape varieties onto ignoble but resistant American roots. The vineyards and the French economy were thus saved and the Phylloxera has been largely forgotten. You can try to replace vines slain by Esca, Eutypiose, etc by *marcottage* or layering—you remember, you bend a branch down underground and up again and the bit underground grows roots. After a year or two (or a month or two, depending on the plant you are doing it to) you cut the branch and you have two plants. It works very well for vines and has the added attraction that the grapes developing on the new plant can be picked the very same year the layering was done. Eventually, however—maybe later rather than sooner, but quite surely—your new plant, which has been formed from a branch of a noble French grape variety, will succumb to the Phylloxera. Layering is a solution for an old vineyard, to keep it going until the whole thing is grubbed up and replanted, but not for a young one like ours. But we did it. We did it because a young Australian vine expert who had spent five years studying the disease and had acquired a doctorate for his researches, gave us his opinion that if the Phylloxera had not been seen for twenty-five or thirty years then it was safe to use susceptible plants and, when pressed hard, he would certainly do it himself! One listens to Australians. After all, it is they, among others, who have forced the French to rethink their winemaking methods, time-honoured practices raised, quite unjustifiably, to the status of an art and proved to be inadequate in the face of New World competition. When we had layered a hundred or so vines, which had not died of anything more sinister than serious neglect in early youth, Monsieur Bougès, our vine supplier (who admittedly has an axe to grind) condemned the practice in uncharacteristically thunderous tones.

This conflicting advice had less serious consequences than might have followed from the downright *bad* advice we received in the summer of 1987. Up at Labouray, the other side of the valley, I noticed a square of vines at the bottom in one corner that was definitely poorly. The leaves were small and turning yellow, virtually no flower buds had formed and the main stocks of the plants were stunted compared with those of their neighbours. What was puzzling was that in the middle of the affected area were several normal, robust plants, just as big as the best to be found elsewhere. The whole patch only took in eight rows and extended to no more than a dozen plants in each one.

I called the technician from the *Coopérative Agricole* who said 'Eelworms' in an uncompromising tone.

'What do I do about them?' I asked.

'The only solution is to pull up all the infected plants, plus those within a metre of them and sterilise the soil. After that you can replant.'

As I digested this stunning piece of news, the technician added: 'Shell supplies the product for sterilising the soil. I'll have to bring the rep to have a look.'

He was back in twenty-four hours with a smartly dressed young man in shiny shoes and driving a shiny new car. I didn't like the eagerness with which they wanted to dismantle my vineyard and sell me expensive chemicals! Was there collusion in the air or did I *imagine* an exchange of meaningful glances between the two men? At that point I sincerely wished the Shell rep, shiny shoes and all, would become stuck in, and disappear into, the heaviest, wettest clay in the vineyard, and decided to disbelieve the eelworm diagnosis and to ignore the prescription. This was not just a fit of pique. The presence of normal plants in the middle of the affected area was curious. Eelworms, like any animal, are mobile, if not all the time then at some point in their lives. If they were not they would all stay in one place on top of one another, they and their children and their children's children, and quickly eat up all the food. The infected plants must have been diseased for some time because many of them were little bigger than our newly planted babies. They should, therefore, have been a rich source of infection. So how could such efficient parasites 'miss' the good plants which they surrounded so completely?

I decided to wait for two years before doing anything drastic and see if the area of 'infection' spread. If it did not then the problem most likely concerned the soil, and this is what I was hoping for. The technician had already pooh-poohed the idea for no other reason than—in his opinion— my leaves looked more like the the pictures of eelworm-infected leaves in his book than any of the other pictures! As the Coopérative Agricole was the only place I knew at that time that could organise soil analyses I did not pursue this line any further in 1987. It was, after all, but one of innumerable preoccupations.

The following summer it became apparent that we had a similar disorder, on a larger scale, at the bottom of the vines on the clay side to the left of the track as you approach the château. By the end of June nearly a quarter of a hectare of anaemic plants was visible, less feeble than the worst ones at Labouray, but with just the same symptoms. In 1988, however, the restaurant was 50 per cent busier than it had been the previous year *and* we had less staff; there was no time to do much more than observe the problem, other than to ask the opinion of anyone who came by who might be expected to know about such things. Monsieur Saint-Martin said it was because the old vines had not been properly pulled up and their roots were still in the soil. This was true; there were *gourmands* or wild vines, grown from old roots, popping up vigorously in the middle of the rows; but the idea that they gave off some evil influence impairing the growth of young vines seemed little better than an old wives' tale, and Monsieur Saint-Martin could not be more specific. The roots *could* have been hot-beds of eelworm or virus infestation, but they extended well beyond the affected patch of vines. Old Monsieur Leglise from Château Lamourette just next door murmured mournfully, 'They talk about Eutypiose but I don't know, I really don't know,' and sighed deeply.

So I was convinced that I was not missing anything really obvious and elementary.

Having waited the two years to see what happened at Labouray, where the affected zone had not budged by a single plant, I called the technician again. The original man had left and I showed the new one the patch of vines on the clay.

'Eelworms,' he said without hesitation, and got out his books.

He was very persuasive. The leaves on the vines, when well selected, looked just like the leaves infected with eelworms in his book. I wondered who the poor bloke was who had provided the material for those pictures. Then I collected another set of leaves and tried to convince the man that this lot looked just like a different set of pictures in the book. He would have none of it and said cheerfully that I was lucky that the whole vineyard was not infected, although in the finish I would probably have to pull it all up. Did I want him to bring the Shell rep out to have a look?

Over the previous two years I had learned a few things, so I said, more or less: 'Stuff the Shell rep. I want two soil analyses carried out: one from the centre of the affected patch of vines and one just outside it, still on the clay, where the vines are normal.'

The technician looked disappointed and shrugged his shoulders, '*Comme vous voulez*,' he said, the tone indicating clearly what a waste of time he thought this was. But he rummaged in his car and brought out a packet of plastic bags and a soil sampler, a sort of miniature version of the hole diggers we had used for planting the vines.

In the middle of the bad patch the technician dug diligently into the soil and emptied his sample into one of the plastic bags.

'Where do you want to go now?' he asked, as if humouring a tiresome child.

We went where I indicated and he dug again. Then he opened the plastic bag containing the first soil sample and ... I promise! ... he emptied the second sample into it!

'There we are!' he said triumphantly and tied up the bag. Now it was my turn to talk to a tiresome child.

'How are we going to show a difference in soil composition between there and here,' I said, pointing to the two places the samples had come from, 'with that?' pointing to the bag.

There was no reply.

'What do you plan to demonstrate with that?' Pointing to the bag again. And once more there was no reply.

This fellow is a qualified agricultural technician, whose job it is to advise farmers on how to do *their* job better, and he was unable to work out that two separate soil samples are necessary to show that two separate pieces of soil are different, or indeed the same! I explained how to do it and he said, 'Oh, I see what you want.'

I checked the labels on the bags carefully to ensure that he had them the right way round.

Three weeks later the senior technician, Monsieur Marot, came to Commarque with the results of the soil tests.

'I knew you didn't have eelworms the minute I saw the leaf samples,' he said. The analyses show a clear difference in the soil down there,' pointing to the yellow, anaemic vines on the clay side, 'easily enough to account for the poor growth. There is an iron deficiency; we can remedy this without difficulty.' So we remedied it. I didn't even bother to have Labouray's soil analysed. The cure worked there as well.

This episode should be taken as a moral tale by all who dream of having a vineyard. Bad advice is easy to come by and to recognise it requires either experience or knowledge—both together is best. For once, all those years I had spent studying obscure beasts proved directly useful in spotting what would, if taken, have been catastrophically bad advice— offered not once, but twice.

* * *

The years of study were proving less directly useful in the restaurant, where our first big group of customers revealed the lack of experience of both staff and patrons alike.

By a group I mean a bus load of customers, and I have to admit that I have never really got used to the way people seem to pour out of a bus and to go on and on pouring. Then they fill the foyer of the restaurant and the queue gets longer and longer outside. It just seems impossible that they will all fit into the dining room, or that once crammed in they will ever all find a place to sit.

The fact that I have counted the chairs six times and checked the number repeatedly against the number given in the letter of confirmation is of no reassurance.

Separate cars are better because even with the most resolute procession, and some of the big summer ones have heralded their arrival with an alarming dust cloud in the middle distance, there are always some people who turn up early and others late. There is the additional satisfaction of seeing the car park, the oak park, even the front of the château, crammed with cars. What an impression of *success* it gives, for example, to hotel guests arriving during the course of the afternoon, even more so to the casual luncher, who is looking forward to a quiet meal on the terrace outside the restaurant and cannot even get close enough to ask for a table!

In June 1987 this was all uncharted territory and that first group was truly terrifying. There were fifty-five people. Marc, in his innocence, had offered them a choice of two menus; this is quite normal, but he had agreed to the organisers' request that we put on *both* and let people choose on the day. Now this might seem fair enough, and it would be in a kitchen with a large staff, but we had a little kitchen and a small staff, mostly untrained.

The preparation of two menus is twice as much work as one, and anyway how many of each menu do you prepare? Will the fifty-five like them equally, or will there be forty-eight of one and seven of the other? There is no way of telling. The only solution is to prepare much too much and hope to flog the leftovers quickly enough afterwards to avoid having to throw them away. Didn't Marc say, '*Avec moi, pas de gaspillage*'?

Actually serving two menus presents an even greater problem. It requires time to prepare and lay out fifty-five plates of food, however simple. Take the first course of a meal for instance: our normal practice now is for the field commander in the dining room, usually me, to give the start signal to the kitchen at the moment appropriate to the complexity of the dish and the temperature at which it has to be served. This is not always straightforward; if you put out Foie Gras ten minutes too early on a hot summer's day it will be a greasy, sticky mess when you serve it. Then there is the 'state' of the customers to consider. Do they have an aperitif to finish off? Are they making speeches? Have they all finished in the loo? The kitchen then dresses the carefully counted plates, which are already laid out, and they are all served in a suitably short space of time.

With a choice of menu nothing can be done in advance of receiving the order from each table. At that point, either half the very small number of people in the kitchen is doing one thing and half another—although half of three people is difficult to organise sensibly—or everyone is doing two things at once! We were saved on that first occasion by the fact that the menus were cheap and simple and by the presence of a young man called Pascal, a 'real' professional, who was to make a solo performance of the waiting that day. He was the fiancé of a girl who had applied, quite out of the blue, for the post of waitress here, before Marc had proposed Martine, but had finally preferred an all-year-round job in the supermarket Leclerc in Langon. Pascal was temporarily out of work and had offered his services as an 'extra' for just such an event as this group. So in theory there was Martine, Pascal and me for the waiting; Marc, Alex and Georgea in the kitchen; and fourteen separate tables to serve.

Pascal and Martine took the orders while I opened the bottles of wine and kept out of the way. Inevitably, the orders came in too fast for the kitchen to cope. Georgea and Alex could manage the Pâté Piquant between them, but poor old Marc was faced with thirty-four Omelettes Basquaises to cook. He had done half a dozen when it dawned on him that they would have been eaten before he had finished cooking the rest. Georgea said, 'Do one big one per table and put it on a silver dish,' and thus saved the day.

But both the main courses involved the last-minute frying of fish and pork chops on our minute cookers, and then the whole kitchen was in danger of total blockage by the washing up. Martine and I abandoned the dining room to Pascal in favour of clearing up the kitchen. There was no room to put out the plates for the main course, no space on the ovens to heat up Pommes Forestières, and—above all—no *system* because Marc had not thought through the procedure necessary to deliver the meal.

We managed to get away with it, however. Some tables were served too slowly, but they were served nonetheless and the customers were a good-humoured lot. I tried to keep them that way by maintaining the flow of wine. Pascal was a revelation. He had a mental map of the dining room on which every table and every order was printed. His unceasing, rapid movement continued for two-and-a-half hours, during which time he was concentrating so hard that he was unable to speak to any of us. My respect for the 'real' waiting profession rose that day and has not wavered since. I know I cannot do what he did. Eight tables is my limit, and at eight tables I am likely to make a mistake; one retrieves them *bien sûr*! But Pascal made no mistakes.

Marc, not surprisingly, was totally exhausted when that first group left and never let himself get caught again with two menus. I have to admit that in later years we *have* done two separate groups at the same time but they have always been quite small, twenty or twenty-five people, and we are cunning about what goes into each menu.

Our second group was a doddle by comparison with the fifty-five. There were only thirty people and none of them was interested in food anyway. They were all owners of 1950s' American cars and their dinner

                    The Vineyard Venture

was just an excuse to sit outside and spend a couple of hours ogling these brilliantly painted, impeccably chromed monuments to bad taste. The diners occupied one side of a long table, everyone facing the row of cars drawn up across the entire length of the courtyard.

After these two incidents, it was now late June, Marc started to get cold feet about the high season, that is to say July and August.

'I may not be able to cope alone,' he said.

This seemed possible. He had already failed to cope alone. None of us knew what was going to happen, but we had seen an awful lot of cars looking for lunch during August of the previous year.

The problem was solved for us one morning by the arrival in the restaurant of a short man with an enormous tummy and a ponytail, who had come to find work for his 17-year-old daughter. He succeeded. We were impressed by his initiative, by the conviction with which he promoted Nathalie, and by Marc's promises to train her rapidly into a state of extreme usefulness. He loved this and was good at it. Perhaps he should have been a teacher! Anyway, he took her in hand from the first day and did not just leave her to peel potatoes and wash up. He insisted on instructing her not only in cookery but also in social graces, cleanliness—he would never let her start work without first having a shower—and would lecture her on morality, workers' rights, and the fruits of his experience. Nathalie was an open, straightforward and hard-working girl and I have no idea what she made of all this, but she had certainly had enough of Marc by the time he left.

In July the staff was completed (what? *more* staff??) by the arrival of Simon, another 'Stephen', but even more omnicompetent: lots of waiting experience, excellent French, highly intelligent and extremely heat resistant. He was able to observe the life of the kitchen with an amused and penetrating eye and kept us posted as to what was, as they say, 'going down'.

* * *

Under no circumstances was Papy Dartigues going to get this year's *vendange* (the grape harvest) so the preparation of the *chai* was already being planned by early summer. This provided my first encounter with an *oenologue* (oenologist), someone who studies wine; more particularly, someone who directs, or advises on, winemakers' winemaking and helps them to do it better. An oenologist is someone who *really* knows about wine, rather than someone who *thinks* they know about wine or, just as common, that everyone *else* thinks knows about wine; there are some wine writers who fall into this category!

It was that first technician, the one who brought the Shell rep to Labouray, who gave me the introduction. Monsieur Jacob was director of the Station Oenologique at Soussac and he came a long way to see me. But he knew the *coin*. His brother had sold out to Yquem, thus parting company with Château Pajot and several perfectly situated hectares of Sauternes vineyard, another one swallowed up by the giant, just before the land started to climb in value with the reawakening of interest in the mid-1980s. Monsieur Jacob lamented this loss… 'if only he had hung on another year or so…', and then turned his attention enthusiastically to the subject of Commarque. He cheered me up enormously.

'This is first class land, you do realise? The presence of different soil types is a big plus. On this side,' he gestured to the sandy patch on the left of the track, 'your vines will give you wine with finesse, and over there,' pointing to the clay, 'the wine will be more powerful—*costaud*. When you mix them together the result will be better than either parcel could produce alone.'

He was equally complimentary about the still hypothetical *chai*. A perfect building was his opinion, and quite big enough even when all the vineyard was planted. He then dropped the intriguing remark: 'With a fine old building like this you'll never have any trouble starting your fermentations.'

I asked how on earth he could be sure of that. The answer went something like this: 'We've noticed that some brand new *chais* are not good places for making wine, despite being built to high specifications and equipped *à point*. The juice won't start fermenting and is then liable to attack by bacteria. The quality of the wine is compromised before it has even been made. We think that despite the fact that we preach sterility, these *chais* are just too sterile. An old building has yeast in its very fabric, in the dust in the air. It is impossible to get rid of it and this seems to be a good thing. We very rarely have problems of this sort in *chais* made in old buildings.'

This was reassuring! 'What about problems with winemakers who are complete novices?' I asked.

More reassurance was forthcoming; 'They never give us any trouble because they listen to advice and do as they are told! The difficulties arise with the older winemakers, who think they know it all and have fixed ideas, often horribly wrong.'

Monsieur Jacob then took a piece of paper and a pencil from his bag and drew our *chai*.

'Keep it simple,' he said. 'Sauternes is easy to make once you have picked the grapes. The difficult thing is finding the grapes in the first place. A small press *there*.' He indicated a spot just inside the door. 'Go to Duluc in Budos—he's very helpful. Beside it you need a *cuvon de réception* for the juice to run into by gravity, dug into the floor—can you do that?'

'Yes.' (Well, Wally and Pirrin can!)

'Leave space for one or two small settlement tanks beside it where you can clear the juice overnight before putting it in the fermentation *cuves* (vats) here and here.' By now we were almost at the far end of the *chai*. 'Don't install more *cuves* than you need to hold the maximum amount of wine you are allowed to make in any one year because in a small set-up like this—I take it you are interested in quality?—you should try and put the whole crop in barrel. Your barrels will fit in over here.'

In my mind's eye I saw the row of new barrels stretching from end to end of the opposite wall, starting where he had pointed.

'Keep the *cuves* small. They're easier to cool. Twenty-five hectolitres is ideal and if they're the right shape they'll fit through the door. Any bigger and you'll find yourself having to knock down the wall to get them in. I'll give you an address. Insulate the roof well. Paint the walls with a good washable paint that won't wash off itself when you clean it. That just leaves the floor; you need to be able to clean the *chai* and clean it again, then clean it once more every time you do anything in it. You will require lots of water and it has to get out somewhere. Ask your builder to lay a concrete floor sloping to the middle here,' and he indicated a line running the full length of the building. 'Install a drain sloping to this end, pierce the wall and make a soakaway outside. Have you thought about electricity?' Well, vaguely... 'Put in decent lighting. Working in half-darkness is a liability.'

'One last thing; cooling the fermentation *cuves*. A *machine à froid* is too expensive at this stage. Get a second-hand milk tank, I'll give you an address, put water in it and cool it down, then arrange to pump it over the vats. And that's all you need! Give me a ring when you've finished the building work and I'll come and check it before you put in the machinery.'

He handed me his drawing, complete with addresses, patted me on the back, said *bon courage* and drove off with a cheerful wave.

I felt well launched, like a good fermentation. This was guidance to give confidence, delivered with the precision and clarity of a master. Monsieur Jacob is to wineries, I thought, what Monsieur Bougès is to vineyards. I looked forward to the prospect of making wine under his direction.

Wally and Pirrin set to work again and dug and levelled and shovelled concrete. They made a lovely sloping floor with a drain and an underground reception tank, the sides of which were raised eight inches above ground level so that no one would fall straight into it. When the concrete was dry they put up a rickety set of step ladders and planks and insulated the roof. Their height meant they barely needed ladders at the lower end of the roof and Pirrin, who resembles a gigantic spider monkey, preferred when he could, to crouch doubled up on the main supporting beams with his knees above his head. Monsieur Arlic, on his first major work at Commarque, installed the best electrical system in the place, with nice, bright strip-lighting. One day at the end of July my oldest nephew Nicky, a medical student, turned up with a friend. They stayed for just a day and three quarters, and spent a day and a half painting the *chai*, a noble contribution to the cause over which we felt slight pangs of guilt at the sight of such paint-splattered exhaustion.

I called Monsieur Jacob to inspect the finished product.

'*Très bon travail*' was his reaction, 'I can see we shall have no problems with you.'

But then came crushing disappointment.

'Sauternes is too far from Soussac for you to belong to our lab. I am going to hand you over to Cadillac. I've talked to Llorca, the director, and you should contact Henri Ducourneau.'

He gave me the phone number, and I never saw him again. Finished was the reassurance of winemaking under Monsieur Jacob's care, and I wasn't even going to get the director of this other place, just some minion! How could I know that Monsieur Jacob was not unique and that at Cadillac rose the fount of all vinous knowledge and wisdom, or so it came to seem, personified by the youthful and dynamic Henri Ducourneau?

Nevertheless, the game had to go on, and it was time to find the machinery. The Coopérative Agricole had the small items: a special wine pump, with expensively designed insides to avoid churning the grape juice and wine too violently, or aerating them excessively. The small tanks, *garde-vins*, for settling the wine also came from there, with *chapeaux flottants* (floating lids) which can be sealed with paraffin oil poured round the edge if you want to keep finished wine in them. I bought one of 10 hectolitres and one of 5. I visited a large shed on an industrial estate in South Bordeaux where I met a man so fast talking that he was almost a caricature of the fast-talking salesman. I left with an enamel-lined, 12-hectolitre fermentation *cuve* in the back of the van, second hand and 'just what you need', he said. It was a mere ₣5,000, comparing favourably with the two brand-new, 25-hectolitre *cuves en inox* (stainless steel vats) that I had ordered from him at ₣16,000 each, plus VAT. They were very beautiful, of a form called *parallélépipède*, that is rectangular when seen from the side. They were also *bouchonné*, meaning patterned all over in little circles, and they were equipped with taps galore.

The address in the Charente given to me by Monsieur Jacob produced a second-hand milk tank without fuss, and Monsieur Duluc at Budos took me round his yard and showed me various large and unidentifiable fragments of machinery all of which, he claimed, could be put together in the appropriate combinations to make wine presses. I now know that he is capable of doing this with his eyes shut. He selected a small, elderly looking wooden and yellow metal-plus-rust affair called a *familial*, and said that lots of small Sauternes producers used them, that it was very reliable and he could get it ready for me in time for the *vendange*—price? ₣6,000. I had had doubts about its visible lack of sophistication, but, although we had allowed up to ₣25,000 for a press, that was before I had been done over by Monsieur David in the shed in Bordeaux. I swept the doubts away. We still have this press. It is not very good, for various reasons, but Monsieur Duluc was right, it is reliable.

The new *cuves* were delivered several weeks later. Monsieur David told us to have a few strong men standing by to help unload them because they weighed 235 kilos each. It was on this occasion that we first met John, the American actor who was to act so successfully as waiter on many, many occasions. That first time he was playing the part of a strong man. He was brought by his friend Maurice. The two of them lived together across the valley in Budos, and we'd first met Maurice, who is English, when he brought his parents to stay in the hotel. The third and last strong man was me.

We had reckoned the delivery man would have machinery for shifting *cuves* and all we would really have to do would be to balance them. The delivery man plainly reckoned it was us that should have had the machinery because his first utterance on jumping down from his colossal lorry was: 'Have you got a transpalette?'

'No.'

'What have you got with wheels that we can move these beauties on?'
And he twitched back a corner of the canvas side on his 40-foot trailer to
reveal a glimpse of the stainless-steel mountains inside.

'Edward's pushchair?' suggested Georgea, and Edward's pushchair it
was, folded flat but not nearly as flat as it was when the *cuves* were finally
in place.

'*Putain*, is that all you've got?' The delivery man sighed deeply and
rolled back two-thirds of one wall of his trailer.

It was crammed from end to end with tightly packed *cuves*. Ours were
by far the smallest and I hoped for his sake that he would find his other
drops were in places better equipped than ours for getting piles of metal
off lorries. Some of the things he had there would certainly need a crane
to unload them.

Fortunately he was a very large man, strong as an ox, and had
patently done what he started to do now many times before. The first
cuve was slid off the side of the lorry with the delivery man alone on
one side and us three strong men on the other. The leading edge settled
heavily on the ground, Edward's pushchair went under the middle and
the full 235 kilograms were tilted forward, then lowered on top of
it. It bent instantly and the *cuve* descended another 2 inches towards
the earth, but somehow the wheels of the pushchair still went round;
somehow, we seemed to push the whole thing towards the entrance
of the *chai*, although more likely it was the delivery man at the front
who was actually pulling it! He had one hand on a sack trolley (I had
suddenly remembered about this!) keeping the front from burying itself
in the ground. The other was thrust through the trap on the front face
of the *cuve*, heaving it forward. So we progressed foot by painful foot.
The step up through the door into the *chai* was crossed by the delivery
man alone. He had no choice. He was at the front, we were at the back
and the *cuve* occupied the doorway in between with a bare inch to spare
on either side!

The second *cuve* came down off the lorry with an unexpected rush,
leaving John wedged underneath to stop it falling forward before the
pushchair was in position.

'All right, lovey?' asked Maurice as John crawled out when we had
taken the weight off him. He was, and the painful progression of *cuve* to
chai was repeated. The pushchair gave up the struggle just inside the door
when the frame finally settled tightly round the wheels which buckled
in sympathy. It was thus impossible to shift the *cuve* another inch. The
operation was concluded rather in the manner we had envisaged before

the lorry had arrived. That is to say the delivery man did all the work while we kept the *cuve* balanced. The only thing missing was the machine which should have allowed him to do this easily. Instead, crouched beneath the *cuve*, he pulled it backwards, rocking on the tiny sack-trolley, while the three of us held the far end up in the air and stopped it falling sideways.

Very handsome the *cuves* looked when they were in position. This is more than can be said for the lawn where the fully laden lorry had parked! The tyre marks were 6 inches deep and it had only recently recovered from the effects of the fertiliser spreading operation.

13

Black Sunday—the Worst Day

The high season was now upon us. The children completed their first year at school, a year which had been running out of steam, with innumerable holidays and a general lack of motivation, for several weeks before the official end of term. They came home to a summer of swimming and playing with the children in the gîte and with all the summer visitors from England.

Thomas was, as the French say, *tranquil*, for he was not to make the big step to College in Langon the following year. It was held that he would suffer in *Sixième*, the first class, because his written French was still not good enough. Monsieur Desautel had sugared the pill by stating that Thomas would not be doing justice to what he called his 'ample intelligence' if he left his care now, and that in a year's time he would make the transition from Ecole Primaire to Collège, taken very seriously in France, with great ease. We agreed, to Thomas's satisfaction; now he could be king for another year! He did remark, though, that as he would be a year older, people might think he had 'redoubled' a class and he would be forever explaining that this was not the case.

What happens in France, if you are struggling in class and not reaching the *moyenne*—ten out of twenty in all subjects, with a bit of latitude, but beware Maths and French—is that you repeat, or redouble, the year you have just 'failed'. Repeat means just that. There will be no change in approach the next time round, no attempt to identify and work on particular difficulties. Any special attention you may receive is dependent on the willingness and ability of the teacher to single you out in an often-bulging class. Once you have redoubled a year, the fact is with you for the remainder of your school career and it carries with it a slight, but definite stigma, despite the fact that 50 per cent of all French children redouble at least one class. Thus in a running race someone might say: 'the only ones who beat me were enormous; I bet they were *redoubleurs.*' I know of one little boy in Sauternes who redoubled his *cours préparatoire*, the very first year of his schooling! How sad to carry that with you for the next ten years. Fortunately he is, to say the least, relaxed about his school work!

Once you get too many years behind where you ought to be, and you will have been pushed on at least once, even though your *moyennes* were dodgy, the system recommends that you leave its confines. This tends to happen at the age of 13 to 15, and the result is either removal from Collège to the Lycée Professionnel ('the LEP') to learn a trade, or a place in a special section within the Collège. There is one at the Collège Toulouse Lautrec in Langon, and I am afraid that the members of this section are often treated as social outcasts by the other pupils. Thomas was to tell us soberly, when he went there the following year, that if a member of the 'SEGPA' sits down at your table in the canteen, you get up and leave! Where oh where are *égalité* and *fraternité*?

That the stigma attached to redoubling is deeply rooted in the collective French consciousness is shown by the failure of Monsieur Lataste, dynamic headmaster of Toulouse-Lautrec, to set up a class of Sixième in two years. The intention was to allow all those who had struggled at Primary School to revise shaky foundations and then progress slowly but surely through the Sixième programme. Many would become, preached Monsieur Lataste with tireless patience and gusto, competent members of Cinquième, the next year up, and so avoid the catastrophe of total failure within the educational system. This enlightened move foundered on the unwillingness of parents, to whom the new option was proposed, to allow their children to join this class, however much they needed it. The majority were thus stigmatised more visibly and ineradicably than they would otherwise have been by inevitable failure in the years that followed.

So, Thomas had already discovered some of the mores of French education, but all that was quickly forgotten in the summer holidays of 1987. In July the three older boys were welcomed with open arms by Langon swimming club, Les Marsouins (the Dolphins) de Langon, where they collected piles of medals in local swimming competitions. Bravo Witney swimming pool and its careful coaching.

This was not a beautiful summer, nothing like 1986. The grass never once went dry and whitish-brown as it had the previous year. The rainfall was above average and there were many dull, grey days. After our rigorous winter we were starting to feel disenchanted with Bordeaux weather, if not downright cheated. It was certainly affecting the hotel and restaurant and it was going to affect the grapes. How depressing it was to hear hotel guests booked in for a week, announce after two days: 'We think we'll head further south and try to find some sunshine.'

Depressing but understandable, doubly depressing when, a quarter of an hour previously, you have told someone over the phone that the hotel is full and there will be no rooms available until next week! For we *were* sometimes full. Not very difficult with only seven rooms, and we had even been full once or twice before the high season of July and August had arrived.

The first time we were able to refuse someone for the hotel (I say 'were able' rather than 'had to' because one cannot help a certain shameful satisfaction in telling someone there are no rooms available), he would not believe it. The French, being at home, exhibit much less forethought about booking their holidays than all the foreign tourists who have had to organise things from afar. It is the French, unfortunately, that we refuse in numbers during the month of August, and sometimes they are downright grumpy about it. I suppose it is the sight of the Belgian, British, Swiss and Dutch cars in the car park that gives them a feeling of being pushed out in their own country. Anyway, the gentleman in question exclaimed, '*C'est pas possible!*' and Marc had to point to the riding boots standing like muddy sentries outside every hotel room to convince him.

We were full of Swiss horsemen and women on what is called a *randonné à cheval* across the Gironde and les Landes and for which we were one of their headquarters. Every evening the boots appeared before the doors while their erstwhile occupants were cleansed of the day's grime, and every evening the boots were minutely cleaned and polished before dinner, a task rendered more agreeable by the simultaneous consumption of Sauternes.

Each morning Georgea and Alex cleaned the rooms after the riders had embarked on their horses for the day and each morning they were fascinated by a 10-inch long cylinder of aluminium foil, found by chance the first day in one of the rooms when it rolled out of its hiding place under a pile of books and magazines as they were being tidied. I am afraid they looked for it after that and it was always there, hidden in the same place. On the last morning it was too much for them. Curiosity got the better of propriety; they took it from its hiding place and peeled off a bit of the foil to reveal ... a single, enormously fat cigar!

The first Sunday in August, we distinctly remember, was hot and sunny. There was a grand Fête in the park of Château Filhot, a celebration of

Chasse, Pêche et Nature, that is hunting, fishing and, of course, nature, although I am not clear exactly how the latter fitted in with the dog shows, clay pigeon shooting and hunting horn competitions. All we knew about it was derived from its extensive advertising campaign, centred around a striking photo of a stag in a misty pine wood. Just the kind of wood found all round Sauternes; just the kind of stag as well. We have all seen them walking among the oak trees behind the hotel and even loitering on our football pitch just beyond the clothes lines. On that day in August, if I had been a stag I would have made it my business to stay well outside the limits of the commune of Sauternes, such was the weight of artillery and hunting beasts concentrated at its heart.

The other hint that that Sunday might not be just like any other was gleaned quite by chance at the supermarket Leclerc in Langon, where I was waiting at the reception for an invoice, or some such, when the phone rang. The caller wanted to know if it was possible to buy a ton of frozen chips for the Fête at Château Filhot. The answer was a crisp 'no', but the question should have alerted me to the fact that Filhot was expecting a crowd and that the Fête organisers were not too switched on about feeding it. This was already Friday morning, and anyway a ton of *chips*!!

The significance of this clue escaped me and, at just before midday on that first Sunday in August, we were sitting comfortably in the shade of the great Wellingtonia having an early salad lunch, in case we had to go and lend a hand in the restaurant. There were a couple of reservations, but nothing the staff, now relatively numerous, could not deal with alone.

On the stroke of noon cars started pouring down the track, escaping, we realised afterwards, from catering based on truckloads of frozen chips. But I am afraid they did not do much better at Commarque. This was 'Black Sunday', the day we lost control of the restaurant.

People came in under the arch in twos, fours and even sixes. The four tables outside on the terrace were filled instantly and a knot of customers began to gather at the door of the restaurant. Martine appeared and beckoned in our direction, but we were still blissfully unaware of what was to come. Simon said, 'I'll get my things on and go and help.'

We continued our lunch and watched Simon dealing competently with the tables outside, giving out menus, taking orders, serving drinks. The customers had been welcomed, installed and had something to do. Those important first steps had been achieved. But from our relaxed viewpoint on the far side of the courtyard, we were unable to see what was happening inside the restaurant where there were more people. Many more people.

Martine had ground to a halt. She had no more menus to distribute. Not that it would have made a lot of difference if she had had enough for everyone and had taken their orders. Marc and Nathalie would have been unable to do anything about it. They were already locked in combat with twice as many orders as they could cope with. At that moment it would have been better for us if we had asked all the remaining unserved, menu-less and already fidgeting customers to leave rather than blundering on like the Gadarene Swine we were! But we didn't think of that. There they all were and there they were going to stay.

Simon came round the back of the hotel at a run and muttered urgently: 'You'd better come quickly, we've got problems,' disappearing the way he had come without further explanation.

I put on my waiting trousers and followed him. Georgea had already gone, telling the children to clear up the lunch. The back way round the hotel means going through the kitchen to get to the dining room. What I saw on dashing through was not reassuring: Marc was standing before the ovens, on which were four large frying pans completely covering every single burner. He had his arms raised in a despairing gesture and was saying: 'But I can't do anything more, there's no more space to cook!'

The restaurant was a daunting sea of faces, and there was precious little food to be seen on the tables. As I crossed the room to ask Martine what needed doing—a silly question really—my arm was grabbed.

'We've been sitting here for over half an hour and we haven't even been given the menu. It's a disgrace. I demand to be served,' shouted an angry voice, belonging to an angry face.

At that moment a wine list descended on the round serving table in the middle of the room. I leapt on it before Martine could get it, gave it to the man, apologised as well as I could, and promised him a menu instantly. Ten minutes later he had it; after quarter of an hour I had taken his order and he had a bottle of wine, a bottle I had made a point of recommending effusively to try and redeem a bit of ground by at least being friendly. It was another half an hour before they got anything to eat. Martine, Simon and I got round the tables and mollified the customers temporarily with wine and aperitifs. But the kitchen was in gridlock.

When tables complain to you individually it is bad enough. It is in fact very, very bad. When they start talking to each other and complaining collectively you know you have lost it completely. Where do you turn next to try and soothe, apologise, promise, amid that expanse of hostile, angry faces? For the French, an assault on the stomach is unforgivable, but for foreigners to do it on French soil is also insulting. To be unforgivably insulted at Sunday lunch …. can you wonder they were upset?

There is surely a happy ending to this story, right? For example, although it was very slow everyone was served eventually and they forgave us afterwards. Or, we gave them all free Champagne, Marc made a speech that was both humorous and apologetic and was loudly cheered. Not a bit of it. Things just got worse. Many people did receive food, but when they eventually got something, it was flung on the plate in panic-stricken haste, prepared with much less than the usual care and with scant regard for appearance. How could it be otherwise? There was at least one out-and-out catastrophe. There were probably others, but this one stays in the collective mind. It must be scorched, like some of the food, into Martine's memory, for it was her table. What's more, the people in question had actually reserved in advance for their 'lunch'.

Four people occupied this table and, conveniently, they all ordered Ris de Veau (Sweetbreads). This was one of the few dishes prepared in advance, like the infamous Lambs Kidneys, which the Ris de Veau also resembled in being thickly brown. It just had to be ladled into a saucepan and warmed up; but there was, of course, no room for another saucepan on the stoves, permanently blocked as they were by frying pans of steak, Magret de Canard, fish and Pommes Forestières. However, a third little oven stood in one corner of the kitchen, never used until then. Its lid was down and it acted as little more than a shelf. In panic I fitted a gas bottle to it, and it worked. The saucepan of Ris de Veau was plonked gratefully on a ring and attention turned to other things. A long, long time later Martine came back and announced: 'I must have the four Ris de Veau at all costs. The customers are *vraiment pas contents*.'

'OK, *c'est bon*, I'll do them now,' Marc said, grabbing the saucepan. Crashing the lid on the floor he groaned, 'Merde. It's Rognons d'Agneau, not Ris de Veau.'

'What shall I do?' asked Martine.

'Tell them we've run out of Ris de Veau but we do have Rognons d'Agneau instead.'

Off went Martine on her disagreeable task. Others might well have burst into tears and gone home at that point, but she stuck to it. The Rognons were dumped back on the gas ring and forgotten about while Marc wrestled with his frying pans. Five minutes later Martine ran back into the kitchen.

'The four are very angry. They say they have driven a long way just to eat the Ris de Veau.'

I have never been able to understand this: how could the reputation of Marc's Ris de Veau have travelled a long way?

'But they'll take the Rognons just so they can have something to eat and go!'

But this was being over optimistic. The saucepan is grabbed again. The little brown dishes are lined up. Nathalie hovered with the boiled potatoes and dried parsley. Marc started to spoon out his little bullets.

'*Merde*, they've burnt! It's all stuck to the bottom. Hang on! I think I can save enough for four helpings.'

And so he did, and our already furious customers, after waiting an hour and a half for melting Ris de Veau, received rock hard, burnt Rognons d'Ageau and walked out. No one asked them to pay the bill!

My personal worst memory concerns the people who grabbed my arm when I first entered the restaurant. Towards the end of the nightmare, when most people had had most of their food, and no one was shouting at us, I imprudently stopped to ask if they had liked the wine I had recommended. Yes, they had, was the reply, but it was most certainly the only thing they had liked. We dishonoured the Bordeaux region. They were ashamed to sit in the room with tourists from all over France who would go home and say: '*This* is the quality of La Cuisine Bordelaise!'

Then the man gave me a detailed criticism of his meal from start to finish, which was, of course, correct in every detail. His discourse was delivered in a loud enough voice to be heard by all the neighbouring tables, and I stood there in the middle and took it. Like the first winter, only a thousand times worse, we had not come to France for this.

The man finished his lecture, demanded the bill with a dismissive gesture, paid and left. Meanwhile, his wife had written me a letter which she left on the table. It was just a summary of her husband's speech, but she had added their name and address and telephone number. The following evening, I summoned up my courage and telephoned them, with the intention of apologising (yet again), of admitting that we had made a complete balls-up of the day, and of inviting them for a free meal, when they would see that we were capable of better. I should not have bothered. I got the lecture all over again, with just as much vitriol as the first time, dishonour to the region and all. Such sins would never be forgiven.

Simon had done marginally better than Martine and I. He had adopted a policy of humorous self-abasement, which, allied to his great natural charm, had worked quite well. He ended the service in a spirit of apologetic joking that had helped to disarm any reluctance on the part of the customers to pay their bills. In fact everyone paid, apart from the four who had been given the burnt kidneys, and at the very end one or two people were even quite sympathetic. I remember some people from Langon making various suggestions, designed to be helpful, as to how we could improve things. They cheered us up a bit by saying that what they had been given to eat had been good, when it finally arrived, and for their part, they would come again because it was such a lovely place. Fortunately, most of the customers that day were not locals, so at least we did not become the laughingstock of Sauternes!

By five o'clock that afternoon we were left alone among the wreckage of that service wondering what exactly we should do about it. At least Georgea and I were wondering. Martine, Nathalie and Simon were polishing the glasses, and Marc had gone to lie down. The lessons to be drawn from this ghastly experience were in fact obvious: the first being that we should have been keeping a closer eye on what went on so as to have avoided the crisis in the first place! I should have taken the hint, so broadly dropped in Leclerc, about the crowds of people who were going to be scattering from Château Filhot that Sunday in search of lunch. What a lack of business acumen is revealed! The following year the fête was advertised again. We organised ourselves down to the last detail to receive a crowd. The menus were carefully arranged for rapid service, large quantities of food were prepared for instantaneous arrangement on plates, glasses were lined up in serried ranks for every kind of aperitif and by ten to twelve we were all standing ready and waiting for the assault. We got precisely twenty people. In 1988 professional caterers were brought in at Filhot. Once in, you couldn't leave the place unless you paid a second time to get back in. The thousands of people in the park were trapped and there was no explosive scattering of would-be lunchers at midday! Somehow, we had failed to hear 'the word' again. We were not part of that circle that knows what's going on. It is a deficiency in this business.

On the more immediate and practical side, Black Sunday taught us a number of quite simple things. For example, we needed to have more menus available and to put more wine in the fridges. By far the biggest problem, however, was that too many of our dishes were prepared at the last moment, hence the blocking of the ovens with frying pans, which were in any case designed for professional cooking surfaces four times the size of ours. What we needed were one or two more interesting dishes that could be prepared in advance. But the question was, could Marc come up with anything? As he was still lying down we were unable to ask him at once, so we finished resetting the tables and retired to lick our wounds.

The question was put to him that very evening, while the memory of what he had undergone was still fresh in his mind and not overlain by a fog of self-justification. He looked totally blank and lifted his arms in the same gesture of despair as he had used at lunchtime in front of his inadequate ovens. Well, could he try and think of something then and tell us tomorrow morning? He looked doubtful, then grumpy. He knew he would have nothing to suggest and he had no books to help him out. In later years we would meet Dominique, who read round his subject voraciously, and positively had to be restrained from trying new things, so constant was his inspiration and enthusiasm. Within fifteen minutes of arriving at Commarque he was cooking six different things at once, and we hadn't even realised that he had turned up with the intention of staying. I found him in the kitchen in the centre of a sea of pots and pans, vegetables, herbs, cutlery and other mess, cutting up aubergines, with an expression of ecstatic concentration on his face.

'What's that for?' I asked.

'It's for a Caviar of Aubergines, and that's a selection of three purées I've made for tonight's vegetables,' he replied. I'm also making a grape chutney (Shutney) to go with the Terrine de Foie de Volaille, and that's a Gelée de Verveine for your Fruits d'Automne, Sauce Sauternes. You see it's rather a nice colour. I hope you don't mind me taking a few of the cèpes I found in the *chambre froide*. I thought you might like to try Raviolis de Cèpes. I'll bring them over to the house when they are ready. You could serve them as an accompaniment to a meat dish or as a starter—oyster sauce goes well with them. I noticed a box of chicken legs, so I was wondering if you would like Poulet aux Citrons Confits? Those are the lemons I am just confiting.

No one had shown him anything in the kitchen. He had not even had time to look at the menu when I'd had left him to settle into his flat a few minutes previously!

Then there was the long-serving Gilles, who looked at books rather than read them, took in the pictures and the names of dishes, and revamped them *à sa façon*, often all wrong, just occasionally excitingly right. But Marc had learned what he had learned and had no new tricks. I thought of the slippery stew he had once produced for supper, announcing with a superior little chuckle: 'Of course, Madame [Georgea] could never produce anything like this. She does not have the equipment to do so.'

I had wondered at the time what equipment he meant; was it the fine sieve he had passed the sauce through to help give it the slippery texture? Georgea would certainly not need that. Or did he mean mental equipment—the *savoir faire*, the years of experience, the mountain of knowledge necessary to make a stew like that? If that was the case, Georgea was about to show him a clean pair of heels in terms of imagination, initiative, inventiveness, understanding and clear-sightedness. He did not take it well.

We all sat down the next day to Georgea's first effort: Estouffade de Bœuf mijotée au Gingembre. Everyone tried it, Martine, Marc, Nathalie, Simon, Alex, Georgea and me. The children were getting it for lunch whether they liked it or not. Everyone liked it, except Marc. Martine was just saying, '*Mmm, c'est délicieux,*' when Marc glared at her and she fell silent.

He muttered, '*Je le trouve fade*'—I find it tasteless.

Simon spluttered and nearly choked with the effort of not laughing, and Alex, who is very blunt, said in English: 'Oh come off it, Marc.'

He understood all right and looked like thunder, but there was nothing he could say. So Estouffade de Boeuf mijotée au Gingembre replaced Bavette Echalotes, thus moving that particular menu onto a higher plane, and Gigot d'Agneau braisé aux Champignons Sauvages, which was to become braisé aux Cèpes in a year or two, replaced Gigot d'Agneau, Sauce du Chef. Don't ask what Sauce du Chef was. We had already been ashamed of that for some time!

Marc, pointedly, would have nothing to do with the new dishes. He never asked for the recipes, nor offered to prepare them. He even served them in a spirit of resolute disapproval. His pride was hurt and he never really got over it. I also think he was quite genuinely tired out, not just by Black Sunday, but by the fact that he had had barely a day off since March, after his prolonged winter holiday in Saint-Jean-de-Luz. The backlog of days was worked off by the end of August, but by then it was too late. Marc had had the 'go' ground out of him, and Nathalie had to take on more and more of the burden of preparation. She never complained, so it was by no means clear to us just how much skiving Marc was doing. The impending *vendange* (the grape harvest) was claiming my attention and Georgea, to avoid the leaden atmosphere in the kitchen and also to look after Edward, preferred to do her cooking for the restaurant in the house.

By October Marc was neither overseeing the preparation of food properly nor keeping a check on his stocks. There was a minor 'incident' with elderly Soupe de Poisson au Fumet de Crabe which was plainly unfit to eat, and when Marc announced one day: 'I have a piece of important news for you. I do not know if you will think it good news or bad—I'm leaving.' I had to smother a cheer.

He had one last, low trick to play on us which we only learned about afterwards from Martine, who admitted that if she had not been frightened of Marc she would have told us before. A friend of his had telephoned to book a group of thirty people for a meal on 31 October, Marc's last day. Unfortunately it was he who answered the phone, and had said, more or less, 'For God's sake don't come here, I'm leaving and I want to go early.'

That just about sums up the spirit of our parting, but one might add his last remark to Martine: 'They'll never find another cook like me.'

We hoped he was right.

More positive things were happening outside the restaurant during this time, and Marc certainly did not occupy all our attention. I had met Henri Ducourneau, Monsieur Duluc had delivered the renovated wine press and we had, at last, made our first wine.

14

Winemaking

One morning in mid-September I came across a man crouching in the vines, munching a grape. He jumped up and introduced himself.

'Ducourneau, Laboratoire de Cadillac, Monsieur Reay?'

It took a moment for me to click as to who he was. Then another moment to adjust to the surprise. He looked so young! A slight, athletic figure, dressed in trainers and jeans, he spat out the pips of the grape he had been eating and grinned a wide, boyish grin.

'*C'est bon,*' he said, 'in a week's time, if the rain keeps off, you can make some good *blanc sec* with these,' and he gestured at the patch of Sauvignon and Muscadelle in which we were standing.

'What about Sauternes?' I asked.

'Too soon to tell. We need some good weather. At any rate you won't be able to pick for Sauternes for at least three weeks and you won't make much this year. A lot of these vines are pretty feeble.'

A tendency to bristle at this lightning write-off of our long-awaited harvest was inhibited by the way it was delivered. Monsieur Ducourneau spoke with the same authority and clarity as Monsieur Jacob had done. I looked at him more closely. He was very pale, and tired looking around the eyes, which belied the boyish appearance. But he gave no other sign of fatigue and we talked for some time. I asked a lot of questions, all of which were answered with the same unhesitating certainty and with a clarity that left me feeling how simple it all was. 'Ums' and 'ers' did not figure in Monsieur Ducourneau's vocabulary, and after a quarter of an hour I understood that this formed part of his arsenal of professional skills. Not all his customers were ignorant noddies like me! He must have had others who were less easy to advise, who had many years' experience and might even take exception to advice that was not to their taste being delivered by this apparent slip of a youth. The manner of a master must help—but not for long if there is no master behind the manner! For my part I was only too happy to accept him as omniscient, given the rapidity with which the unknown quantity of our first *vendange* was coming upon us.

Monsieur Ducourneau promised to return in a few days with the student oenologist who would be collecting my samples of juice and wine for analysis three times a week. I could go to the lab any time I liked, he had explained, but during the busy period of the actual grape-picking, when I would have difficulty in getting away from the place (in fact a permanent condition here), this *stagiaire* (someone on a course) was there to do the travelling for me. A very snooty young man Monsieur Medeville turned out to be. Plainly the son of big vineyard owners, he thought we were a bit beneath him and that he had no need to run around after us on menial errands. But he had no choice, and I asked his advice and he liked that. As time went on and the questions became slightly less elementary, he would say, 'I'll check with Monsieur Ducourneau', and would even phone me with the answer if it was urgent. At the end he admitted his *stage* had been a real eye-opener and that Monsieur Ducourneau was *incroyable* and *vraiment branché* (really switched-on!) Monsieur Medeville left with a newfound humility that can only have been good for whatever property he was to direct in the future.

An inkling as to why Monsieur Ducourneau looked so tired was forthcoming when I went to the lab for the first time with a little bottle of something I wanted his opinion about. It was a day when the student was not due to come our way. The entrance hall of the lab was a kind of waiting room, not unlike that of a large and busy medical practice, except that it was not the people waiting in it who were the patients. The patients were all the bottles the people had brought with them. Really it was more like a baby clinic because only a few of the patients were actually ill. Most were just being checked up on!

The 'mothers' came in all shapes; there were old men in carpet slippers and caps, with grubby used bottles still bearing their labels. There were men in blue overalls with muddy boots and there were very smart men, and ladies too, in fitted wellies and padded jackets, carrying shiny new *cageots* designed to carry special small sample bottles, corked with special small corks. Most of them seemed to have arrived in four-wheel drive vehicles, whereas the carpet-slipper types had very old Renault fours and Deux Chevaux. Many just left their bottles with the lab's standard analysis request sheet slipped over the necks but others, like me, wanted to see 'The Man'. They sat in the chairs round the wall, talking or reading the farming journal *Le Paysan* thoughtfully left there for the purpose. When the door opened, to the right of Reception, and Monsieur Ducourneau appeared, in they shuffled or strode, according to their type, clutching their samples and pieces of paper with the results of analyses, to hear him pronounce. Some of them were old enough to be his father (or mother), and even grandfather, but he had their winemaking in his hands. What a responsibility!

At a tasting of experimental wines a year later the man next to me said, 'What I like about this place is their [the *oenologues*'] decisiveness. There is never any doubt about what they think and why they think it. Above all they don't hesitate to take decisions about *your* wine.'

I agreed, but added that it was not a big deal to be decisive about the little bits of wine I produced. The man looked very serious and said: 'Ducourneau behaves in exactly the same way with the biggest member of the lab as he does with you. The answer comes out *clack*, *clack*, even when the sample in front of him represents ten million francs worth of wine.'

So that's why he looks so tired!

The following year Monsieur Ducourneau taught me about fermenting dry white wine in barrels, keeping it on its lees and stirring it, a process which adds 'body' to the wine. To do this requires clear juice, not the sort of thing that tends to come out of my antique press. So the juice has to have all the bits taken out of it, rather than just being left to stand over night, which only allows the biggest 'lumps', or *bourbes*, to settle to the bottom of the tank. A *debourbage* with enzymes is necessary. The morning following this operation the opaque greenish liquid of the night before is divided into clear, appley-green juice, about three quarters of the total volume, and dark brownish *bourbes*. You take off the clear juice and ferment it and throw away the rest! After I had done this once or twice, I calculated how many dustbins of grapes I had just allowed to pour into the drain, so well-constructed along the middle of the *chai*, and then how much I paid the pickers to pick the grapes that had filled those wasted dustbins. I was so horrified by the result of this calculation that the next day I kept all the *bourbes*, put them in the small, second-hand *cuve* that I had bought in Bordeaux, and set it fermenting. The day after I added more, so I finally had several hundred litres of this stuff bubbling away when Monsieur Ducourneau came round on one of his tours of inspection. I told him what I had done.

'Show me it,' he said.

I showed him. He tilted the glass of opaque, brownish-ochre liquid and looked at it closely, then took a large mouthful. I already knew it tasted foul, but Monsieur Ducourneau was not bothered by that. He was assessing specific flavours, the *goût de bourbes*. He spat into the drain.

'You should add seventy grams per hectolitre of bentonite, six grams per hectolitre of gelatine and forty grams per hectolitre of caseine, in that order. You will recover about fifty per cent of the volume fermenting. Put it in a barrel as soon as it has cleared to give it some flavour and we'll' taste it in a couple of months and see if it can be mixed with the rest.'

So I added 70 grams per hectolitre of bentonite, 6 of gelatine and 40 of caseine, in that order, and recovered … exactly 50 per cent of the volume that had fermented! The rest was voluminous, liquid-jelly-like lees! Two weeks later, into a barrel it went, and six weeks after that Monsieur Ducourneau tasted it, grunted, asked how many barrels we had altogether.

I told him and he measured out the correct proportions of *vin de bourbes* and the rest and mixed them together. The result was indistinguishable from the rest alone; so we got 300 more bottles of dry white wine that year than we had expected.

Not every *oenologue* is a marvel of analytical skill and the repository of all knowledge. Monsieur Ducourneau has a 'plum' job as one of only two Oenologue-Conseils in a Centre d'Etudes et d'Informations Oenologiques which is full of junior oenologists and laboratory assistants as well. He did not get his post for nothing! I once visited the lab of an Oenologue-Conseil in Langon when the usual supplier of some substance needed for the Sauternes had run out and was met with incredulity by a young oenologist (he said he was an '*oenologue*'!) when I explained what I wanted.

'You never use that in white wine,' he said.

'I do,' I replied. 'It works very well.'

He shrugged his shoulders and found me what I wanted, but I know he thought I was just a loony Englishman with no idea of what I was doing. When I mentioned the incident to Monsieur Ducourneau, he merely said: 'There are people who are not properly up to date.'

An Englishman, who had written a book on Sauternes, came to stay in the hotel just before the *vendange* was about to start. He was to be enthroned as a Chevalier of the Commanderie de Bontemps, an honour reserved for those who have rendered service to Sauternes, at the annual Fête du Soleil. This is a great publicity event and a kind of pre-harvest festival in which folklore, eating and administration are combined. It includes a prolonged ceremonial dinner and the Ban des Vendanges is proclaimed, the official date on which picking can start—always much earlier, I have noticed, than anyone would ever want to begin! This man explained to me the different kinds of rot, both noble and ignoble, which were visible on our bunches of grapes, but was surprisingly ignorant about recent developments in Sauternes winemaking techniques. He had never heard, for example, of the *chambre froide*, a device installed by a number of the great châteaux in the previous couple of years, and which was going to save Sauternes for ever more from the effects of bad weather. Or so said the men who were busy installing them. I know this because they all stayed at Commarque.

The *chambre froide* is a giant freezer with a running temperature of minus 8°C, rather than minus 18°C or minus 24°C, the temperature at which ordinary food freezers operate. The bunches of grapes, once picked, are laid out on shallow trays, hundreds and hundreds of them, and stacked in the *chambre froide*. The juice is then partially frozen, frozen enough to get rid of excess water in a rainy year when the Noble Rot is not accompanied by the sunny afternoons needed to concentrate the juice. The partly frozen grapes are loaded into the press and the water stays frozen long enough for the press to squeeze out a juice much richer in sugar than it would have been before the grapes went into the *chambre froide*. This process is called cryo-extraction. Fortunately for the mystique of Sauternes and its claim to be a *vin blanc unique au monde*, the removal of water is not the only beneficial effect of the fungus that causes Noble Rot and the *chambre froide* is incapable of reproducing the others. What it does do, is to ensure that 'real' Sauternes can be made from correctly rotted grapes which contain too much water, and no more than that.

This fact has not always been understood. Some people hoped that it would no longer be necessary to spend all that money on painstaking selective picking with successive passes through the vineyard. Why not just pick the lot and bung it in the *chambre froide*? The reason is that in years when you really need the machine, when the weather is cool and wet in the autumn, Noble Rot tends to be mixed with a variety of ignoble rots which must be scrupulously sorted out and thrown away before the grapes destined to be made into Sauternes can be allowed into the wine press. Far from eliminating the need for selection, the *chambre froide* demands even greater care, for in concentrating the sugar it concentrates the evil taste of any evilly rotted grape that is left in the mixture. After that all the gelatine, caseine and oenological skill in the world is powerless to remove the *goût de moisissure* (the taste of mould) in the resulting wine.

So the wine duly fails its exam and is denied the *Appellation Contrôlée Sauternes*.

This is not just something that *might* happen. It did *happen*, discretely in certain great châteaux in the early days of the *chambres froides*, more openly later on to a number of smaller producers when a public *chambre froide* service was opened in Langon. The people in question obviously had no Monsieur Ducourneau behind them to help avoid such a costly blunder.

When I told our about-to-be-crowned Chevalier of Sauternes of the existence of these machines, he looked astonished, then worried, and finally asked if there was anything else that had happened recently which he ought to know about. I pointed out that I was hardly the person to consult on this and suggested a talk with an oenologist might be helpful before he set about updating his book in preparation for a new edition. He looked worried again and agreed. I wondered then how much the writings of other experts would benefit from such exposure. As quite a few wine writers have passed through Commarque, I got into the habit of suggesting to them that they would find a periodic talk to an *oenologue-conseil* a helpful and illuminating experience. This may be cheeky but the reactions have been interesting. One or two were offended by the implied criticism of their expertise; the offence may have been justified but, judging by the reaction of that good scholar Anthony Rose, I doubt it.

'You're absolutely right,' he said. 'I'm going to make an appointment to see Denis Dubourdieu.'

Nothing like heading straight for the top; Professor Dubourdieu of the Institute (now Faculty) of Oenology at Bordeaux University is the whizz-kid who has explained to us all, among many other things, how and why stirring dry white wine on its lees makes it better, so enabling the method to be improved. He has also discovered, by a fascinating mixture of classical biochemistry and wine-tasting skill, what substance makes the characteristic aroma of the Sauvignon grape, *le goût de buisson*, and why it is so fugitive. Now winemakers can rationalise the treatment of their vines at the end of the growing season to preserve this delicate chemical. Denis Dubourdieu practises what he preaches, and his Château Reynon Vieilles Vignes has been a reference for all who aspire to make dry white wine.

So how did Mr Rose get on with the King of Kings?

'I've learned more about wine in two hours than I have learned in the past two years!'

If he did, I should think most others would too. He also received some interesting opinions about some of his colleagues, but these are best left unrepeated!

At the other end of the scale there are some wine writers who wouldn't know what to say to an oenologist even if they met one. The most abject case I have come across was preceded by a visiting card which announced its owner as a writer on 'Art, Architecture and Wine'. Writing about the subject was clearly not synonymous with knowing anything about it, at least in the case of wine. But the gentleman came with the backing of one of our most influential newspapers which was to print his inanities on vineyard visiting and holidays in Bordeaux across three pages of one of its weekend magazines. He spoke not a word of French and was unable to drive, thus guaranteeing that he would find out very little in Sauternes at any rate. The inability to drive might also explain a certain haziness about distances between some of the vineyards he wrote about, and the hotels he suggested from which to visit them; thus for Château Haut-Brion and the other Grands Crus Graves in Pessac and Leognan on the south-west outskirts of Bordeaux, he recommended the Domaine de Fompeyre at Bazas, some 60 kilometres distant and indeed 15 kilometres from the nearest vineyard of any description! He mentioned Commarque but said we had a Basque restaurant. This means he had never even glanced at a menu, let alone set foot in the dining room, for this was three years after the departure of Marc. The only restaurant he recommended in Sauternes had closed down eighteen months previously! Of Sauternes wine he was as innocent as a babe; he asked me, during our brief discussion of the subject, what I meant by Noble Rot! When the president of the Syndicate, the same old intolerant Lamothe, accompanied by the then Director of Château Yquem, turned up on his first evening to carry him off as honoured guest to a grand reception at Château Sudiraut, I found him in his room clad only in his underpants. The two local dignitaries were obliged to stooge around in the courtyard for a good quarter of an hour before he stumbled out of his room, apologising in English while they gazed at him in surprised incomprehension! What an ambassador for England.

The real con in all this is that the man need not have budged from London to write his finished piece. A few brochures and hand-outs from the Office de Tourisme in Bordeaux, the English versions of course, would have allowed him to write a better-informed article than the one that appeared, if only because the brochures would have been up to date. As it was, he was treated as the Honoured Guest wherever he went, including—and this really sticks in the gullet—at Commarque, where we were expected to put him up for nothing because of all the good publicity he was giving us and the rest of the region!

* * *

Monsieur Arlic appeared one day with a great quantity of central heating pipes which he proceeded to weld together into a complex, abstract pattern. It resolved itself when he asked me to help him place it on top of the three fermentation *cuves*. Each one had a rectangle of perforated pipes sitting on its roof on feet made from other pieces of pipe. Between each *cuve* there was a tap, and a pipe hung down the side of the first one, to which, Monsieur Arlic explained, I should connect the pump which would supply the cold water from the milk tank. A man staying in the hotel dealt with the complicated adaptors necessary for this, and he bought and paid for all the pieces himself, absolutely refusing to be reimbursed. His wife said I shouldn't bother to argue, he had thoroughly enjoyed himself.

The press was delivered just two days before we planned to start picking. Monsieur Duluc swung it off the back of his lorry on a crane, and it settled heavily into that long suffering grass in front of the *chai*. I wondered how they were going to move it, for it was a good deal heavier than the two *cuves* that had caused us such trouble. The technique used was a triumph of applied mechanics, but not good for the lawn; Monsieur Duluc and his assistant produced a pair of 8-foot metal poles which they used as levers, bouncing and rocking the quarter ton of wood and metal in the direction of the *chai*. The narrow door was passed in two grinding movements by lifting the back end with one lever and heaving it forward with the second, shoved sideways through the legs and braced against the wall on the inside of the *chai*, which duly lost a couple of feet of new paint. Monsieur Duluc explained how it worked, gave a brief demonstration of its clanking, squealing mode of action, and now everything was ready for our first winemaking efforts, even the grape pickers.

It was Alex who first introduced us to that group of casual bohemians which was to provide, throughout the years we have been at Commarque, most of a thoroughly competent team of *vendangeurs*. But that was the following year, when Alex left to seek her fortune in the Dordogne. Back in 1987 she and Pirrin and Wally needed work, and grape picking was the only thing available, a job which Pirrin had already learned to detest over several years.

We also had John and Maurice from Budos; an English boy called Guy, in the honourable line of Stephen and Simon; Georgea; and Joel, a young man who was the uncle of one of Robert's friends at school. He lived with his brother and his brother's family and, during the *vendange* a year or two later, he was to be seen one morning gazing anxiously every few minutes at a column of smoke, rising above the trees in the direction of the village of Sauternes, the direction of his home. Shortly after his failure to return to work after lunch, we learnt that he had burnt his house to the ground that morning, as he had dimly suspected, by stuffing the stove full of paper!

Some good came out of the disaster because the people of Sauternes revealed a heart-warming solidarity for the homeless Sore family when the Mairie made an appeal on their behalf. They had lost all their possessions in the fire, down to the last pair of socks, so anything, but anything, was welcome to help them re-establish a home. Socks they received aplenty, and every other article of clothing as well. Madame Guicheney, the headmistress, completed it with brand new winter overcoats for the two children.

'Really nice ones,' said Robert, breathless with the news, and delighted for his friend David.

Bedding, furniture, toys, the Mairie rapidly filled up with offerings, and when a new oven arrived, still in its box and without a trace of its donor's name anywhere on it, there was a general feeling that the right thing had been done by the Sores! They were re-lodged, and eventually their house, which belonged to Château Filhot, was rebuilt better than before by Henri de Vaucelles, who was perhaps the only person not finally completely happy with the episode. It was after all *his* house which had burnt down in the first place!

Our pickers were completed for that first *vendange* by a local girl, a friend of Nathalie. She had asked if she could bring along her mother who had twenty-five years' experience of *vendanging* and who arrived on the first day, her only day, clad in calf-length overcoat and suede boots.

The first day's picking was undistinguished. We had had to delay for a week, not because the wine press had not been delivered, but because of the rain Monsieur Ducourneau had feared. Many châteaux were in the process of making wine so poor that they were unwilling to proclaim it as their own by sticking their labels on it. Instead, they would sell it in bulk for anonymous bottling elsewhere, at extremely modest prices. But we were full of optimism as we sallied forth with our new buckets and dustbins and our new clippers to pick healthy, ripe, unrotted grapes for dry white wine. At least that was what we were hoping for, and that was what I had explained to everyone, giving examples, what is more, of the kinds of bunches we wanted and what should be thrown away. By the end of the first rows more grapes had been thrown down between the vines than had found their way into the buckets, for the *bouyroc* was everywhere, giving those orangey-brown, vinegar-smelling grapes, full of fruit fly maggots, that we had seen the previous year when the harvest had been abandoned to Papy Dartigues. The disease had got hold earlier this time, spread by the bad weather and helped by insects and birds coming out of the woods at the ends of the rows and eating into the grapes, so helping the disease to get started. Nevertheless, we filled the press by mid-morning with grapes that were convincingly yellow-green and scrupulously mould-free. This was quite an achievement considering the ineptitude of one or two of the pickers!

The foreign novices were fine. They had been lectured ad nauseam on the horrific consequences of getting hold of the wrong grapes and could be seen frowning with concentration before every bunch. Slow they might be, but the selection, or *trie*, was carefully made. This could not be said for Nathalie's friend and her mother. An inspection of their buckets, which I had almost passed over as an insult to their experience and status as locals, revealed that they had picked everything: little green hard grapes from the tops of the vines, bunches full of *bouyroc*, and bunches already attacked by the Pourriture Noble which should have been left for the Sauternes. Fair enough! They had probably been defeated by my accent. So I explained what we were after all over again. Had they understood? *Yes, yes, no problem, sorry about the misunderstanding.* They had not realised how careful I was trying to be. We continued. Quarter of an hour later mother and daughter had shot ahead of the rest of us, and my suspicions were aroused. I arrived in time to find them emptying their very full buckets into a dustbin, from which rose a small cloud of dust, the dust that signals so clearly the presence of abundant Noble Rot. The more it billows the better one is pleased when picking for Sauternes, but its presence is a guarantee of failure for dry white wine, which will lack aroma and probably fail its exam because of high volatile acidity (vinegar!) as a result. The offending dustbin had to be sorted through and half the grapes thrown away, to the accompaniment of an embarrassed silence.

I called Alex and Joel across and asked Alex, whose French is excellent, to ask Joel, who has the local accent and any local vocab we might have lacked, to explain to Nathalie's friend and her mum once again what we wanted them to do. He did so, and there was much head shaking and murmuring about how difficult it all was. The final straw came in the afternoon when we went up to Labouray. The second row of Sauvignon up there has some fifteen or twenty plants of *Cabernet* Sauvignon, with red grapes, planted by mistake, along its length.

Mother and daughter had charge of this row and carefully picked all the red grapes. Georgea, who had to sort this one out, was not even able to save the white grapes mixed in with the red because Maman, after carefully lowering her bunches into her bucket as instructed, to avoid damage to the grapes and consequent oxidation, had crushed them flat with a suede-booted foot. Why? So that she could fit more in and not have to walk all the way back to the dustbin before finishing the row!

She called it a day that evening, so removing from me the onus of suggesting she might care to go picking somewhere else, saying that she had never been asked to select like that and it was far too complicated for her. This was plainly true, but struck us as bad for the legend of Sauternes; who does all that one-by-one selection of beautifully rotted grapes if not someone with twenty-five years' experience of grape picking?

If the few days it took to finish picking for the dry white wine were undistinguished, the Sauternes picking was even more so. The weather did not improve and our barrel or so of Sauternes was achieved at great cost both in picking time and rejected grapes. With hindsight I know that we should not have waited so long, nor made such an effort of selection; taking only the less weak among a weak crop of grapes does not make a fat lot of difference! We should have picked earlier and more generously. The time spent waiting for an improvement that never came was simply time for more grapes to go bad, as it so often is in Sauternes! That's why Nick Ryman had said, when I told him we were going to Commarque: 'Hah! You've bought Sauternes? It's the hardest wine in the world to make!'

Despite all that, we were able to witness, for the first time, the semi-magical process by which wine makes itself. For we do not really make wine ourselves. All we do is to provide the conditions that will allow this self-propelled and often unruly display of microbial life to unfold in the best possible way; but it will do it with us or without us, although not always to our satisfaction. The science of Oenology is, I suppose, the science of making it satisfactory, and part of that is knowing when to leave well alone.

Four weeks after starting the fermentation of the juice destined to be dry white wine, it had transformed itself from a semi-opaque, pale brown, yeast-smelling slurry to a clear, pale greenish-yellow liquid, quite recognisable as wine—and I had done precious little to help this astonishing change! The starting process had included tipping a saucepan full of frothing yeast into the juice, a kind of yeast that produces more aromatic wine than that found naturally on the grapes. But this will quite happily get going and make wine for you if left alone to do so, and that is an example of interfering to improve what will otherwise happen naturally and spontaneously. For the rest I just watched anxiously and made sure the temperature stayed between 17 and 20°C with my milk tank of cold water and Monsieur Arlic's sprinkler pipes, which worked perfectly.

I put the wine in barrels and the flavour improved. Monsieur Ducourneau came on one of his tours of inspection.

'It isn't very fruity, but you *will* be able to market it.' He said, after tasting it. Of the Sauternes he said merely: '*C'est un petit Sauternes.*'

They both passed their exams and were issued with the *label*. This is the Appellation Contrôlée, the right to the name Bordeaux (for the dry white) and Sauternes, not the actual labels you stick on the bottles, as I thought when I had first heard the term. I was taking advice on how to bottle the dry white when Monsieur Ducourneau said: 'It must be tested for iron and protein before bottling,' and went on to explain about the dreaded Casse Ferrique and Casse Proteique which can afflict wine weeks or even months after bottling. One day the wine is clear and sparkling, the next, *plaf!*, it has turned milky white or got great lumps floating in it! Iron has formed insoluble complexes or protein has coagulated.

The tests were done. Protein was fine. It always is because I add an unlikely, grey sludge to the fermenting wine, a volcanic clay called bentonite, which grabs all the proteins and then sinks to the bottom of the *cuve* to be thrown away as part of the lees when its job is done, leaving no trace of itself in the finished wine. But we had iron, dangerously large amounts of it. Where on earth had it come from? There were two possibilities: occasionally an iron-rich soil in a vineyard gives rise to iron-rich wine, but more commonly it is rusty machinery which is to blame, especially rusty wine presses. Despite the new paint on the metal bands holding the cage of our old press together, there was rust inside it, especially on the huge screw along which the wheel travels. In future years we would spend several days preparing the press to avoid this disaster and it never happened again. But what could be done about iron in the wine *this* year? Treat it with Potassium Ferrocyanure (a name that sounds disagreeably like 'cyanide!'), leave it for ten days, then filter it. I did it and our wine—our precious, so-longed for, laboured-over, worried-about wine—turned bright blue with Potassium Ferrocyanure and was undrinkable. Some days later great bluish plates of crystals started accumulating at the bottom of the tank, but when the wine was filtered the blue colour all stayed behind on the filter plates and the wine regained its former colour, but … did I imagine it? Was it not just a little less fruity and fragrant than before?

'Yes,' I was told. 'Every treatment, every interference with the finished wine, entails a slight loss of quality.'

So, what we put in our bottles was not quite as good as what had come out of the fermentation *cuve*. A little potential had been lost and all because of a question that should have been asked but was not. I could not have imagined it, and Monsieur Ducourneau could not have foreseen that I ought to ask it, but might not! What dangerous ground for novices this is.

And what of the Sauternes? Well it tasted, slightly, of Sauternes and smelled, slightly, of Sauternes, but it was not at all the sort of thing with which we had imagined relaunching the château's reputation, so we did not bottle it for sale. We bottled it for cooking in the restaurant. With the arrival there of Georgea, Gilles and la Cuisine au Sauternes it was just what was needed for the *au Sauternes* bit of la Cuisine, and lasted for the next two years. It did not, however, make a major contribution to the prosperity of the vineyard.

15

Dogs and Robbers—and Gilles

Winter 1987 went off a lot more smoothly than its predecessor had done. For one thing, Monsieur Jeantet's central heating was working, except in our bedroom—still the coldest room in the house and destined to remain so. The pipework to supply the radiators, installed in the full flush of optimism in the roof space above us, has remained up there, un-extended and useless to this day! But it was a much milder winter.

The boundary was walked on Christmas Eve and we could measure Edward's growth over the previous twelve months by the fact that he did not have to be carried a single step of the way, and was thus even more exhausted at the end than he had been the first time. During the Christmas holidays the children learned to help in the vineyard with that routine annual task of 'getting down the wood', that is disentangling the pruned branches from the wires, making them into bundles, carrying them out of the vines, and burning them, keeping enough for barbecues and as kindling wood. It has to be said that they did not like doing this and have not grown fonder of it since. The trouble is that we have the largely customer-free period from mid-December to March to finish the accounts for the hotel, restaurant and the vineyard, and complete the winter work in the vines before the customers start to return in the second half of March. We still had Alex for the occasional room, help with the vines and so on, but in January and February there was not much money around to pay for many hours, especially with the Saint-Martin brothers out pruning. There was only Georgea now in the restaurant kitchen and me *en salle*. So we had a tight schedule, admittedly aggravated by what was to become our annual visit to England during our official *fermeture annuelle* in February! We needed the children's help. Never more than an hour at a time, but with Georgea and Robert in one row, and some stamping down of piles of *sarments* by

Edward to make them easier to carry, the twins in the second, Thomas in the third and me in the fourth, we did eight rows in that hour. Later it was Edward and Robert to a row, Francis, William and Thomas each to a row, plus Georgea and I, and that made twelve per hour, sometimes fifteen with those who finished first helping the last. As for carrying the bundles out and burning them, the progress made each year as the children grew led to a constant overestimation (for once!) of the time required to complete the job.

The children were not to enter into the life of the restaurant just yet, with the exception of Thomas, who had already started an early career as occasional waiter with great success. Martine was always full of pretend indignation at the size of the tips he received, and on one occasion a couple on whom he had waited in some large group returned alone months later when he was at school and demanded: 'Where is the little waiter? We have come all the way to see him again!' …. and left him fifty francs. Martine remarked that life would be a lot easier if *she* got tipped for not being there.

So, the winter of 1987 was easier than the previous one, but we were not finished with surprises yet. While on holiday in England and despite the vigilance of Alex, who came in every day, left lights on, fed the hamsters, and made sure she and Pirrin were visible about the place, we were burgled; a shutter prised open, a window broken at the back of the house and the television and hi-fi gone. The gendarmes came out, took statements and looked round but found no trace either of the thief or of the stolen goods.

We were burgled for the second time two weeks later. It happened just after a *fiançailles*, or engagement party, for about thirty people on a Sunday. This was our first group, as it were, on our own; just Georgea as cook, with Alex to help her dish up—almost her last task here. A week or so later she produced her friend Joan to replace her and took off with Pirrin and Wally to work for Mr Jenkin-Lee who was building a veritable holiday village at his château in the Dordogne! I did the waiting together with Martine, who was not yet 'officially' employed for the season but came down from Bordeaux for the day. It was Georgea's menu, not bad for a first attempt!

Le Velouté de Saint-Jacques

La Salade Landaise aux Deux Foies (a bed of varied lettuce with prunes, walnuts and pine nuts). Then slices of dried duck's breast (magret seché), smoked duck's breast (magret fumé), confited duck's gizzards (gésiers), and hearts, the whole array topped with two croutons, one bearing Foie Gras, the other Terrine de Foie de Volaille au Sauternes, almost a meal in itself)

Filet de Bœuf au Sauternes et au Roquefort

Le Plateau de Légumes du Marché

Fromage de Brebis de Léogeats (a prize-winning Pyrenean style sheep's cheese, made just down the road by a real Basque, André Michelena, absolutely delicious)

Le Kilimandjaro (an ultra-rich ice-cream of chocolate, praline and thick crème chantilly)

Café

It was the Terrine of Chicken Livers, used here in the salad, that really woke us up to what good stuff Sauternes is for cooking. The original recipe called for cognac, and it was with cognac that Georgea had made the terrine on several occasions in England. At Commarque we carried out a terrine blind tastin;: one made with cognac, a second with cognac and Sauternes, a third with Sauternes alone. The day was carried comfortably, without a single dissenting voice, by the Sauternes-alone terrine. It was not sweet. It was … difficult to describe in English! At any rate, smoother and richer than the others; the French would say *plus moelleux*, and it was without a slight harshness given by the cognac that we had never noticed before, but which was quite clear when tasting the two together. On the whole, Sauternes enriches and deepens the flavour. If your dish actually strikes you as sweet, apart, of course, from desserts, you have probably used too much.

The Fiançailles was a great success. Just after we had cleared everything up, said goodbye to Martine and Alex and returned to the house, at about six o'clock, I remembered something I had left behind and ran back across the courtyard to fetch it. On opening the door of the restaurant a strong draught was immediately obvious, and I found the back door of the kitchen wide open. Thinking nothing more than 'that's odd', I shut and locked it, found what I was looking for, probably the remains of a bottle of wine for supper, and returned to the house. The next day I was working in the *chai* when Georgea came in.

'Have you got the grill in here?'

'What on earth would I want the grill for?'

'I've no idea, but you're always taking things from the kitchen and not putting them back' (true!) 'so I thought you might have it.'

'Well, I certainly haven't.'

'Then it's been stolen!'

It had too!

I must have missed the burglar by a second the night before, and he would have been able to slip away across the park behind the restaurant without anyone noticing. The gendarmes didn't even bother to visit the scene of the crime this time, but certain unofficial enquiries were being conducted in the neighbourhood, mainly by Bernard Dartigues and his friends, for ours were not the only minor break-ins that had been happening. In the meantime, we decided to get a dog.

Commarque is a place that cries out for dogs. Up until then we had rather thought that five children, a hotel, restaurant and vineyard were enough to look after, but this was different. We had the uncomfortable feeling that prowlers could easily snoop about the place unsuspected and vanish instantly if necessary into the trees and bushes and away along the numerous tracks which surround the property. Georgea made enquiries and was horrified by the price of dogs. It was Joan who had the answer. She had several dogs and was soon to start breeding basset hounds. She knew the local dog world. All we wanted was a friendly mongrel capable of barking a lot; we weren't going in for the French passion for guard dogs trained to the peak of perfection in the art of killing and maiming, so Joan suggested the dog refuge near Illats, in the middle of the woods, run by an eccentric old lady.

I had no idea that plans have advanced so far until Georgea returned one afternoon from a shopping trip with all the children in her old Peugeot 304—like Daniel's, but not the estate version—and known as 'Mum's Ferrari'. As the car entered the courtyard my first impression was that it was slightly more down on its elderly hunkers than usual. Looking inside it I had quite a shock. The front was filled as usual, but in the back there were no children visible, just an enormous doggy backside and a great banner of a tail wagging ever so slightly against the window like a jammed windscreen wiper. The car stopped. Georgea, Thomas and Edward got out of the front and the back doors opened.

'Don't let him out!' yelled Georgea and Thomas together.

Too late! From a three-child launchpad, pressed firmly down into the back seat, bounded one of the biggest dogs I have ever seen. A towering golden retriever-type-monster with a head the width of a young cow's, and paws like horses' hooves. To yells of 'Tommy, come here!' he hurtled across the courtyard, jumped the wall down to the swimming pool without even touching it and that was the last we saw of him until nightfall. We heard him though. From all four points of the compass his deep-throated, long-carrying wuff could be heard. One thing was certain: all the local baddies would know he was here, or they would if he ever came back!

He did come back and he had been noticed. When Bernard came to talk to us about the break-ins he told us that one of his men had been following a trail of empty wine bottles, *his* wine bottles, stolen from *his cave*, things like Châteaux Petrus, Yquem and Lafite, which had led through our bottom gate and up to the edge of the field planted by Bernard. He had just spotted another precious but empty bottle when he saw Tommy coming straight for him along the edge of the field. There was nowhere to run, so he stood frozen to the spot as this huge and unknown dog bore down on him.

'*Putain*, I was scared,' he told Bernard afterwards, but Tommy had sailed straight past him without even a glance, just giving him a whack in the stomach with his tail as confirmation of his size and power.

Bernard had come to tell us about the burglaries. They had all been carried out by someone he had employed on the recommendation of a friend in Bordeaux. *A really good worker*, this friend had said, *and he needs a job*.

'Unfortunately, he forgot to tell me,' went on Bernard, 'that he was a compulsive thief.'

This man had left smartly when his crimes had caught up with him, leaving the caravan he had been living in full of stolen goods which did not, as it happened, include our television, hi-fi or grill. Some of Bernard's friends, themselves victims of his attention, had tracked him down to La Rochelle but the gendarmes didn't want to know.

'*Les gars* [the lads] are not happy at all,' Bernard said, and there was talk of an expedition to La Rochelle and of private justice!

The main purpose of his visit was to say that he suspected some of the stolen property had been sold to the inhabitants of Léogeats and if he found any of our things he would let us know at once. He must have been very persistent because, nearly a year later, he announced that he had found the hi-fi—sold to a friend of his just down the road for five hundred francs, a real bargain.

'I told him he can't keep it and he isn't very pleased but if you go and see him, he'll give it back to you.'

He did, reluctantly. As it was a brand you don't find in France and I had the instruction booklet that came with it, he had to concede that it was mine. He also admitted that he had found it odd that the fellow who sold it to him had had it in the first place. It was even more odd that he himself could have been unaware of the hue and cry after this man, and ignorant of the nature of what he was buying!

Meanwhile, Tommy was proving to be a guard dog of overweening arrogance, although he behaved perfectly with the children and at first with anyone actually in the house. This was just as well. He was big enough to have swallowed Edward whole! His first offence was to jump on Joan. 'Jump up', the usual expression, is not appropriate in this context. Tommy was so tall he was already 'up'. He lunged at her on his hind legs, put his front paws on her shoulders and knocked her flat, ripping an earring from her ear as he did so. After that he ran off and, while Joan was shaken, she tried to put his behaviour down to over boisterousness. We wondered what might happen if Tommy tried to 'play' with a customer.

Within a few days he would not let anyone into the place. This is not wholly satisfactory in a hotel, and the crunch came when a prospective customer drove slowly into the courtyard in his Mercedes, windows rolled down, looking round for the reception. What he found was Tommy, head down, coming at the car with about as much *accueil* as an enraged bull. The driver's side windows went up just in time to receive Tommy's front paws and to protect the driver from the contents of his enormous mouth. Tommy was definitely not playing this time. The car drove away as fast as it could, seen off the property, and well beyond, by a bounding, snarling mountain of a dog, trying to eat the tyres. I am surprised the people in the car did not make a formal complaint, and Tommy went back to the refuge, looking as docile as a lamb, that same evening.

The lady from the refuge turned up a few days later with an animated black bundle under her arm, a most appealing puppy who would grow, she explained, into a biggish dog, 'more or less' a Brie shepherd dog or 'Briard'. Freddie did as she predicted, very rapidly. He was intelligent and lively, unruly and disobedient, and in one respect he was a great sinner: Freddie had no lady friend in the neighbourhood but manifested a well-developed libido. It was imprudent for ladies, of the human kind, to bend over or kneel down in his presence, or even in his absence, because he had a telepathic awareness of these desirable postures. Ladies working in the vineyard were most at risk, as many of the tasks there demand bending and kneeling. Georgea and Joan both had their share of attention, but it was Celia—of John and Celia our partners—who Freddie found totally irresistible. They came down for the *vendange* in 1988 and Freddie would be seen, a lusty, single-minded black form, streaking out under the front arch and vanishing up a row of vines. Moments later there would follow the agonised cry of, 'OH! BUGGER OFF FREDDIE!' and Celia's not a bit like that really.

As he grew older, Freddie became aggressive. Maybe we are not good with dogs, maybe we are just unlucky, but he went for one of the twins' friends, who had the presence of mind to roll himself up into a ball and keep very still until we arrived a few seconds later. He was a pest when people arrived for the hotel, and finally he had a serious go at Thomas, who had done nothing more than approach him unnoticed. Thomas managed to defend himself with a chair until Georgea arrived, but that was enough. Freddie too went back to the refuge, to the grave displeasure (with us) of the lady who ran it.

William missed Freddie, and as Georgea was not happy alone here without a dog, we agreed to get him one for his birthday, but we said it would have to be small. Even small ones have big teeth, and Timmy, who came from another refuge, having been found wandering in the streets of Bordeaux, bit Monsieur Jeantet a week or so after arriving. Even if plumbers are traditionally fair game, along with postmen, we still built Timmy an enclosure outside the kitchen door so that he couldn't bite anyone else! As Christian Jeantet remarked to him reproachfully: 'I've never done you any harm!'

And there were all those tempting legs in the hotel to snap at if we let him loose. He was an excellent guard dog, to the extent that he barked at everyone who entered the courtyard. He disliked strange men in particular, and must have been ill-treated when he was little; his attitude to long stay hotel guests was ambivalent: he would *like* to make friends, and sometimes did, but had difficulty in renouncing deep suspicion and his duty as a guard. Cats sent him wild, he was untrustworthy with children (except ours) and he loathed Monsieur Arlic. The only person he hated more was Gilles, but we think Gilles kicked him surreptitiously once or twice!

* * *

Our new cook Gilles was about to arrive. We had returned to Madame Bercovici to find Gilles explaining that Madame Reay-Jones was now in charge.

'Ecoutez-Monsieur-Reay-Jones-it's-the-best-way-to-get-your-restaurant-as-you-want-it'—and that we were after someone young, *not* 38 years old, who could work under her overall command, but was sufficiently clued up to cope on his own when there were not many customers. Madame Bercovici 'understood-exactly-what-we-wanted-and-would-find-him-for-us-at-once'.

This was April; there were many more cooks looking for work than the last time we had tried to find one, and Madame Bercovici was quickly back in touch with a charming young man who was quite useless. Being wiser by eighteen months than when we had first had dealings with Madame B., and therefore less prone to believe her every word, we had determined to adopt the original system we had planned for selecting a cook. This involved getting him to prepare something of his choosing for us to eat and to make up menus at the prices charged in the restaurant. The young man could think of nothing to cook for us. Had he got any cookery books? Yes, he had the manual they had used at college. So we told him to select something from there and cook it for us'

Two hours later he produced a piece of boiled fish with sliced vegetables on top of it. We suggested to him and to Madame Bercovici that he needed a little more experience working with other cooks, in a big kitchen before thinking of going off to work on his own.

Madame Bercovici contacted us again with, 'A-young-man-*très-vite*-in-his-studies-with-a-year-or-so-of-experience-at-some-good-addresses.'

Gilles telephoned that same day and made a good impression. His manner was polite and confident, he would be very pleased to come and see us, we would like him to cook for us? Very well, he would bring his knives.

I met him at Langon station the following morning. He did not go with the voice on the phone, but then he had been travelling most of the night and was unshaven, dishevelled, if not somewhat homeless looking! A short, sallow-complexioned, hollow-eyed young man with broken front teeth, he *was* somewhat homeless, despite having his own flat in Saint-Etienne. He had left home, we learned later, in less-than-ideal circumstances, at the age of 14, preferring boarding at cookery school to the daily drama of living with his parents. He was to live, belatedly, a part of his missing adolescence at Commarque. But he could cook when he wanted to.

Gilles impressed us, temporarily, by the arrogance with which he dismissed Marc's menus and the lack of hesitation with which he wrote out his own. For a lad of 19 he seemed very sure of himself. The dishes he cooked for us impressed us more permanently; we asked for a starter, a main course and a dessert. He looked in the *chambre froide*, then asked if we could put him up for the night so that he could make us Nougat Glacé au Grand Marnier. Intrigued, we said '*Bien sûr*, but what about the other things?'

'I will serve you in the restaurant in a *petit quart d'heure*,' he replied and turned his back on us.

We raised our eyebrows at each other and ten minutes later seated ourselves at a table, resisting the temptation to go and see what he was up to. Five minutes later, smack on the *petit quart d'heure*, Gilles appeared behind a most appetising aroma, bearing his Salade de Foie de Volaille à l'Estragon (Chicken Liver Salad with Tarragon). It tasted as good as it had smelt—and looked, decorated with little fans of radishes and carrots and 'tulips' of tomato. Next he hit the bullseye of Cuisine du Terroir with his Magret de Canard au Sauternes, which has become, with variations, more or less our culinary logo—and it's so simple!

The following day he bowled us over with his Nougat Glacé, a kind of ice-cream of praline, orange and chocolate, laced with Grand Marnier, beautifully presented with fans and flowers of fruit in *crème anglaise*. He claimed to have the original recipe from its creator. It is just possible and is less of a cliché than the usual story, 'it's my grandmother's recipe', which of course sounds a lot better than, 'I got it out of my cookery book'. Nougat Glacé has itself become a cliché. Nearly every frozen food supplier to the trade lists it and I have tasted several. None of them has anything to do with the plateful of heaven that Gilles dished up that day. It was not *always* to be quite so good; he was erratic. Once he prepared a batch without any visible chocolate, although he swore on the head of his mother (whom he loathed) that there was chocolate in it! Perhaps there was—just the one or two squares that happened to be left when he had suddenly remembered what he was meant to have done with the chocolate he was busy scoffing upstairs in his apartment after work. Food did disappear mysteriously with Gilles; not only chocolate, but pâtisserie, whole *gratins* of potatoes, cream, strawberries, and other items like saucepans, which then surfaced mysteriously in the dustbins, charred black, and dozens and dozens of glasses! Gilles never had any idea what had become of any of these things. But Marie-Laure once told us that whenever he washed up glasses, happily not very often, he put the dustbin beside him for easier disposal of the breakages ... one for the bin, one for the drainer, one for the bin, and so on!

On that first visit here he had accompanied his triumphant Magret with some rapidly sketched-out menus that sounded great until you stopped to consider the ingredients which would have to go into them. Gilles was not economical, but then he had never been asked to buy raw materials, had worked mainly in restaurants much pricier than ours, and was in any case very young. This in no way prevented him from giving us the benefit of his opinion on what we should and shouldn't do, what our customers might and might not like, how many or how few of them we were going to get, and how he would prefer to be left in peace to get on with the restaurant on his own. Not on your life boy! We've been through that one already. We did not, of course, say anything remotely like that; Georgea mildly pointed out that it *was* our restaurant and we were interested in what went on in it. The reply was: 'I could find you a *grand cuistot* (slang for 'cook') who would do you for a *brique* (F10,000) a month and not let you set foot in the kitchen.'

So presumably we should think ourselves lucky that *he* would let us at least look in from time to time! I tried to greet this with a tolerant laugh, but Georgea wondered afterwards if we were going to get on with Gilles. A few days later he took me aside and asked me did I realise what a very good cook, a very, *very* good cook Madame Jones was? I replied that I had an inkling, but he was not finished.

'*En plus*, she's faster than most of the ones I've ever worked with, yet she's English!'

We hadn't realised that; about being fast I mean.

'I always thought Marc was a bit slow.' She replied when I mentioned it to her.

Thus, Gilles started to develop a healthy respect for Georgea, who was the only one capable of putting the wind up him. If this sounds like an outdated approach to personnel management, then all I can say is that usual criteria cannot be applied when dealing with Gilles. He was an extraordinary mixture of childish bad manners (or rather absence of manners, because no one had ever taught him what good manners were), deviousness, kindness, generosity and talent. One moment, we would be marvelling at his latest creation, or thanking him for playing soldiers with Edward all afternoon—something he enjoyed every bit as much as Edward—the next we would be listening to him cursing and throwing saucepans, or catch him pulling ape-like faces through the kitchen window at customers on the terrace!

Georgea's first clash with him came after two or three weeks, when we were starting to prepare for our first wedding. It was a complicated affair and the preparations had to be organised, so in comes Georgea first thing and asks brightly: 'What are you planning to do this morning?'

He ignores the question. This is unwise. Georgea repeats it.

'*J'ai plein de trucs à faire*'—I've got loads of things to do—he grunts, without looking up.

In the face of such rudeness and lack of cooperation, *la patronne* explodes. There follows the first nose-to-nose confrontation, Georgea advancing, Gilles retreating, a uni-directional two-step to the music of raised voices. Georgea always won, but we did have to have him over to the house once and threaten him with the sack after some appalling performance with a customer.

The fact is, he suited us. He worked hard, most of the time; what he did was good, sometimes very good. He played computer games with Francis, soldiers with Edward and football with everyone. He set, with Georgea, the style of our restaurant. We keep using so many of his dishes: la Petite Marmite de la Mer au Sauternes; Pavé du Saumon au Vin du Château (dry white wine this time); la Gibelotte de Lapin Sauternaise; la Salade de Moules et de Coques; Mousseline de Poissons, de Homard; de Saint-Jacques au Beurre d'Herbes; Beurre Rose or Beurre de Ciboulette.

He obviously interested the Michelin Guide inspector, who ate anonymously one lunchtime and then solemnly announced himself. He asked hundreds of questions, made copious notes, cross-examined Gilles (Georgea insisted on staying right out of the way), inspected the hotel rooms, the swimming pool and turned slowly in circles in the middle of the courtyard writing as he went. I asked diffidently if all this meant we were going to be in the Guide. Not a bit of it! He would write his report, send in all his pieces of paper, and a dossier would be opened. The matter would be carefully considered in committee and a decision would be taken thereafter. Naturally we rushed to look in next year's edition. Naturally we weren't in it.

A year later another Michelin inspector turned up, as tall, thin and solemn as the first had been short, fat and solemn. I asked him why he had come and he replied: 'We like to keep an eye on places we are interested in.' Adding, 'I wanted to see how your *travaux* were coming on.'

I said I wasn't doing any *travaux* so what exactly had he in mind? He positively swelled with solemnity.

'I am not at liberty to divulge the nature of the improvements we require.' He announced. 'Should you wish to know more you may consult the dossier in Paris, but under no circumstances will the information be made available outside the four walls of the Michelin office.'

So, of course, I rushed off to Paris on the next train to find out exactly what we needed to do to get in a guide that would certainly transform our performance. Or did I? Well … no. I have to admit I didn't.

Another example of evasion of the fundamentally important? Only partly, I plead. *Travaux* implies structural improvements, not just the buying of smarter plates or better salts and peppers for the restaurant, or even the provision of a less rustic and more weatherproof loo. These were things we would have to do to get into the Michelin Guide. People who knew had told us so. But *travaux* meant more than such trivial adjustments. It meant, I was sure, getting a bit closer to the 'norms' governing hotels and restaurants, making changes we could not possibly afford. What was the point then of going all the way to Paris, even supposing the château could cope with my absence, to find out the impossibility of measuring up to the Michelin requirements? I never went and every two years a solemn inspector came and asked after our *travaux*. Finally I told him, to a gratifyingly surprised and disappointed response, that it wasn't worth coming any more, there would be no *travaux*; we had no money to rise above our present station.

None of this has anything to do with Gilles except that it was just as well, even if irrelevant in the long run, that he had arrived by the time that first inspector sat down to his lunch. But you could never tell what he was going to do next. I'm sure we never knew the half of it, and our waitresses only let on when they couldn't cope with him anymore. Martine scratched him deeply around the eyes; Joan's daughter Sheriden—a strong, athletic girl who worked here off and on as a waitress and preceded Marie-Laure, our longest-serving and best-ever, in 1989—laid him flat on his back with one punch. Marie-Laure herself had cause to bring her knee up sharply on one occasion. Fortunately for the peace of the restaurant all these ladies were capable of looking after themselves and Gilles never bore grudges nor even remained out of temper for very long! But his moods changed like April weather: a difficult order, a late arrival and the crashing and cursing could start. I wonder what it was that led him to break the pipes of the vacuum cleaner against the kitchen wall, or how the *chambre froide* got all the dents in its door. Like the disappearing chocolate and cream, he never knew anything about it. He was also incapable of managing his money and would come in proudly wearing a pure wool jumper he had just had made for himself, for F700, or show us an expensive watch he had bought in Bordeaux. Two days previously he had been asking me for a written confirmation of his salary to send to his bank manager, because he had 'big problems' at the bank.

One last Gilles story before we leave the poor boy in peace, not that peace is likely to come his way. Late one afternoon during the *vendange*, Marie-Laure came into the *chai* and told me that the pickers, some of whom we did not know well as it happened, had complained about the lunch. The Garbure, a kind of hearty soup made with cabbage, bacon and confited duck, had been inedible, salty *and* thin and watery. I tried it. It was. Worse was to come. Gilles had told everyone that 'Madame Jones' had made it! While Marie-Laure said she had not believed him ('Madame would never make anything like that'), this was too much for Georgea when she came in from the vines. She had just spent the whole afternoon working alongside all these people, quite unaware that dissatisfaction, even resentment, was in the air. Might they not be saying to each other: 'So that's why they go off to the house and eat alone instead of with us, to avoid the disgusting stuff they expect us to put up with.'?

In fact, we didn't have time to sit over wine and coffee like the *vendangeurs*. Georgea prepares the supper, I keep the press rolling. That's why we didn't join the others for lunch! Georgea decided Gilles could not be allowed to get away with this one. Particularly as it had been impossible to pin his many recent crimes on him; all we had got was that infuriating shrug of the shoulders and '*je n'en sais rien*'—I dunno anything about it.

The problem was to get him to admit that he had made this soup, and the weakness was that there was a little of Georgea's left over from the last *vendangeurs*' lunch several days previously. This would certainly have been mixed in with Gilles' salted water and probably gave him the idea of blaming it all on her in the first place. Georgea went down to the kitchen that evening and found him poking around on his knees in the *chambre froide*, getting out vegetables and salads. She pretended to check the stock of meat.

'Did you find the container of *vendangeurs*' soup left over from the last time?' She asked, innocently.

'Yes.'

'Was there enough or did you have to make some more?'

'No, there was only a bit left. I made some more.'

Splendid! He's put his foot right in it, much further than Georgea had hoped for.

'Oh yes! There it is. What a lot there is left! Didn't they like it?'

Gilles, still on his knees, stiffens slightly as he senses a trap closing round him. Georgea tastes the soup, pretending not to know what it's like.

'Yeuk! It's awful Gilles, far, far too salty.'

'*Ah bon?*' says Gilles, keeping his eyes down.

He cannot now blame it on her because he has already admitted that there was only a bit of hers left! Now she lets go.

'You know full well it is! You know it's inedible because everyone complained about it and couldn't eat it.'

'They *did* eat it.'

'How much did you make then for God's sake? There are only ten of them. *And* you told them I made it!'

Gilles, still kneeling down in the *chambre froide*, bangs his head on the floor and groans, 'All right, I lied! I lied!'

It does no real good though; it just relieves, temporarily, Georgea's bottled up and so often impotent irritation with him.

Let us remember his triumphs: all those children *demi-pensionnaires* he delighted with his special *crudités* containing radishes made into mice, and lemons transformed into pigs. The banquet he prepared for the last night of a wine group staying in the hotel.

'What shall we do for the main course?' asks Georgea. 'They've had practically everything.'

'Carré de Veau Choisy,' says Gilles, without hesitation.

'What's that?'

'Ah-hah! Leave it to me. It's *hyper-bon*. They'll love it!'

It *was hyper-bon* and they did love it.

The annual lunch of the Algerian war veterans of Sauternes, Bommes and Léogeats. How pleased we were to get sixty-odd people from just up the road. When the bus arrived the men vanished as one into the oak park, made an orderly line with their backs to the restaurant and peed with ceremonial solemnity before rejoining their wives to sit down at table. The meal was a triumph, and that was thanks to Gilles. At the end, the president of the Association stood up and made a speech of thanks in which he apologised for not having thought of Commarque sooner for their celebration, but with the reputation it had had in the *coin* over the years, well! He was sure we understood and hoped that they had made amends. I was clapped. Then Gilles and Georgea had to come in and be clapped as well.

The Fraisiers and Framboisiers, served at so many baptism and communion lunches …

La Mousse Glaceé au Citron Vert, the pleasure he took later in teaching William how to make it *and* all his other lovely creamy puddings: Mijotée de Veau au Basilic, la Feuilleté Gasconne, la Cuisse de Canard au Vin de Graves! …

Bravo!

16

The Great Running Saga

The summer of 1988 started abruptly in the middle of June. Before that it had been cold and wet, showing every sign of being as miserable as 1987, with all that that implied for the vineyard and the hotel. Nevertheless, several novelties appeared in the local fauna that spring, so perhaps it was a little better, or perhaps we had just never noticed them the year before in the desperate scrabble to get started.

The first was the arrival of the hoopoes on the lawns of the courtyard. These exotic-looking birds are a rarity in England but we have seen them here, in increasing numbers, every year. Freddie adored them; he felt he had a sporting chance of catching one—if he could just stop himself barking—since it took them a moment, with the problems of vertical take-off from the ground, to fly out of his reach. He never succeeded and his efforts failed to discourage the hoopoes from visiting us every day. They are striking creatures, with plumage boldly striped in black and white, orange-pink face, neck and breast, a high crest which opens and closes like a fan and an exquisitely thin, curved beak. Their call may be heard all day long, even when they remain invisible, on one note either in threes: boo-boo-boo, pause, boo-boo-boo, or fours, boo-boo-boo-boo, pause, boo-boo-boo-boo. It is monotonous, very monotonous, but less of a bore than the nightingale!

What! How can that be? Nightingales have the most wonderful, melodious song; everyone wants to hear it. True ... but no one wants to hear Schubert's *String Quintet* all night long, every night, either. During May the nightingales don't stop, and they aren't the only ones. In spring and early summer, the night sounds at Commarque, even though 100 per cent natural, are sometimes loud enough and varied enough to satisfy the most confirmed city dweller!

One who cannot be faulted for excessive decibels is the owl who took up residence under the arch by the restaurant, tucked up somewhere in the corner beside the chimney. There is little enough room there under the roof; he must be almost *in* the restaurant, but he (or is it she?) has been there ever since. The first indications were the small piles of what he had been eating on the ground, just to the right of the menus: beetle shells, balls of fur, little bones. We cleared them away regularly as they would surely not be appreciated by the visitors from the likes of Paris, Brussels and Zurich. Then one night, I saw him swoop out of his corner on white, silent wings, fly straight under the centre of the arch and out over the vines to the woods. It seemed impossible that a creature that size could fit in where he had come from. But he must be comfortable there for we see him regularly.

Equally predictable are the bats that emerge abruptly every dusk from the air vents down to the cellar at the end of the house, and then hunt round the courtyard. If you stand still, listen carefully and are lucky, they will make a catch so close to you that you can hear the tiny clack of their teeth snapping together round their prey. There is usually one during the day hung up asleep just inside the cellar door. As soon as you open it he drops down just in front of your face, before vanishing down the steps into the darkness. The first, and only, time it happened to Joan, it was too much for her. She refused flatly and for ever more to set foot in the cellar. This was a pity because we often need to go down there to fetch wine.

The least loved members of the local population are the toads. Damp conditions from early spring to early winter bring them out in numbers. They don't mind people and seem quite at home in the courtyard. They are indifferent to the Freddies and Timmys of this world, who are prone to yap incessantly at them from the safe distance of several inches, but won't touch them. They are also, and this is more serious, quite unconcerned about the feelings of people who do not like them, such as those squeamish Parisians who are apt to visit us in the summer and won't tolerate a vast, gravid toad in the shower! Toads, unlike bats, birds and even hornets, have no hesitation in passing doors and crossing man's indoor territory.

We have some unloved insects as well, but it is grossly unfair of those young lady bathers to demand the removal of the Praying Mantids close to them on the sunny wall beside the swimming pool. In any case they don't move for hours at a time, and are certainly not interested in acres of female flesh. It is the arrival of a male stag beetle, that's the one with the big nippers, that causes the greatest panic. They are quite harmless, although if one happened to fly into you (unlikely, unless you are confusing it by flapping towels and running round in circles), I suppose it might hurt a bit. On the other hand, there are some genuinely nasty horseflies ...

With all this nature from which to draw inspiration, it is not surprising that Monsieur Desautel should have used that summer term to try to develop an awareness in his pupils of some of the operations of their own bodies, as well as providing them with all the benefits of healthy, outdoor exercise every day. Under the umbrella of *Science de la Vie*, the children in his class started a programme of monitoring their pulse rates and breathing in relation to different kinds of activity. He did it well, and their interest was engaged. Notebooks were filled, charts, histograms and graphs were drawn. All this was good practice in Maths, presentation of data, working in teams, etc, etc, but the consequences of embarking on Monsieur Desautel's pulse-counting exercises were destined to be altogether more far-reaching, and of much greater duration, than anyone could have imagined.

The term came to an end and the notebooks were put away, to be forgotten about until La Rentrée Scolaire in September. A fine summer ensued and the twins and Thomas won piles more swimming medals. In the hotel we received the first visits of some of those customers who were to come and stay every year, a bus company in Bordeaux started to send us groups, we hosted two weddings, were having no difficulty in selling the dry white wine, Château de Commarque Sec 1987, and were in the process of buying many more barrels than in the previous year for a much more promising looking grape harvest, when Thomas pioneered the way to secondary school, Collège, in Langon.

After meeting Monsieur Lataste, the headmaster of the Collège Toulouse Lautrec, back in the autumn of 1986, and Maïté Bodis who had so successfully taught the boys French, we were keen to try and get Thomas into the Collège which they had represented so well, even though the children of Sauternes were supposed to go to the other Collège in Langon. This was easier than we had expected. Toulouse-Lautrec had the best exam results in the Gironde, at least partly because Monsieur Lataste quite openly exercised his power to admit pupils with a good academic record, on condition that he was asked to admit them! I telephoned him. He remembered us.

'Of course, *parfaitement*. Just put "preferred choice" on the application form and leave the rest to me.'

It was as simple as that. Once Thomas was in the others could follow. Later on it did become more difficult because Toulouse-Lautrec was

bulging at the seams, the 'Other One' had places available, and the
Rectorat in Bordeaux was unhappy with the imbalance. But by then we
could invoke 'a brother already at the school', better still for Robert:
'three brothers already at the school', and by the time Monsieur Lataste
left to take up a post in Bordeaux, we could truthfully say, when it came
to Edward's turn, 'four brothers have already been at the school'. Egalité,
as is so often the case, is relative!

Back in Sauternes that September, Monsieur Desautel's physiological
exercises were being resumed; how fast and how far was it possible to
run, or trot, without an increase in pulse rate? How long did it take
for the pulse rate to return to normal after running, or trotting, for
one, two, five, ten minutes? How high would the pulse rate rise after
sprinting?—and so on, all done in class time, across and around the
school playground. Then one day Monsieur Desautel took everyone out
on a trot-and-stop, measure-and-trot, measure-and-recuperate exercise in
the park of Château Filhot, just opposite the school.

How lucky the children were to have such a beautiful, peaceful place in
which to work. The park is an eighteenth-century nobleman's landscaped
paradise with a lake opposite the palatial château, an amphitheatre of land
around it planted with ornamental trees, tracks through the woods, round
the lake, and out into the vines beyond the wrought iron boundary fence
towards Sauternes and the school. There cannot be many primary schools
so favoured! In the park of Château Filhot, the exercises developed into
short cross-country runs, speed carefully controlled, breathing regular,
recovery time monitored, absolutely no question of racing—and everyone
enjoyed it, even the stoutest, least athletic child. One afternoon Monsieur
Desautel announced that he wanted to take the whole class to a 'U.S.E.P.'
cross-country meeting.

'U.S.E.P.' stands for Union Sportive des Ecoles Primaires (the Primary
Schools' Sports Union). At Collège and Lycée it becomes 'U.N.S.S.' (the
Union Nationale des Scolaires Sportifs) with departmental, regional and,
later on, national championships. No one seemed to know what was
involved in a 'U.S.E.P.' cross, but Monsieur Desautel had the entry forms;
it all seemed very official. A bus was hired and sundry parents went with
the children and Monsieur Desautel as *accompagnateurs*. We were not
among them, something kept us at Commarque as usual, but we heard
all about it that evening.

There had been scores of children in the races: seventy-eight in Robert's,
130 in the twins'! There had been races for each year, and separate ones
for boys and girls. The older you were the further you ran, but half the

course was covered at a trot behind men with a rope stretched between them—*les lièvres* (the hares). They had forbidden pushing and shoving, encouraged everyone to run at an even steady pace and then leapt aside with a cry of, '*Allez les enfants*!' to let the real race develop.

So how had the children done? They had enjoyed themselves. The whole class had enjoyed itself. That had been obvious from the way they had all tumbled off the bus when they got back, but what about the results? Well, Francis was pleased as punch because he had come thirteenth, Robert had even managed ninth—and William an unruffled thirty-fourth. Other Sauternes children had been in the top ten of their races, some had been well down the field, but no one had come in anywhere near last!

Funnily enough the results seemed far less important than the manner in which the races had been run. Rather than trying all-out to beat the other runners, the children had treated the races as an application of Monsieur Desautel's lessons. They had measured up to others, knowing that they knew what they were doing, they were in control of themselves. I asked Francis if he could have run any faster. Oh yes! He seemed quite surprised by the question! They had all run how Monsieur Desautel had taught them: steadily, not allowing the effort to cause loss of rhythm, not worrying about the erratic speeds, the puffing and panting around them, checking their recovery at the end of the course; a good exercise, a great afternoon out, but not really a set of races.

That had been on Saturday. The following Monday evening the twins and Robert announced that they were going to a 'big' cross in two weeks' time and Monsieur Desautel was changing the training completely. There was to be no more gentle trotting, no more controlled-breathing-and-let-the-rest-of-you-get-on-with-it. Monsieur Desautel was out to race and the class was out there with him! All us parents received a circular letter about the Cross du Sud-Ouest, organised by the newspaper of that name, at Gujan-Mestras on the Bassin of Arcachon. The name of this cross comes from the paper, but it is also the biggest cross-country meeting in Southwest France, with a section devoted to schools as well as races for the athletics clubs. It lasts two days, bringing in competitors from all over France, from Spain, Belgium, even further afield, and there are literally thousands of runners. Another bus was hired, picnics had to be arranged, a call for *accompagnateurs* was issued. Sauternes school was to make a day of it. When the racing finished there would be a visit to a boatyard making the traditional flat-bottomed *peniches* that work the calm waters of the Bassin, and afterwards a visit to an oyster farm.

The boys wanted one of us to go but that presented the usual complications. Gilles and Martine had departed for the winter; Martine, in fact, permanently, preferring a job in Bordeaux, sorting carrots, which kept her closer to her daughter Zelya. She visited us several times, bringing gifts of large bags of first-class carrots, but said it was a cold, monotonous job! However, it was the end of November, the weather was freezing and wet, there weren't many people around. Georgea said the place would survive for a day without me so I went to the Cross du Sud-Ouest, Martine stood in for me in the restaurant and we received our first bag of carrots.

That 'U.S.E.P.' cross of 1988 at Gujan-Mestras resembles nothing less than a Boys' Own magazine tale of juvenile heroes (and heroines) and is scarcely less improbable! There were hundreds and thousands of children, all in a state of high overexcitement—for were there not television cameras on the final straight, loud-speaker commentary, oodles of prizes, the chance to be interviewed for the Sud-Ouest newspaper and for the telly, and, best of all, a chance to put one over your old enemies from the school down the road? Fifty-four schools were represented that day. The biggest ones, from Bordeaux and Arcachon, entered several hundred runners, the little ones, like Sauternes, had twenty-five.

This is a serious sporting event and it is very well organised, despite the appearance of that milling, shouting, hyperactive rabble. Order was imposed by loudspeaker, thousands of numbers were pinned to thousands of T-shirts and the first races were called to order. Monsieur Desautel gave his final briefings to an attentive and, I must say it—for it is not often said of the children of Sauternes these days—well-disciplined group. The first Sauternes performers, which included Robert and his friends, to be followed by the girls of his year with his neighbour-in-class Adeline, moved over to the starting field. They tried to keep warm in the biting wind by jogging backwards and forwards beyond the 70-metre-long start line set up beneath an enormous Sud-Ouest banner. Two-hundred-and-eighty other competitors arrived for Robert's race and it was all acutely nerve wracking. But Monsieur Desautel was there with his little group as the loudspeaker announced: '*Garçons nés en 1980*', Robert's year, and, '*A vous monsieur le Starter.*'

I ran up the course to stand at the point where it narrowed to a 5-metre-wide cinder track, in company with the mother of Marc-Antoine, the little boy who had befriended Robert on his first day at school. Back at the start the runners made a jostling line three deep, the hares spread out across the line of advance, the loudspeaker boomed, a silence, punctuated by cries of 'Allez Libourne', 'Allez Arcachon', descended on the field, the starter raised his gun and—it failed to go off! A little surge forward at one end of the line was quickly brought to order and now they were away, a sudden dash by 280 children, just as suddenly checked by the hares, and then a gentle jog towards us with shouted orders, encouragements and reprimands from the five fit-looking men in front carrying the cord.

The Sauternes boys had been in the middle of the line, carefully positioned there by Monsieur Desautel, but it was impossible to see them now, swallowed up as they were by the crowd. The field started to narrow as it approached us; two hares dropped out, then a third, when the cord was but 15-metres long. Now they were in the funnel leading to the cinder track and there was Robert, right at the front, deathly white, an expression of grim concentration on his face, elbows out and chest nearly touching the cord. The 280 starters were already spread out in a long, irregular line and, by the time the back markers had straggled past, the hares had long since disappeared into the pine trees through which lay the course. Marc-Antoine's mum and I took a short cut, running hard for the finishing straight, spurred on by a wave of cheering for the invisible but fast-approaching runners in the woods. We had still not reached the track when the first of them came round the bend out of the trees into view of the stands and the TV cameras, where the commentator was working up an atmosphere worthy of the Olympic Games. We reached a gap in the crowd at the fence alongside the track and saw the front-runners clearly for the first time. Ahead of all, by a good 15 metres, gaining ground with every stride was … Robert!

He was just showing me his victor's watch, Conseil General (County Council) T-shirt, the first of dozens he has received, and the carrier bag of other winnings, when the Girls' 1980 race reached its climax beside us. Sauternes did not win this one, but we did the next best thing: Adeline was second and her friend Aurélie Rougié was third! Not bad out of 250 starters. While they had been in the woods and Robert was showing me his prizes, the cameras had been on us. We appeared on the local TV news that night and I was wearing a granny mac!

In Garçons 1979 Sauternes was represented by Antoine Boisseau, son of the Sauternes pharmacist, a blond-haired little boy with long, long legs. All the Sauternes parents, together with the children who had already run, were by now in a line along the white fence fifty metres from the finishing post, well placed to cheer home our athletes. As the swelling crowd noise announced the approach of the leaders, a lone bobbing head could be seen above the spectators, still alone as the powerful body and legs of an exceptionally big 10-year-old came striding into view. But glued to his shoulder—invisible previously because of his much smaller size—matching him stride for stride, came Antoine. Competitive, crafty, the honour of Sauternes at stake, he jostled his adversary, his head an inch from the boy's shoulder. They drew level with us and he passed him, a foot in front, a bare metre, but the power of his opponent was too great; he finished superbly to win by a clear 5 metres but, *quand même*, another second for Sauternes!

We parents had slipped easily by now into the winning mode. After a first, two seconds and a third we were expecting results, quite unreasonably given the circumstances, but we got them!

The next race was, of course, *Filles* 1979; Hélène Roumegoux (Sauternes) had swung gracefully into the straight and crossed the finishing line before the second runner, in a field of over 300 competitors, was even visible! That means a lead of at least 150 metres! Stunning!

Then it was Francis's and William's turn—*Garçons* 1978. The number of children running had become ridiculous, and the dense throng at the start meant that if you were not well placed, you would never be able to push your way to the front. But Francis, like Antoine, is highly competitive, was already noted for his speed on the football pitch, and had all those earlier results to spur him on! Word reached us from the other children out in the woods that he was leading the race. I ran towards the bend to get the earliest possible view of him, and yes! there he was, well clear and going easily. We've come to expect it. The sensation was now one of relief, not amazement. But hold on! There was a lad coming up behind him like a train!

'Watch out behind you!' I yelled. But there's so much shouting and cheering he didn't hear me.

He looked over his shoulder just in time to see the boy catch up with him. He accelerated. There was a sprint finish for fully 50 metres, side by side they went, the commentator was beside himself with excitement and—Francis lost by the width of his bony little frame! Disappointment, and disgust with himself at his lack of tactical skill, are tempered by the pleasure of discovering how good he is at this game. He knows he *would* have won easily if he had been watching what was happening behind him.

William was forty-third, out of a field of over 400. For a man not much interested in this sort of thing that's pretty good, and would have earned the heartiest congratulations were it not for the extraordinary things happening in front of him. The full 'glory' was finished now. In any other of the fifty-four participating schools the fifth place obtained by Sauternes in *Filles* 1978 and the ninth in *Garcons* 1977 would have been wildly acclaimed, but in the Sauternes camp these achievements were accepted calmly as no more than just desserts.

For the rest of that winter, the season of cross-country running, Sauternes school participated in every available 'U.S.E.P.' cross. There were days when the children won every race for which they were entered. The most spectacular performer was Hélène Roumegoux. Without apparent effort, with an easy, natural step, she would leave the opposition floundering far behind her on every occasion. The sight of the children out training became a familiar one in the village and the tale of their prowess spread beyond the confines of the circle of pupils and their parents. One consequence of this was that by the end of January there was a Sauternes 'kit', provided by no less a body than the Sauternes Wine Syndicate. Monsieur Lamothe had therefore suppressed his innate contempt for the 'brats of vineyard workers' once it dawned on him that they were capable of providing good publicity for the name of Sauternes. Everyone was issued with a 'Sauternes-Barsac' T-shirt, decorated with a bold logo of grapes and vine leaves. But where does Barsac fit into this? The problem was that the full title of the Syndicate is le Syndicat des Vins de Sauternes et Barsac and the Barsac element insisted on being represented, despite the fact that Barsac has its own school, one of many finding itself without results now in 'U.S.E.P.' crosses! There was dissension among some of the Sauternes parents, perhaps ancient rivalries expressing themselves, but free equipment is free equipment and 'Sauternes-Barsac' it was that marked the T-shirts. It didn't matter. The race commentators, binoculars in hand, would announce, on spotting the familiar strip: 'And here comes another *petit* Sauternais (or *petite* Sauternaise) leading the field,' never, 'here comes a *petit* Barsacais!'

Tactics developed along with a vivid team spirit. Inevitably other schools were out to 'get' Sauternes and tripping was not uncommon in the crowd behind the hares. It was then or never—you cannot trip up someone you are unable to catch! The result was that the 'stars' were surrounded and protected by the other team members, just part of the development of a strong sense of community, extending to the whole school, pupils and parents alike. However, the most important, and unforeseen, consequence of this adventure was the effect it had on other kinds of schoolwork. Children hitherto anxious, reticent and underachieving in class found confidence, a willingness to plunge in, even an increasing interest in French, Maths, History, etc. I don't mean just the winners, although Hélène, who comes from a family with more than its fair share of problems, fairly leapt ahead in 1989; nearly everyone was infected by success! Let anyone who doubts the value of sport in education read the lesson of Sauternes Primary School and its cross-country running. No one was more delighted and surprised by it than Monsieur Desautel himself. He remarked that he had passed nearly the whole of his professional life before grasping it—and thank God it had finally dawned on him.

After Easter he announced that he had a plan 'of interest to everyone' and invited all the parents to a meeting. In class he had hinted he was plotting 'the most exciting experience of their lives' to the children. A good community spirit means a good turnout at meetings, and everyone came. Monsieur Desautel, to general surprise, then delivered himself of an emotional little speech in which he explained that Sauternes school was certainly his last post before retirement and that in, as it were, the autumn of his career, he had come to know a satisfaction in his work that he had never previously experienced. His class was the most rewarding one he had had in nearly thirty-five years of teaching, and he wanted to say a thank you to the children for what they had given him. The tone lightened as he went on to say that *en plus*, as 1989 was the bicentenary of the Glorious French Revolution, it was in every way a suitable year for celebrations. His plan, he then announced, preceding his words with a significant pause in which you could have heard a grape drop, was to fly the entire class to Canada for a bicentenary run of 1,789 kilometres, a revolutionary distance, around Quebec, finishing at Niagara Falls. Monsieur Desautel then sat down to a stunned silence. The questions all started at once. How much would it cost? Where would they stay? When was he planning to do it? Wasn't it dangerous? Who would pay for it? Monsieur Desautel rose to his feet again and raised his hand for attention. He had done his homework. He had made contacts. The outline of a workable plan was there: a set of camping cars would be used for sleeping, with stops at schools and community centres. The route was already sketched out and he had an agreement in principle from most of the proposed stopover sites. Cost of air travel, insurance, the way to run such a long way with such small people, he had dealt with all of them. And the cost? A little over F200,000 for a trip lasting two weeks. By the end of the meeting he had everyone in the palm of his hand. The natural organisers started organising, fundraisers raised funds and the realisation of this next to impossible project was achieved in the weeks that followed. Money was the chief difficulty—when isn't it? The solution was to present the trip as a publicity exercise: the great châteaux of Sauternes and Barsac, *all* the châteaux of Sauternes and Barsac, were invited to contribute. In exchange, their labels, logos, names in lights, whatever they chose to provide, would be conspicuously displayed on the camping cars. In addition, there was to be TV coverage in Bordeaux and Montreal, Canadian newspapers would be covering the story, there would be spots on the radio and civic receptions. The names of Sauternes and Barsac would be writ large in Canada. Canada is next door to the USA, and Americans of all stripes are among the very best customers of Sauternes! The Syndicate backed the operation; Monsieur Lamothe now adored the children of Sauternes, and the châteaux, great and small, coughed up with gratifying readiness. Yquem came in late but on a scale commensurate with its position and there was just one notable abstention, which shall remain shamefully anonymous. The parish council, county council, sports suppliers and others made their contributions. There was a resident doctor (Madame Boisseau) and resident pharmacist (Monsieur Boisseau!). The trip was organised down to the minutest detail, as it needed to be, and off they all went at the beginning of July.

There was a grand send off at Bordeaux station: TV, press, the children all in their 'Canada tracksuits' with a maple leaf and Sauternes motif—to be seen for years afterwards on children in the *coin*. The whole class was there except one little boy, Gaël, whose mum could not bear to be parted from her angel for two whole weeks, and therefore deprived him of an experience he would have remembered all his life. For the reality of the voyage was neck and neck with the expectation it had aroused. Well perhaps the civic receptions were a bit much! We have a video of the mayor of—was it Laval? La Tuque? Grand Mère—rabbiting on and on and Robert said he was bursting to go to the lavatory the whole time! They visited Indian villages, Fort Lennox, a ghost mining town, 'just like a film set', the parliament in Ottawa, saw whales in the St Lawrence and still had time to run 1,789 kilometres, in five-minute relays. They were fêted wherever they went and the only regret was a slight hitch in the timetable which prevented the final visit to Niagara Falls. They returned safe, sound, grubby and exhausted.

Two small incidents give a flavour of the trip; Gregory, *enfant terrible* of the class, was running in front, arrived at a T-junction and shouted over his shoulder to Monsieur Desautel pounding away in the middle distance behind him.

'Which way now?'

'Straight on!' Monsieur Desautel yelled back, not really paying attention—it's only Gregory after all.

Gregory, obedient, when it suits him, to the word of command, hops over the barrier and runs unhesitatingly into the St Lawrence!

The camping car travelled through a magnificent landscape of pine forests. *This* is Canada. Europe has nothing to offer on such a scale. Madame Rougié, the mother of Aurélie, glanced into the back of her camper to see her charges—Francis, William, Antoine and Co.—intently playing 'Uno', which they have been doing, to their entire satisfaction, for the past hour and a half—and shouted exasperatedly: '*Mon Dieu*, les enfants, show some interest in what's going on outside, and don't spend the whole day playing that stupid game!'

Not everyone has the same idea of the 'experience of a lifetime!'

Two years later Monsieur Desautel retired and was elected Mayor of Villandraut. Running at Sauternes School came to an abrupt halt and has never been resumed. As a farewell treat he organised a little relay—from Villandraut, just down the road and home of the only French Pope, to Avignon, the Pope's other home! But while the school stopped running collectively, certain pupils found themselves unable to abandon what Monsieur Desautel had so successfully begun. Francis, Antoine, Hélène, Robert and Aurélie joined the Club d'Athlétisme Bèglais (C.A.B.) a well-known Bordeaux club, and tried themselves against the club runners of Southwest France. No hares now, no little fat runners you can shove out of the way. Aurelie found it hard and gave up, Hélène moved away from Sauternes and we stopped seeing her on the circuit. The others won championships. In the end there was only Robert left, single-mindedly devoted to middle distance running, he became Gironde champion at 1,000 metres and vice-champion of Aquitaine. Whatever happens, Jean Desautel, trot-and-stop, measure-and-stop, measure-and-recuperate, will not be forgotten at Château de Commarque.

17

The Best Day

In 1990 we appeared for the first time in an influential and widely read guide, *les Auberges et Hôtels de Charme de France*. The publication of the 1990 version produced an effect beyond our dreams and beyond any expectation that might have been aroused by the two boys who had announced themselves as inspectors one morning at breakfast. Not that they were at all unprofessional. They were knowledgeable, enthusiastic about the necessity of 'making places like this work' *and* they were enthusiastic about Commarque. But they lacked the magisterial solemnity of the Michelin men. The ease with which they took us aboard seemed too good to be true. Where was the automatic rejection of the early days? Anyway, it happened. We got into the guide.

From the beginning of March, the telephone started to ring with a new and refreshing frequency. Responding to letters of enquiry became a more arduous chore. We had an outstanding Easter with the hotel full for a good ten days and nearly everyone buying 1988 Sauternes and 1989 dry white wine. This was a wonderful boost at the leanest time of the year when all those winter debts have mounted up and there is still virtually no income. During March and April there is a continuous stream of demands for taxes of great obscurity and ingenuity, generated by the previous year's activity. Income may be seasonal but expenditure most certainly is not! The other consequence of being in the guide was that we collected unheard of quantities of deposits for holidays in the summer. It looked as though a turning point had been reached.

The description of Commarque in the *Auberges et Hôtels de Charme* was spot on. 'Simple and rustic' were the rooms, it said; no unreasonable expectations could be aroused by that. People would come because they could cope with simplicity and rusticity, in the interests of enjoying the beautiful surroundings and good food: 'Succulent traditional cuisine, served with a smile for very reasonable prices'—*Eh oui*! That's what it said. Many of the entries had nothing about the quality of the restaurants; they were just mentioned, with their prices and specialities. We were favoured indeed. The impression of having been accurately written up was strengthened by the sale, during the summer, of all forty of the expensive copies of the guide we had bought, in rash enthusiasm, back in the spring. We looked forward to a rosy future in the *Auberges et Hôtels de Charme* as we dealt with coaches sent by Sudinter of Bordeaux, with a succession of marriages, baptisms and confirmations, and watched the perfect ripening of the abundant grapes in that year of years. For 1990 was also a grand year for Sauternes.

Our neighbour in the vines, Monsieur Leglise of Château Lamourette, who has seen seventy vintages, says there has been nothing like it since 1929. The year had prepared itself from the start: fine weather for the flowering, enough rain at just the right time, a hot summer and, above all, a wonderful autumn, the afternoon light sharper and clearer than that of summer and the dusty heat replaced by a temperate warmth which does not discourage exertion, especially grape picking! The best thing in such autumns is the colour. The vines, the acacia trees beyond them, the creeper on the walls of the château and the fiery red ornamental trees in the distant park of Château Filhot, they all seem to be lit from within— how could this not be a successful time looking like that? If 1990 is our best year, 25 September is easily identifiable as the best day we ever had at Château de Commarque.

* * *

On 25 September the sun was beginning to break through by eight o'clock, just as the first hotel guests drew their curtains, and stepped out into the courtyard for the pre-breakfast stroll. This particular stroll has been taken unprompted by so many people over the years: out through the front gate, turn left round the tower in the north-east corner, past the vines by the car park, checking that the car hasn't disappeared over night, and back under the arch by the restaurant. It only takes about three minutes but it seems to sharpen the appetite, and the crunching of feet on the gravel warns me that it is time to make the coffee. I am probably the only winemaker in the Gironde, perhaps in the whole of France, who has to give breakfast to his hotel guests before starting grape picking.

On 25 September 1990, the stroll took a little longer than usual for most people because they interrupted it to examine the grapes. It was difficult not to stop and look, even if you had seen this sight before, because these grapes had been attacked by Noble Rot and were beautifully rotted, that is to say it looked impossible to do anything with them except throw them away! In fact they were just right for making into Sauternes, and not just ordinary Sauternes. They were close to perfection.

This was not just a day for making good wine. We had thirty-five French wine buffs in the restaurant at lunchtime and two minibuses of Japanese tourists in the hotel that evening. The two parts of the enterprise were working together in the way we had planned, under the benevolent influence of the weather. We were going to be busy.

Fortunately, the period of *les vendanges* breeds a solidarity which extends beyond those directly involved in them. The guests arrived early for breakfast so as not to hold things up, or so that they could come and listen to the briefing of the grape pickers. Marie-Laure, the waitress, also arrived early to clear away so that I could escape, and even Gilles was up early. He was cooking quails in Sauternes with great intensity long before Georgea could extract herself from the house to come and mastermind the preparations for lunch. He was in a good mood, which was not always the case on busy days. There would not be an 'atmosphere' in the kitchen that morning. He continued to brown quails, oblivious of anyone trying to get past him, making a noise like the rhythm section of a jazz-group through his teeth when he was not noisily slurping gulps of his special tea. He invented the quails in Sauternes, and it is for such things as this that we put up with an occasional atmosphere and the rhythm section.

Brigadier Hoskins, who was staying in the hotel, ate an enormous breakfast. He was going to try grape picking. He had announced this the previous evening when the *vendangeurs* were cleaning their buckets and clippers, although he could see how they looked after a day spent crouching or bent double in front of the vines, and they were all less than half his age. One does not become a brigadier for nothing! There had been some derisive betting on how long he would last, but not even the kindest estimate got it remotely right. Brigadier Hoskins was to pick all that morning and lunch with the other *vendangeurs*, rather than lying down in his room. Then he picked all afternoon. I reckon he was picking for England and St George, but he did a good job for us as well and contributed to the best wine we ever made, the *Crème de Tête* 1990, for this, do not forget, was our best day.

When the brigadier came in that evening, he was nearly bent double and he asked to stay on two extra days, 'Because the weather is so wonderful.'

We think it had more to do with not wanting to move on to his meeting in Toulouse with French army colleagues until he could stand up straight and walk once again like a brigadier!

I escaped from breakfast in time to see Robert and Edward leave for school. They pedalled up the track between the vines, into the dazzling haze to the east. The mist was lifting rapidly now and the vines had become a sea of brilliant pin points as the sunlight picked out the moisture on the yellow, translucent leaves. The lawns around the walls were beginning to steam. The boys had become dark blobs against the golden trees on the horizon as a distant rumble announced the approach of Isabelle's ancient van. It pulled over to let the bicycles pass, then continued along the track at its habitual snail's pace. The suspension was sagging and the spectre of final collapse lurked in every pothole!

Isabelle and her husband Victor were our two ace *vendangeurs*. She was the only real Sauternes local among our pickers because I had had trouble with the locals, all of whom had fixed ideas about how the job should be done which did not coincide with my own! I prefer people I can indoctrinate myself. Ten brigadiers would be ideal but, failing that, I had a group of Marie-Laure's friends. That day there would be Dinky, Stephanie, Flo and Sabine. They are all intelligent, hard-working drop-outs who are unwilling, or unable, to hold down regular jobs. They subsequently formed, with Marie-Laure and others, a street entertainment group and revealed an interesting array of talents. There was John, of John and Maurice from Budos, who would have to leave the vines at a quarter to twelve to put on his bow tie and help Marie-Laure to wait at lunchtime, and Michael, an English sculptor, with his wife Lisa. They find penury in France a better bet than penury in England. Joan, the chambermaid, would be out when she had finished the rooms. She is English as well, and even after ten years, she still called the *vendange* the 'vendarge' and hated it! But she did it so well.

We were one person short, fortunately replaced by Brigadier Hoskins, because Sébastien had been sacked the week before during our last passage through the vines. We had finally understood why he always selected the tallest bucket, previously a disinfectant container and not a *vendange* bucket at all. He would rush up his row of vines with this bucket, turn it upside down at the end and sit on it, gazing raptly at the vine in front of him, stoned out of his mind! It was the sheer weight of grapes left in his rows which finally alerted us to the fact that he rarely picked anything at all.

Isabelle and Victor jumped down from the van and strode over to the door of the *chai* in front of which Dinky and Flo were sitting on a stone smoking, having laid out the buckets and secateurs and piled up the *bastes* (plastic dustbins without lids) into which the grapes are tipped. Isabelle wore Doc Martins for 'vendanging' and an extremely baggy pair of dungarees to make bending easier. She then made it difficult again by putting on a large, leather belt from which hung various accoutrements, including several clean cloths, changed each day, for wiping sugary fingers, etc., a stone in a leather pouch for sharpening her private clippers, and a water bottle, at least I think it had water in it. Victor strapped himself into a weight-lifter's corset; he had a bad back. This is a man who had in his time followed the grape harvest across the world. He said there was nothing, anywhere, which resembles picking for Sauternes. These two could be relied upon to fill bucket after bucket with individually selected grapes and so lift the sugar content of the juice to dizzy heights. That day their concentration and dexterity were scarcely necessary. The grapes were *all* so sugar sweet that even Sébastien would have been able to pick a decent bucket full.

John's unreliable moped puttered down the track and died on the bend by the front gate. He pushed it resignedly into the car park and went off with his backpack to hang up his red velvet waistcoat, his waiting trousers and bow tie beside Marie-Laure's black mini-skirt in the entrance to Gilles's flat, which served as a changing room. By the time he got back Stephanie and Sabine had shot up to the château in their tatty Renault Five with the flat tyres, leaving a pall of dust behind them, to the irritation of the smart, elderly French couple, hotel guests like the brigadier, who were exercising their poodle round the vines. Michael and Lisa were last, as usual, but their unhurried arrival, followed by unhurried movements throughout the day, would be compensated by the thoroughness and care with which they work. We were lucky indeed to have an *équipe* of pickers like this. Joan has horror stories of what went into the buckets at certain great châteaux where she had worked. Mind you, the rows of vines can be very, very long. Worse than that, a vineyard owner from the other side of the river, not in Sauternes, told me sadly that he had had to abandon hand-picking and go over to harvesting by machine because of the *mauvaise ésprit* (ill will) of his *vendangeurs*. Not only were they uninterested and careless but also violent and, finally, destructive. In Sauternes we do not have the option of machine picking. The rules decree, as if anything else were possible, that the grapes must be picked manually by *tries successives* (that is by successive passes through the vines) picking just those grapes that have been attacked by the Noble Rot and leaving the rest for later *tries*.

The briefing was simple on 25 September: we wanted 100 per cent rotted grapes and no *pourri plein*, that is rotten (*pourri*) but full of juice (*plein*). Only grapes which had lost enough water to have started to shrivel would do.

The little crowd of *vendangeurs* and spectators straggled across the track and past the swimming pool to the patch of vines that had been left untouched the longest. It was ten days since we had last picked here. Several hotel guests were there helping to carry the *bastes* and lending moral support to the brigadier, although not all had pure motives. Dinky was holding several hundred francs worth of bets!

From my position at the back of the field I saw Flo and John reach the first row of vines and stop dead. Flo leant forward and pointed, then beckoned to the others. There was a visible quickening of interest. John called back to make me hurry.

I was immediately worried. Had all the grapes been eaten by birds? Had one of the telegraph poles fallen across the vines? ... What on earth was the matter?

Nothing was the matter. Everyone was looking at a sight which is to be seen perhaps two or three times in a generation: the vines had had the leaves stripped off their lower branches to expose the grapes. That morning they were strikingly more visible than we had ever seen them before because they formed a uniform black band stretching away from us and curving down with the fall of the land. The band was composed of hundreds of bunches in which every grape was *flétri* (shrivelled) to perfection. Purplish-brown and mouldy from close-to, the effect en masse was this startling black strip which had stopped Flo and John in their tracks. Every row was the same. There would be no sorting that day, no 'tickling' of individual grapes. We would pick everything and still make our best Sauternes ever.

Isabelle took charge of the brigadier, and the other hotel guests gathered round them. The rest of us selected our rows and started picking. Normally we pick two to a row, one *vendangeur* on each side, to avoid missing anything. That day this was unnecessary, the grapes were so visible that, just for once, a one-sided view was quite appropriate.

The brigadier's followers soon departed and the companionable silence that always seems to accompany the first hour or so of picking fell over the vines. The only sounds, apart from the birds, were the snipping of the secateurs and the plop of the bunches into the empty buckets. They, and the *bastes* at the ends of the rows, filled up as quickly as if we had been picking for dry white wine. Dinky was the first to complete a bucket. He always went like lightning all morning and then struggled in the heat of the afternoon. This was partly because he was carrying too much weight, but after lunch he was generally carrying too much red wine as well. Three weeks before, when picking for the dry white wine, he had risen from the vines and yelled '*Regardez!*' at the top of his voice.

Heads had obediently appeared all over the vineyard and there he was, a kind of modern fertility symbol with arms outstretched above his head, holding aloft three immense bunches of grapes, each at least eighteen inches long, with which he had completely filled his bucket!

Clouds of dust from the mould on the grapes billowed out as the buckets were emptied gently into the *bastes*, very gently: we must not break the grape skins yet. By half past ten the *bastes* were full. This alone was remarkable. It can take the whole morning to fill the nine necessary to make a press-full of grapes. But that is when sorting and selection are called for and, on 25 September, they were not.

Michael helped me to fill the press and then left me alone to listen to the elderly machine groan, creak, and rumble as it did its work. It was so elderly that it couldn't be left alone. More modern presses operate without any human assistance whatsoever. Mine, on the other hand, requires constant attention: apart from the fact that it will not switch itself off but will simply shoot drive bands all over the *chai* when it cannot advance any further, it is capable of squirting juice sideways and up to the ceiling if left to function alone. Once it has started I am obliged to listen to its noisy clankings for the rest of the day, except when emptying the skins, stalks and pips at the end of the pressing. It is very tedious but supportable when the results are good. On 25 September they were so good that they were difficult to believe.

The press started turning but nothing came out except clouds of dust. This is a good sign. It means the grapes are not blown up with juice, but then that day we knew that already. As the grinding rhythm continued and still no juice appeared, I start to wonder if we had left our picking too late. The week before, Château d'Arche had extracted only 300 litres of juice from sixty *bastes* of grapes, about 4,500 litres! They had mistimed their *trie* by just one week.

The wheel had moved over a quarter of the way along its screw before the moisture started to gather on the wooden slats of the press's rotating cage. The dust was still billowing out of the machine but stopped suddenly as thin, blackish streams of juice started to fall into the tray (*la maye*) fitted beneath the press. The noisy work continued and at last the juice started to pour from the pipe under the *maye* into Wally and Pirrin's reception tank dug into the floor of the *chai*. By now I could put a burette under the pipe and collect enough liquid to see if it was as good as it looked.

I dropped the hydrometer into the juice and then tapped it on the top because it didn't seem to want to go down properly. It bobbed up again. This was puzzling so I pushed it slowly down again. There was no resistance. I hadn't picked up a piece of stalk squeezed out of the press or anything like that. I let go and the hydrometer slowly rose again, and went on rising. It did not stop until the bulb at the base was beginning to show above the liquid! The machine was telling me the juice was so concentrated that it was unable to give me a reading! The sugar content could not be measured because it was off the scale. At this point in the morning's toil Georgea appeared in the doorway.

She was unimpressed by my raptures over the juice, having her mind on her own affairs. Her position as an Englishwoman providing lunch for thirty-five Bordeaux wine enthusiasts was hardly less perilous than sitting in a lion's den with her head firmly in the owner's mouth. Had they known that the Chef de Cuisine of their chosen restaurant was English they would probably not have made the reservation. Old legends die hard and, let's admit it, some are well rooted in truth! Apart from this the Bordelais are considered by the rest of the French population to be particularly chauvinistic and know-it-all. The thirty-five would be unforgiving of any weakness and parsimonious in their praise, even if well satisfied. Gilles may have been responsible for the quails but Georgea carried the overall can and in any case the Velouté de St Jacques, which started the meal, was hers and so was the *plat de résistance*—le Gigot d'Agneau braisé aux Cèpes. The wild mushrooms are abundant here and this was their season. The plates would even be garnished with *cèpes* picked on the property; not many, however, for the good places are secret, even on our own land, and jealously kept that way by the locals.

Georgea was full of Gilles's Mûrier (Blackberry Gâteau). It was magnificent, decorated all over with flowers made of strawberries and blackberries, and filled with a dream of a Crème Chantilly, laced with the liqueur Fraises des Bois. The blackberries *all* come from our own brambles—we are certainly not short of these! Marie-Laure had made some beautiful table decorations out of autumn leaves and John had perfected a new method of carrying five dishes at once. Everyone was surpassing themselves today.

The demands of plate counting, which Gilles could never manage without Madame Jones to help him, claimed Georgea and she disappeared back to the restaurant leaving me to listen to the rich vocabulary of squeaks and rumbles now issuing from the press. The juice trickled, then briefly poured before the machine was switched off and thrown into reverse.

Just as the press started to unwind for the fifth and last time the pickers arrived with the second load of grapes. The timing was perfect as befitted the day, and, what was more, they arrived just in time for lunch.

Everyone looked very hot. Joan was puffing a lot and the brigadier looked boiled. He made a point, however, of grabbing the hose and leading the ceremony of cleaning up. The buckets and *bastes* were piled in pyramids and the secateurs spread out carefully in the sun to dry. Isabelle had her own elaborate procedure with all her cloths. Large quantities of water were drunk.

The lunch table was set outside, behind the restaurant kitchen, in the shade of one of the great oak trees which grow behind the hotel. The *vendangeurs* were a bit grubby to eat in the restaurant itself. Besides, they added a great deal of local colour to the scenery and were visible to everyone entering the restaurant! There are not many vineyards that feed their pickers these days, but we do have a restaurant from which to do it, and it is not as if we are feeding a hundred people.

The meal was simple and large: there were foot-long sandwiches filled with pâté and gherkins, bowls of salad and a kind of paella of vegetables and pieces of fish that Gilles had found time to concoct during the morning, under the strict instructions of Madame. As we know, in the past he had been less than wholly committed to these lunches and had even tried to blame one of his more miserable efforts on Georgea. That day his paella was highly praised. Litres of red wine were washed down with litres of lethally strong coffee, a self-cancelling cocktail which, everyone claimed, helped them to concentrate all afternoon.

Meanwhile, I had my sandwich and paella in front of the press which could not be allowed to stand idle. I missed the arrival of the thirty-five, but, when taking my plate back to the kitchen, I heard roars of laughter from the dining room, which suggested that things were going well. In the kitchen conversation was non-existent; everyone was working flat out, so I helped with the washing up for ten minutes while the press was unwinding. Isabelle had taken over with characteristic energy, having abandoned her lunch, and had a mountain of plates and cutlery beside her. When the mountain had been safely removed and then rebuilt all clean behind her, I was thinking about prodding everyone back to the vines to restart the picking. At that moment there was a prolonged burst of applause from the dining room. Marie-Laure had carried in the Mûrier to enthusiastic acclaim. Anyone with business in the kitchen tended to hover when these cakes were being served (along with the Fraisiers and Framboisiers), because when the leftovers came back, Georgea would divide them up carefully into equal portions for everyone. Eventually Marie-Laure returned with a big smile but no remains of Mûrier. The diners would like to congratulate the cook on the Gâteau and would we please leave it on the table so that they could finish it! Several people groaned audibly.

The *vendangeurs* were already wandering unprompted back to the buckets. There is no doubt that when the grapes are good the pickers are more buoyant, more energetic, infected by success. But it was very hot. It was going to be hard that afternoon and the strength of the juice would rise even higher. Hats were now *de rigueur*.

Flo and Stephanie had wide straw ones. Flo tied hers under her chin which made her look like a 6-foot 2-inch milkmaid. Sabine had a very large knotted handkerchief about which she was slightly self-conscious, and Dinky a totally inappropriate black trilby. He wore it at a jaunty angle which he changed in accordance with the direction in which he was moving, thus maximising the protection it gave. Isabelle and Victor had started the day wearing business-like blue caps which they now had on back to front to protect their necks and I was curious to see what John would produce when he had finished in the restaurant. Michael and Lisa, being English, had boaters which were greatly admired, and Joan a large, pink affair worn to a wedding a couple of years previously. It looked ludicrous bobbing along the rows of vines. Georgea would appear later wearing one of the floppy white hats the twins had had as babies. She should not really have been picking at all since there was another load of customers in the restaurant that evening, but that day was a successful day, and success breeds energy.

Only the brigadier was hatless, and it was he who needed a hat most of all. He had not been prepared in advance for this, and he could hardly put on his brigadier's khaki cap, which we knew he had with him because Joan saw it hanging up in the wardrobe of his room with his uniform! The problem was solved with one of Edward's baseball caps … the brigadier even wore it back to front.

The habitual rhythm of picking was more or less resumed, a little slower than in the morning, accompanied now by a murmur of conversation. The crickets were going full blast in the bottom field and the sun was beating down, bleaching the colour from the ageing vine leaves, out of a sky of the clearest blue. Bursts of laughter and noisy conversation announced the fact that the thirty-five had finished their lunch. They were not in a hurry as they had a visit at Château Guiraud, just up the road, in half an hour's time. So, being wine buffs, they were looking for us. We wouldn't have dreamt of saying we were busy and couldn't stop to talk to them. These people had come a long way to eat at Commarque and had just spent a gratifyingly large sum of money in the restaurant. The wine trade is famous for generosity with its time and its products, and, in any case, it is bad publicity to be churlish; a *mauvais acceuil* soon gets known. Apart from this the *vendangeurs* were delighted by this little bit of attention. For a moment they had lost their image as an anonymous group of heads seen irregularly above the vines, and they were all being treated as experts, including the brigadier!

He was looking flustered in the midst of a knot of Frenchmen all asking him incomprehensible questions and was rescued by John who, having polished his last glass, had appeared in dark glasses and ... how camp can he get? ... a sombrero. The visitors all knew him by now and their enthusiastic greeting indicated that he had put on a fine performance for them in the restaurant.

Before bailing out the brigadier he couldn't resist introducing 'le Général Hoskins' to everyone and there followed the comical sight of the brigadier doffing his back-to-front baseball cap and shaking hands solemnly with this group of suddenly respectful and somewhat perplexed Frenchmen. It is, of course, only *British* senior military personnel who are likely to be found grape picking in Sauternes!

I had a brief conversation with Monsieur Lacampagne, the man who had organised this group, with whom I had spoken several times on the telephone but not met until now. He had spotted me giving out orders so he naturally asked me if I was a field marshal. He was in an excellent mood but looked dangerously overheated by food, wine and sunshine. He shook my hand vigorously and told me how delighted his comrades were to have found Château de Commarque and how well they had eaten. I was to be congratulated on my Chef de Cuisine. I replied that it was my wife.

'Then your wife is French *évidemment*?' The question was almost a statement of fact.

'Not at all, Monsieur, she is as English as I am.'

He dropped my hand and took a step backwards.

'*Ce n'est pas possible, monsieur*,' he said. '*Une Anglaise* would not be able to cook like that.'

I feigned indignation (we have had this before) and said that I would be very pleased to introduce him to my wife if he did not believe me.

He apologised profusely and walked away shaking his head at this terrible blow to his prejudices. It was difficult to decide whether this incident was gratifying or irritating! In the spirit of the day satisfaction gained the upper hand and Monsieur Lacampagne restored his peace of mind by summoning his troops for the visit to Château Guiraud. It would certainly be prudent to put these men in a cool place for some time. A strenuous bout of hand-shaking preceded their departure, except in Sabine's group, where there was much ceremonial kissing. I noted that Sabine had removed her handkerchief.

The last hours of the afternoon passed without incident; the press was filled for the fourth and final time, the *bastes* and buckets were sterilised by Isabelle ready for the next day, Dinky fell asleep outside the *chai* with his trilby over his face and was kicked awake by Flo, who wanted a lift home. Georgea went off to collect our three older boys from the school bus and, at that moment, when I was on my own with the press at a critical stage in its cycle, the Japanese guests arrived. There was no one to greet them but me and I was covered in dust and sticky juice. There was nothing for it but to switch off the press and face them, filth and all.

There are no tourists like Japanese tourists, at least among the ones that I have encountered. These have ranged over the years from a bus load of lost Slovenian wine-makers to a drop-head Bentley full of Swiss millionaires; from American cyclists so stout that their bikes spent most of the time travelling riderless from place to place on a trailer while their owners rode in minibuses, to two lean North Africans who were delivered by taxi and then did all their tourist visits on foot, at a steady 20 kilometres an hour, as training for the Bordeaux marathon.

From the moment each pair of Japanese feet touched the gravel, their owners were looking round, up and over their shoulders, unable, it appeared, to take in their surroundings rapidly enough. Everyone had a camera, everyone started photographing as if the courtyard would evaporate before they were able to record it. They scattered, walking backwards, sideways, or turning in circles, photographing as they went. One fell over a chain between the plane trees in front of the hotel rooms, another sat down in a half barrel of geraniums. Just one seemed exempt from the frantic need for visual input, and she was the guide. She was extremely anxious on behalf of her charges and her anxiety took the form of an aggressive bossiness: they must have all the best rooms, and she hoped they were clean enough and comfortable enough. This was said, not unreasonably, while eyeing me up and down with deep suspicion. She must have someone to help with the luggage; did I realise how important some of these people were? She pointed to a small bespectacled man photographing half-a-dozen of his companions and informed me that he was managing director of the fourth largest company in Japan. (I forget the name, she certainly told me.)

Feeling a slight shadow pass over my flawless day I pointed out that the hotel was rustic, rather than luxurious, and hoped that it would suit her distinguished guests. The guide unbent sufficiently to say that this was their day (just one?!) for exploring rural France and she thought they would find it 'an interesting change from their usual itinerary'. I kept to myself the thought that they could have found better representatives of rural France than us and instead offered my services as a porter.

I found out quickly why the guide was so anxious for help with the luggage. These people were all equipped with suitcases like young cabin-trunks and they felt as though they were filled with gold ingots, or possibly crushed Japanese cars. They came fitted with wheels but that wasn't much help on the gravel. I had got two or three of these chests out of the first minibus when Georgea returned. She took in the scene instantly and I could see her muttering to Thomas, William and Francis, who dropped their school bags and advanced on the mounting pile of suitcases. The twins were only 12 and Thomas 14, but they were at least as big as the distinguished guests and, with the guide dancing round and yelling orders at us, we started to drag the luggage to the rooms.

Some of the guests joined in, which calmed the guide down. She was definitely more worried about what *they* thought than about incorrect luggage distribution and, as *they* seemed relaxed and happy, *she* could stop over-acting her part as their attentive guardian. I noticed three cases moving under the impulsion of not one but two distinguished guests, one pulling on the handle, the other pushing from behind! Eventually all the cases found a home and the visitors vanished abruptly into their rooms. Silence fell over the courtyard.

Marie-Laure arrived for the evening service, just as Gilles wobbled through the front arch on his incredibly expensive racing bike, the wheels of which were so narrow it was almost as hard to ride through the gravel as the suitcases had been to drag through it. We retired for supper, knowing that they would look after the needs of the guests.

The day was by no means finished yet. After we had eaten, Georgea took up her post in the restaurant kitchen and I returned to the *chai* to clean up. Cleanliness precedes Godliness in wine-making and this job would take from one-and-a-half to two hours. Thomas came with me to carry out his speciality: cleaning and disinfecting the reception tank. The distinguished guests were all sitting outside the restaurant in the gathering twilight drinking Sauternes. The tables were laden with cameras and the courtyard was filled with the noise of Japanese. I wondered if this sound from the other side of the planet had ever been heard before in the long history of this corner of La France Profonde?

We had just got the pipes connected together for pumping the juice out of the reception tank to settle in a *garde-vin* overnight, when the guide came to ask if the visitors could see the winery. She had obviously expected the answer 'yes', because they were all just behind her. They gathered round, cameras flashing, and then they noticed the opaque, brownish liquid filling the reception tank and the noise of astonishment, in Japanese, echoed round the *chai*. The guide spoke loudly and they all fell silent and backed away, making a ring around Thomas and me with the reception tank behind us. She had called them to order, what discipline! She spoke to them again and two or three answered. I realised that they wanted to ask questions, so I asked whether anyone spoke English.

Several said yes, several nodded. I heard someone say, 'English better than French.'

This did not please the guide, who rattled away bossily in Japanese and spoke to me in French. She wanted to keep a tight control of the situation: all questions had to go through her.

Everyone wanted to know about that horrible-looking juice. How do you turn it into wine? How long will it be before it looks like wine? How long until you can drink it? I replied that it should be a clearish, golden wine in three to four weeks and they did not believe me. But as all things were possible that day I was able to convince them easily: I went to the barrels of dry white wine which we had started fermenting about three weeks before, and filled a glass with the new wine, already nearly crystal clear. The transition from opaque, yeasty ferment to clear, greeny gold wine has always seemed to me quite mysterious and magical as it happens each year without any assistance whatsoever.

I placed the glass of wine on a stool in front of the reception tank and put beside it a glass of the new Sauternes juice. I pointed and said, 'From that to that in three weeks.'

There was an explosion of chattering and the two glasses were photographed a hundred times, then a hundred times more, this time with Thomas holding them. After that the distinguished guests each had a glass of dry white wine and I saw from the guide's beautiful smile, hitherto well-hidden, that the success of the evening was now assured. They left for dinner. Thomas finished his reception tank and departed for bed and I had just finished sterilising the press, it was now nearly ten-thirty, when Marie-Laure came in and announced that the guide wanted me to come to the restaurant. Nothing was wrong, they just wanted to talk to me. I looked at her in horror.

'What! Like this?'

I was by now covered in squishy stains and well soaked by backfires from the pressure cleaner which had squirted off the unpredictable curves and angles of the press.

'Well, you know what she's like,' she replied. 'She said could you come as soon as you have finished.'

I followed Marie-Laure out, as obedient to the guide's commands as her tourists. As I walked into the restaurant, there appeared to be a veritable sea of Japanese faces looking at me! They had rearranged it in a most surprising way: the tables had been moved into a long line across the dining room and they were all sitting behind them facing a single chair placed in the middle of the empty space where most of the tables should have been! The chair was for me. I was going to be interrogated; the only thing missing was the blinding light!

The guide was still firmly in control: all questions, and there were plenty, passed through her. A number of people actually made notes. The questions were surprisingly simple and had little to do with trying to understand the structure or habits of another culture: how long had we been here? how many children do we have? can they speak French? how big is the vineyard? do I like making wine? ... all the world is indeed strange.

Question time continued for some twenty minutes, then there was silence. The guide thanked me and spoke in Japanese. The distinguished guests rose to their feet as one and the sound of applause filled the restaurant for the second time that day. I retired from the room waving with both hands and 25 September neared its conclusion with the sound of clapping ringing across the courtyard.

We sat, Georgea and I, under a clear night sky, still comfortably warm at eleven o'clock, and tried to assimilate the day. It felt like the culmination, the objective, of the four years we had been here but we could never have imagined it four years previously. I do not mean the numerous details like the eccentricities of Japanese tourists, the unlikely presence of a grape-picking brigadier, nor even Georgea's direction of the lunchtime banquet. (Our imaginings had never included Georgea as the

Chef de Cuisine of a restaurant after all!). I mean the underlying spirit of that day; it was the fulfilment of the dream which had enticed us out of England, safe, comfortable, dull, *cold*, England—or so it seemed! That day we had laid down our future in potent grape juice and assured our present in satisfied customers as never before. It seemed improbable that we would ever surpass 25 September 1990, although of course we would be trying—the next day, the day after that and the following year.

The *chai* was full of wine now. Monsieur Ducourneau had come by the day before, looked at the two-high row of barrels running the length of the right hand wall and said: '*Tiens!* It's better garnished now than it was a couple of years ago.'

The hotel was also full, with our Japanese guests, and even if they were only here for one night—this was nearly October after all—we were to be full again the following weekend. Georgea had forty-five people for lunch on Sunday and I was to take a little party of English visitors to Saint Emilion for the day. We would visit Château Ausone, Château Beauséjour-Bécot, la Grave-Figeac and the people we met would be as generous with their time and their wine as they always were.

We don't want to leave the impression that all was now perfection at Commarque. Far from it! The buildings were still gonky and we were still underfunded. Not everyone who came here liked it. The word 'château' conjures up a highly specific image for certain people, an image of luxury: chandeliers in a baroque dining room, formal gardens, lots of waiters. Château de Commarque, with a dining room in an old winery, rustic courtyard surrounded by la France Profonde—and there is nothing more rustic than that!—and one-and-a-half waiters, does not correspond in any way with this image. But the prices don't correspond either and the disappointed few seem to overlook that. Every couple of months someone says: 'It's not what we expected; we don't want to stay.'

And for years we worried and asked ourselves what we could do about it. Better to remember all the people who like it enough to return year after year and to take comfort from the well-heeled West End estate agent who remarked, as he watched two disgruntled Parisians drive off in their BMW: 'I pity the poor sods who don't like it here!' Then picked up his towel and sauntered across the courtyard to the swimming pool.

18

1991—the Biggest Year

Even before the best day had dawned in September 1990, it was clear that the first seeds of our undoing had been sown and were already germinating, beneath the long shadow, no less, of Mr Jenkin-Lee!

As the Crème de Tête 1990 gathered flavour and tannin in its barrels, and the bookings for 1991 started to come earlier and more abundantly than ever, we began to look forward to the issue of the 1991 version of *Les Auberges et Hôtels de Charme*, the guide which had had so dramatic an effect the previous year, and to talk about how many copies we ought to buy. But the order form did not arrive and by February we were wondering if they had forgotten to send it to us—but perhaps it was just coming out later than in 1990. The book certainly hadn't yet appeared at Leclerc in Langon. Then Georgea found it one day, just before we were due to go on our annual pilgrimage to England.

'I knew what had happened,' she said, 'and I really didn't want to look.'

She did though and found what she had feared. We were no longer in it.

I telephoned and asked why. The reply was unclear. Compiling the guide is the responsibility of a lady in Marseilles.

'*Monsieur*,' she said, 'I think you will find you are now in our new guide to *chambres d'hôte*.'

'*Madame*,' I replied, 'I know we are not. I discussed this possibility with your inspector and it is clear that Commarque is a hotel and not a *chambre d'hôte*.'

She changed tack abruptly; '*Monsieur*, I have received letters of complaint about your services. It is for this reason that you have been excluded.'

Oh horrors! And there we were thinking we had done so well by the people who had come through the guide.

'Would you please tell me what kind of complaints, *madame?*'

'I cannot remember, *monsieur*. I will have to search my records.'

'Please do! We must know what we have done wrong or we can do nothing to put it right.'

Three weeks later no complaints had been forthcoming so I rang once more. We went through the same spiel again. The lady promised to fax me copies of the letters of complaint. She didn't. I phoned a third time. She said she had been very busy but would do her best. This too produced nothing so I wrote to the editors of *Les Editions Rivages* in Paris—and did not receive a reply. By now we were well into our busiest ever season and the matter was temporarily swept aside. The effect of being booted out was barely perceptible in 1991. So many people were still carrying their 1990 versions that we still got more people from here than from any other single source.

That year continued to develop well on the hotel front, with the holiday department of Air France second in line as a source of customers, largely owing to a policy of cut-price fly-and-drive holidays. This gave, we found out from a customer in mid-August, return flights *and* the hire of a car for duration of your holiday, for substantially less than the normal price of air travel alone. Unfair competition perhaps and, unfortunately for us, it was not to last! The only thing we had against Air France was that they paid in arrears and the money had to be prised out of them with a crowbar. As their bookings occupied more than a third of all the rooms between mid-July and the end of August this might have been quite serious. But Sudinter was positively pouring coaches our way and even small groups of wine buffs for the hotel. Sudinter paid impeccably. You sent in the ticket given by the driver or guide on arrival and the cheque came back like clockwork within ten days. Cash flow was thus assured and the restaurant kept busy.

Preparations for the new season were progressing well, with the exception of that, as yet, more galling than damaging omission from the *Guide des Auberges et Hôtels de Charme*, when disaster struck the vineyard during the night of 21 April. It struck not only our vineyard but the whole of Bordeaux, having prepared itself for several days with a keen north wind. While we went to bed blissfully unaware of what was afoot outside, people more in the know were making frantic, and unavailing, preparations for what was to come. For once there were not that many who knew more than us, certainly not the weather forecasters, who missed that lethal frost as completely as their English counterparts had missed the hurricane that swept through the south of England in October

1987. As late as eleven o'clock that night, when the temperature had already dropped to -2 degrees in a brilliantly starlit, diamond-hard sky, the Bordeaux meteorological service was stoutly defending its view that it would cloud over and the temperature would drop no further. There were some that did not believe them and a few with the means to do something about it. Monsieur Moueix, owner of the celebrated Pomerol cru Château Petrus, producer of fabulously expensive wine, is a weather buff. He knew the forecasters were wrong. As the temperature fell below the danger point of -4 degrees, the point at which even the best kept and totally weed-free vineyards start to suffer, he called in helicopters to fly over the vines and keep the air moving. It didn't work.

That night the temperature dropped to minus seven and a couple of days later Monsieur Moueix announced that there would be no Château Petrus in 1991. Bordeaux lost 400 million bottles that night and slipped unnoticed into a recession from which it took many years to emerge. The start of the recession went unperceived, because in 1991 we were all near the top of that heady price spiral that accompanied the great years and high demand of the late eighties. In Sauternes that year the price of a tonneau rose to ₣50,000—and just five years earlier the Marquis de Lur-Saluces had enthused over the sharp rise to ₣24,000! The following spring it was to rise to ₣55,000 before crashing to half that, to 25,000 … 22,000, 18,000 for unstable 1993s, and even less … and even nothing at all for the unsaleably awful. But that was still three years away. Bordeaux was on a high, even the Reay-Jones at Château de Commarque were in better shape than ever before, with wine to sell and bookings bounding ahead. We could weather one bad frost. Bad? The lab at Cadillac announced in its end-of-year newsletter that there had been no frost like it since 1869. Sounded about in line with our usual luck, we thought!

That April morning in 1991 was brilliantly blue and white, and quite beautiful. The vines glittered in the dazzling sunshine and as I saw off a friendly businessman who had stayed the night he asked: 'Is this OK for the vines?'

In my innocence I answered 'Yes'. By mid-morning I had realised my mistake and by mid-afternoon the gravity of what had happened was clear. As the frost melted in the spring sunshine the crisp, sparkling green-and-white foliage on the vines first drooped, then collapsed, and finally shrivelled and turned black from the tips of the cold-blasted shoots to their bases. By the end of the following day there was not a green thing left in our vineyard. *Still* we didn't appreciate how profound was the damage. Vines grow again. They put out secondary shoots from the buds in the axils of the ones that have already grown. These will bear fruit, later perhaps, but even in 1990 Commarque had been slightly frosted and look at the recovery we had then. But in 1991 the frost was of a different order of severity. The primary shoots went all right; along with their flower buds, exceptionally advanced after an exceptionally mild spring. The axillary buds went too, slain in their covers as surely as if they had been exposed like the little leaves. On many of our vines just leaves developed that year, and on some growing on the lower, colder, clay soil, the leaves issued only from the main stock. The branches of these plants had been killed as well as the foliage, and the afflicted vines were creeping slowly back to life from their oldest, most stable centres. A few of them were unable to produce fruit even the following year and it took until the end of May 1991 for a trace of green to reappear in the vineyard.

Miraculously, many plants managed to flower and the grapes developed. Optimism grew. So what if the 1991 crop was bound to be small and late? It's amazing how much catching-up vines can do and the crop *could* still be very good. Why not one of those marvels where quality is matched by rarity and the price leaps up as the years go by? In fact, this wouldn't suit us that well. We didn't yet have enough stock. But others would cope, given their cellars bulging with good and prolific vintages. Even Commarque was better off than ever before. We had bottles of 1989 (very good!) and lots of half-bottles to sell expensively in the restaurant. People bought whole cases at F80 a bottle and there were tons of 1990 dry white, which was equally popular. Best of all for the bank balance though, we had enough 1990 Sauternes to sell some in bulk and bring in a bulk amount of cash in mid-June. A year later the wisdom of this sale was in question but, once again, what is the use of hindsight? In June 1991, for the first time in our five years at Commarque, all the bank accounts moved into the black—when the bank draft from the SICA de Barsac arrived. John and Celia, Georgea and I toasted ourselves in champagne and John got quite excited about the bit of return he was at last going to get from his involvement with Commarque. We felt insulated from imminent financial danger; the vineyard was starting to generate its long forecast return, the hotel was booked as never before, the restaurant had bus loads every week. None of us felt, could have felt, the gentle shudders in the foundations of our enterprise.

* * *

Lots of things were changing in 1991, including the personnel. We had finally parted company with Gilles the previous October, on moderately bad terms. He had burnt one too many saucepans, pulled one too many ape-like faces and, more seriously, had stopped trying when it came to cooking. There must surely be someone, somewhere, easier to live with and just as competent who would like to work here? The answer was, surprisingly, not really! Perhaps it was the measly salary, and there was also the isolation. Whatever the problem, Gilles was back two years later, behind a splendidly oily letter telling of his newfound maturity *and* the new *hyper-bon* recipes he would bring us. Marie-Laure had left too, and certainly not through heartbreak at the departure of Gilles. *Très juste*— barely tolerable—was how she described working with him. She had already announced that she wouldn't stay if he did. But finally her street entertainment group was starting and she needed to do her own thing. She too was to return—the group had to eat—and bailed us out *in extremis* as early as September! What an eventful, or ghastly, summer that was.

Back we went to Madame Bercovici for a cook. Could she find us someone more or less normal this time *and* who could cook?

She-understood-*bien-sûr*-and-would-find-us-a-reliable-young-man-in-a-few-days. But time passed with no result, so that Georgea was obliged to carry the can all through May and into June. Bernard, Madame Bercovici's choice, only arrived on the 12th and Georgea was tired out before the season had properly begun.

We had been luckier with the waitress. Valérie Vigouroux ('Vigorous Val') had been an easy choice when she had answered our advert in the *Sud-Ouest* newspaper. Polite, efficient, smart and experienced, she settled that particular problem nicely for the season.

Bernard was a young man of great height and extreme leanness, had he been a plant one would have called him 'etiolated'. Affable, jokey, fast-talking, blond hair *en brosse* and a bag of nerves. This was not immediately obvious. His manner in the kitchen was confident; he sliced with astounding rapidity and was both courteous and cooperative, an agreeable change indeed. He asked apologetically if he could raise the big kitchen table, on which most of the work was done, in order to avoid having to stand with his ostrich-like legs far apart where everyone would trip over them. He duly jacked it up on breeze blocks, thus allowing him to stand with his back straight and his face close enough to the work surface to make out what he was doing. Work was accompanied by a constant patter of jokes and comment, delivered so fast we missed the half of what he said and mistakenly believed he was as confident as he sounded. Valérie was primed to ping the bell for help when people arrived, at least until Bernard knew all the dishes properly. But he never learned to cope with more than a couple of tables. Georgea was called incessantly, only to carry out two minutes' work then stand around with nothing to do. She did not like this. Bernard was also quite unprepared for being consulted on new dishes: 'I don't have ideas, I execute,' he said.

But surely he had a few recipes from other restaurants which would fit in? When pushed he did produce one gem: boned, stuffed legs of duck, a perfect one-person roast, popped in the oven when the order was announced, crispy and succulent when served three-quarters of an hour or so later. The trouble was their preparation. It took Bernard a whole morning to do fifteen or twenty of these elaborate little parcels. Being rather good, they went fast. Twenty-four hours later he would spend another morning preparing another fifteen, thus leaving Georgea to do everything else. She didn't much like this either, but drew some comfort from left-over pieces of his excellent Marquise au Chocolat. The weeks passed, however, without serious mishap, although he admitted that he was unhappy about being so isolated and would never have come if Madame Bercovici had told him Commarque was in the middle of nowhere. His confidence grew a little but he still revealed an alarmingly shaky hand when the service got 'hot', and a total inability, or unwillingness, to produce vegetables. Hot dishes were served with a lettuce leaf and a slice of tomato. Even a formal ban failed to stop this low practice and plates continued to go out behind our backs—to the discomfort of Valérie—garnished in this shabby way. Bernard did, however, distinguish himself at a couple of hair-raising weddings. The *pièce montée* collapsed in the first one. The restaurant got as close as it has ever been to being smashed up in the second.

Pièce montées are cone-shaped mountains of profiteroles, sometimes several feet tall, glued together with caramel as hard as Araldite—it needs to be to hold the things up. We don't make them ourselves because the process takes too long. Some of those you can buy probably don't taste much better then Araldite—not that I've tried it. They are, however, almost obligatory for celebratory meals, sometimes alongside a 'proper' dessert. They are served with the champagne, they accompany the speeches and toasts and have plastic models on the top appropriate to the occasion: a couple in wedding gear for a marriage, a baby in a cradle for a baptism and so on; a bit yukky, but traditional. If they are not kept cool the caramel can soften and cause sagging—or worse. One hot, hot July night in 1991, so hot that the milk tank in the *chai* was being used to generate the cold water needed to slake the guests' thirst, I went to the cool bathroom of room four to recover the *pièce montée*, a monster of over 300 choux pastries. It had collapsed sideways, leaning against the pedestal of the basin in drunken and sticky disarray. It could have been funny, but the bridegroom had asked for this sagging mess to be served in ten minutes. Served means presented, held up for admiration and applause, shown to all the aunties and godparents before being whisked away for demolition. There wouldn't be much clapping for this pathetic wreck. I rushed back to the kitchen for help. We put the thing in a large box for support and smuggled it in round the back of the hotel. Bernard took command.

'Put it on the oven, keep warming it gently and dismantle it completely,' he ordered. 'I'm going to make a cone of cardboard and foil and stick it together again—well some of it. You'll have to make sure it comes back in here for serving. Whatever you do don't let the bride and groom get their hands on it.'

I believe he had done this before...

The gods were with us that night. The guests were all dancing, the lights had been dimmed and no one was in a hurry. The one problem was the streams of guests arriving at the kitchen door with empty carafes for more water. All other service ceased in the interests of stopping them before they reached the kitchen. A first wall of waiters stood there grabbing carafes—it was impossible to get into the restaurant to serve as we should because of the wall of dancers gyrating in semi-darkness. A second wall of waiters and kitchen staff surrounded the guilty secret. There was a nasty moment when the groom came and shouted some cheerful instruction to me (middle of second wall), but somehow he saw nothing, suspected nothing.

The reconstructed *pièce*, barely two-thirds the size of the original, was heralded with rapturous applause, strongly led by the staff, paraded at lightning speed and whistled off to the kitchen before anyone could get a proper look at it. A tentative 'Shall we help serve it ...?' from the bride was easily countered.

'Thank you so much but there are too many people to serve without the proper equipment in the kitchen.'

A very old lady did say to me: 'Young man (!) I didn't see the *pièce montée* properly before you took it away!'

'*Mes excuses, Madame*, but in this heat it was beginning to melt and we were afraid it might collapse!' I was able to reply, with perfect accuracy.

The second affair was more serious. A large family lunch had revealed itself as a reconnaissance for a wedding, and not the usual run of weddings either. It was to be a two-phase operation; the family, complete with all their elderly friends, made up the first phase. This was a sit-down lunch of some five or six courses for about sixty people and it went off very well. Phase two was for the younger element, who would supply their own drink, dance the night away and consume a Buffet Campagnard (a rustic supper) with loads of *charcuterie*, cheese etc. But we added gazpacho, salads and iced puddings and generally made it far too nice for the brutal crowd that turned up that night. Bernard surpassed himself with a huge silver butterfly on which he laid out, in magnificent array, serried ranks of charcuterie.

We hadn't much liked the look of the groom, a thin-faced man of about 30 with a handle-bar moustache and fierce eyes. Apprehensions were further aroused when the drink was delivered. Seventy people were expected but enough wine and whisky arrived for at least 150. When the groom himself turned up he came in at a run, leapt onto a table and delivered himself of a succession of war-whoops, beckoning those nearest to jump up and join him. I called a halt to this, not without difficulty, and then spent an exhausting eight hours stopping him and his witless cronies from running amok. Rich and spoilt I suppose they were, thoughtless and loutish I know they were. This is the only time anything remotely like this happened but it leaves a permanent and disagreeable taste and a determination never to allow the possibility of a repeat performance.

The windows of the restaurant were used as doors and Georgea's banks of busy-lizzies were irreparably trampled flat. Food was thrown everywhere, the bottles of Château Commarque displayed in the foyer were stolen, our honoured guests peed and threw up all round the back of the restaurant and in the carpark. They broke the signs under the entrance and ripped a basin off the wall of a hotel room. The final straw came at about five-thirty when some oaf drove the tractor, against which dozens of folding chairs were propped, out into the vines and left it there with the engine running. I announced it was time to leave. This was not well received. I insisted. There was a slanging match. I did OK, even in French, and they went, but not without exacting petty revenge. To this day the vineyard sign at the end of the lane is badly twisted on its stout metal post. I have no idea how they managed this because I was quite unable to untwist it, merely straightened the sign so that it pointed down the lane once more, not into the ground.

When the last drunken guest had driven his car too fast up the track— what a harvest the gendarmes could have reaped that night—I put on the lights of the restaurant. The floor appeared to be covered in mud, alternating with puddles and strewn with broken glass from end to end. Fortunately tables, chairs, lamps and ornaments had all been removed at an early stage, on instructions from the bridegroom 'to make more space'. Forty or fifty wine glasses and several carafes had contributed to the glass scattered everywhere. Later we found another twenty or so glasses smashed outside. I hoped the puddles were nothing more than wine and other drinks, and of course the mud resulted from the constant crossing and recrossing of the flower beds. It smelt awful. So, at 6.30 the following morning I started to clean up. At 6.45 Bernard came down to help. He hadn't slept too well. By nine o'clock the restaurant was fit to start resetting for lunch and I was free (oh joy!) to spend the morning repairing the damage elsewhere. A busy lunch followed and the hotel was full in the evening. It took me—all of us—several days to recover.

'We're not doing that again,' Georgea said.

Monsieur Bellot, the father of the groom, expressed shock and distress when I phoned him but he never came to see me. I expect he preferred the alternative version of events he would have received from his son, whose hopes of his ideal wedding reception we had undoubtedly dashed.

We decided to limit weddings to fifty people, to put a time limit of 4 am, and to ask for large deposits to cover damage. Naturally we lost bookings, and we eventually succumbed to the temptation of another large wedding. The people who came to see us about a reception for 100 to 120 guests were extremely reluctant to take no for an answer. Very well behaved they would be. There would be no problems and they would leave on time. The money was most tempting, so we said 'yes'. It was a success. Commarque had never looked more beautiful. A stripey marquee occupied the corner by the restaurant and there were round tables all dressed in pink the whole length of the terrace. We had six in the kitchen and six serving that night, for a six-course dinner—the full works: Foie Gras, Salmon, Pièce Montée etc. The waiting staff long remembered the four hours spent in unceasing procession to and from the kitchen bearing plates. The kitchen staff long remembered the spectacular piles of washing up and serving 102 Tournedos au Sauternes et au Roquefort, and then eight children's portions without Sauternes and Roquefort. Our cook would remember, above all else, peeling and shaping by hand 425 even-sized little rugby balls of potatoes for roasting with herbs—his idea, not ours. I recall having a nasty turn about 1 am and having to sit down. But the people behaved impeccably, left at the allotted time and we all went briefly to bed, leaving a great deal of mess still on the terrace. Just before dawn it rained, and the morning clear up was thus rendered three times more difficult than it would otherwise have been. Learning from previous occasions, we closed the restaurant that night and collapsed.

But it still took days to recover and when we came to calculate the effect of closing the restaurant, of blocking the hotel for the wedding—for you can't expect anyone else to sleep in the place when a party like that is in progress—it didn't work out so profitable after all. Enough was enough and we only did little weddings afterwards, and on our own terms.

Meanwhile, what of Bernard and his nerves? He had been more than efficient at those two weddings but they had taken it out of him, as they had taken it out of all of us. But he wasn't tied to Commarque and he wasn't made of the same stern stuff as we are! On 15 August I had a mild altercation over the inevitable vegetables.

'We must have a new vegetable tonight for the *demi-pensionnaires*, Bernard.'

'That's it,' he cried. 'I can't go on!' He ripped off his apron and rushed upstairs to his flat. He rushed down again, having changed out of his cook's gear, and ran over to the house. He was back in another half a minute, bolted upstairs again and ten minutes later, with all his belongings about him, he strode up the track. We never saw him again.

'What did he say to you?' I asked Georgea.

'I didn't catch all of it but he said he couldn't stay because he had to go and have treatment for his head, something like that. Just great isn't it?' And off she grimly went to the restaurant to sort out the day's work on her own.

On the morning of 16 August, the 15th being a bank holiday, I phoned Madame Bercovici.

'*Mon-Dieu*-what-has-got-into-that-young-man-I-need-to-have-a-word-with-him,' she intones and, of course, understands-our-problem. But she was unable to do anything about it. In mid-August she had no one looking for a place, but as she wouldn't own up to that we wasted precious time waiting for her to solve our problem. Meanwhile, the impossible happened. The day Bernard vanished I said to Valérie—reliable, solid, steady-as-a-rock Valérie: 'You won't leave, will you?'

'Certainly not,' she declared. 'I'm safely here until the end of October. You don't need to worry about me.'

Three days later she failed to turn up for work. There was no explanatory call, and we were worried in case something had happened to her. She couldn't have thought it was her day off, could she? She didn't arrive the next day either and her phone seemed to be permanently engaged, or off the hook. That morning we got a letter from her ... and, she'd left! A dream job she had applied for at the start of the year, with no chance of it coming up until at least the end of 1991, has suddenly been offered to her: Chef de Rang at Novotel, permanent rather than seasonal, stable, definitely promotion. Of course, she can't refuse it, but she can't face us either so she has just evaporated. Later, when she has to see me to get papers signed, it turns out the damned job didn't even start until September. She could have seen out August, given us a chance to find someone else, been paid her 10 per cent in lieu of holidays, to which she would have been entitled. But she couldn't bear the prospect of the coals of fire she foresaw heaped upon her head if she had returned to Commarque. How wrong can you get? We hadn't time to waste in recriminations. We were up to our necks in it now!

The next three weeks were less than enjoyable. For Georgea they rank among the least favourite weeks of her life. A job she had taken on only out of necessity now became totally overwhelming, grinding the energy out of her day by day as she was forced to ignore the children and neglect the house in order to cook endlessly, on her own, in the heat of high summer. She started at seven in the morning and finished at eleven at night, or later, doing this thing she had never liked and now came to dread. We have been able to laugh at most of the disasters that have befallen us at Commarque but not at the last two weeks of August 1991.

At first we awaited Madame Bercovici's call daily, and called her daily. Then we realised that we would have to take the matter into our own hands. An advert in the *Sud-Ouest*, a tour of the temporary work agencies produced nothing. The former generated a small but extremely select response from social misfits and other unfortunates. The agencies owned up to never having cooks available, let alone in August. I was, however, let off the waiting hook to a degree and Georgea obtained some incompetent help. It was Joan's daughter, Sheriden, who came to the rescue. She herself, available briefly between jobs, came and helped with the waiting, the children's meals, the washing, but she couldn't stay long.

'I might be able to find you some people,' she said.

'Do they know anything about it?'

'They've been working in a posh hotel in the Landes.' Now that would be something!

The following morning, I found two pretty girls standing outside the restaurant.

'Sheriden sent us,' one of them said. The answer to our prayers? The perfect solution? Not exactly. We had two more weeks to put up with before that arrived, but they helped a bit. One became waitress and was good but very slow. One wondered how she had managed at the place where her contract had just ended. Still, if you smile enough and are pretty enough you can get by.

'Gosh, Nigel,' said one of our English visitors, watching Irène admiringly as she showed people to a table, 'that agency of yours is fantastic. Everybody you get here is good looking!'

Georgea's girl was nearly useless. Her first job was to peel and slice potatoes for a Gratin Dauphinois. It took her nearly two hours and she did not get quicker with practice. It drove Georgea wild watching her, almost wilder than if the girl had not been there. However, she could hold things during the service, get out the plates, burrow in the *chambre froide* to find things and just eased the strain a bit. But neither of them could stay beyond the first few days of September. They were students and they had to get ready for the impending academic year. Meanwhile, we were no nearer a longer-term solution and even if the pace of the season was slackening, Georgea's would have to slacken more or she was going to become ill. There was also the winemaking to prepare for.

At this point two minor miracles came to pass. Sheriden bumped into Marie-Laure and Marie-Laure needed some work to ease her group along. They were finding bookings even harder to come by than they would be at Commarque in 1992! She was back in control the very next day and it was as if she had never left. There were even guests staying in the hotel whom she knew from the previous year.

The second miracle followed the new advert I put in the paper, calculating that the end of August meant the end of many summer contracts and therefore some hopes of ending Georgea's purgatory.

'I can't keep this up much longer,' she said, and it was visibly true.

At this point Dominique strode unhesitatingly into the kitchen, exuding confidence, competence, enthusiasm and know-how from every pore. Georgea gratefully left him to it. We have never come across anyone else like him. He *knew* so much. In fact he was very highly qualified, with the equivalent of a couple of degrees, positively an academic among cooks, and this had led to problems with more ignorant, and consequently jealous, employers. Not that Dominique was in the least big-headed or over assertive. He was just a 'Superior Being' and not all his colleagues liked that. For us he was heaven sent and so competent that he relieved Georgea not only of the grinding toil but also largely of the responsibility of running the restaurant. I have to say that this was helped by the dismal fact that in 1991 the season slowed down much quicker than it had in the previous two years, as the first of a series of cold, wet autumns set in—with all that that implies for the wine.

So, Dominique was free to experiment, to add to, to garnish and to provide menus described by one appreciative diner as 'full of little surprises'. Not that he was faultless. He worked ankle deep in mess. His plates were ornate, and to pull that off they must be immaculate; occasionally Dominique's had splots on them and bits of stuff where there shouldn't have been any. Some of his arrangements were too complicated and plates were fiddled with until the food got cold. We Brits seem more bothered about this than the French. Anyway, it made Georgea twitchy. Not all of his creations succeeded. Like many modern and inventive cooks, it seemed to us, he sometimes made things that lacked flavour; elegant they may have been, interesting to look at, thoughtful in the use of ingredients, original. But none of this really matters if the result does not taste as good as the name sounds! But let's not carp. He was quite shocked when Georgea took the broom and started to sweep up on his first day.

'You're the patron,' he said, 'that's not your job, it's mine.'

And he did have some lovely things. He taught us Sauce Grand Veneur and game Grand-Mère and things to do with oyster sauce that we would never have thought of. His main effect was perhaps to stimulate Georgea, who is untrained but quick on the uptake, to try experimenting more and therefore produce dishes that were more truly hers. So why didn't he stay for ever and ever? The trouble was we could not employ him through the winter, although we hoped he would come back in the spring and do a season. He liked us and wanted to return but he had to find something in the meantime, and he found what he deserved: a permanent job in a first-class restaurant. He kept in touch. He told us when he became Chef de Cuisine of a new smart place in Bordeaux. Last time we went by it had gone the way of so many new restaurants and had shut down. He will have found something else because he is very good, very hard-working, very intelligent and very normal. Cooks combining all these qualities are not that common and are in demand. Dominique should go far.

* * *

The 1991 vintage at Commarque was, meanwhile, a dreadful flop. I had already decided not to make any dry white wine. There were simply not enough grapes and then we did have a fair bit left over from 1990. What of that small quantity of gorgeous Sauternes? It just didn't happen. While some of the Cru Classés, and others well situated on the higher ground to the north of the village, got in some good *tris* and made small amounts of fine Sauternes, we were still waiting for our grapes to concentrate themselves properly. There was Noble Rot but it was not advanced enough for picking. Then cold, wet weather took over; I waited for too long. We should have picked earlier and more boldly. The resulting wine would not had been worse and there would have been more, for we were obliged to throw away even some of the few grapes we had. We ended up with one-and-a-half *tonneaux*, or six barrels, or 1,800 bottles of light, if not thin, Sauternes that no one wanted to buy in 1992 and I didn't really want to keep. What of those wonderful prices? That ₣55,000 a *tonneau*? It certainly wasn't for wine like this. It was for decent 1990, a reward for the patience of those who had hung onto it. With all the stocks of good wine still available why should anyone want the poorer 1991s at any price? So there was no bulk sale in 1992, not even a little one, and that was only one of the things that went wrong that year.

19

This is My Broth

At the start of 1992 there was still a feeling of forging ahead. We had after all broken all records in the hotel and restaurant the year before. The fact that we had a small, poor-quality crop of wine was a hiccup, but we could put that right next time round. Even the awful experience of those weddings, and of Bernard and Valérie, could just be bumps on the road to stability and success. We could put up with a lot if we could see progress. Dominique had restored, in part, Georgea's faith, not to mention her energy. Based on the accounts for 1991, we could make forecasts for 1992 which were, well, quite convincingly dynamic; a coherent case could be made for a modest expansion of the hotel and repayment of part of the excess investment made by our partners. In short, we went looking for a loan.

We could not have started our search for money at a worse time! A lending bonanza was coming to an abrupt halt in France. The banks were licking wounds inflicted by their own excessive generosity over a number of years. They had done, as the bank manager said, '*n'importe quoi*' and lost a lot of money. Now they were making it their business to ensure that this did not happen again, and the easiest way to do that was not to lend anyone anything. At any rate, they only lent to people who could cover themselves a hundred times over and didn't really need to borrow in the first place. The truth of the old adage that banks never lend you money when you really need it has been proved over and over again! The bank manager, charming and helpful Monsieur Duperrieu, who 'understands' us because he too has a vineyard, or his wife does, did his best but, 'my bank doesn't do "that sort" of loan'.

'Two or three years ago,' he said, 'you would have got what you want with barely a glance at the accounts.'

As it was I was to pass three years, with the assistance of various helpful but ineffectual gentlemen, in the fruitless preparation of dossiers, visits to well-groomed men in offices both plush and scruffy, mainly in Bordeaux, and hours and hours of fax time to John and Celia in England. How much more useful it would have been if the time had been spent on MARKETING. It was during these exercises that we discovered the weight of mortgages hanging round the neck of Commarque. It must have frightened off some of the banks without even a glance at our figures. But one must not underestimate the fact that banks are businesses; the banker to whom you present dossier and business plan is no more than a salesman like any other. He lives by selling money. He is charming and encouraging. He finds your enterprise both interesting and courageous and yes, it has lots of potential! He visits, sometimes with a little trail of nondescript people in tow. How pretty the place is! How delicious your wine! We can see you have the whole affair well in hand. The weeks pass and you hear nothing, then a flurry of questions, most of which you thought you had already answered. They are tedious questions about the S.C.I. (the company that owns the château you may recall), the S.A.R.L. (the company that runs the hotel and restaurant), the rent the latter pays the former, who runs the vineyard, how much rent does that pay, can we have the last three crop declarations? And so on. The weeks pass silently once more. You telephone. 'The dossier is pursuing its normal course.'

More questions and more silences. The fellow knows it won't pass la Commission if he puts it forward. It's simply not up to the criteria now being set. But if he says so we shall clear off to another bank and he will have lost his customer for ever. So he can't say yes, but he won't say no. We might well become more prosperous after all; we might decide we can put up more solid guarantees; the criteria might even change. So each dossier takes months and months before the penny drops that it is going nowhere, just getting fatter, so fat that soon it will be too heavy to move at all, let alone pass a commission!

While this time-consuming and discouraging activity got under way in optimistic mood, the truth about the 1991 wine was becoming apparent, along with several other disagreeable truths. That winter, loss-making Air France Travel was dismantled. The profitable bits, Paris and the Côte d'Azur, were retained and all the rest was dumped in a new company. The cheerful lady in charge had been with the old company and was 'sure it would work out fine'. I don't think we got more than two customers from her that year and not a single one since! So that was our second-best source of trade gone. There was, however, news from the number one, *Les Auberges et Hôtels de Charme*; one evening in March a vaguely familiar couple turned up for the hotel, dined in total isolation and then revealed themselves as inspectors for the publishers *Editions Rivages*. I knew I had seen them before. He was the man with whom I had discussed the new *Chambres d'Hôte* guide in which we hadn't figured.

'A dreadful mistake has been made,' he said. 'We don't quite know how it happened but we think Madame G. who looks after the guide mixed you up with Mr Jenkin-Lee. He's given us a lot of problems with his place in the Dordogne.'

The plague on him! More than five years after he left the place his influence lingers like a bad smell.

'How could she have mixed us up?' I asked.

'The trouble is she's been looking after five guides at the same time, more or less alone, and has been a bit overwhelmed. We shall do our best to make amends and you will certainly be in the next edition. I shall do the write up myself.'

They looked a bit dismayed when I said it might be too late, that being out of it had hurt us badly—and you might think I was exaggerating. The guide had been our number one source in 1991. But it was already clear that this was not going to be the case in 1992. Whether it was that those two-year-old guides were being thrown away, to be replaced by the latest version, or whether it was the effect of the recession I cannot say. Probably it was both. The fact was that bookings were down and precious few were coming via the guide. The phone rang infrequently, letter writing diminished and Easter, the first time we expect to be full after the winter, was to be a brief affair, limited to a long weekend. We were not the only hotel to suffer a reduction in trade that year and the hotel trade was by no means alone in its difficulty. Sudinter sent us *one* group in 1992. At the end of the year I asked if we had done something wrong, fallen out of favour, been replaced by another restaurant? 'Not at all,' came the answer. 'It's just that we've suffered a great reduction in business this year...' So there went our top three meal tickets, all at the same time!

In 1993 we were back in the *Auberges et Hôtels de Charme*, but the effect was not the same. Money was tighter. All those second, and third, holidays were being suspended. Easter was no longer a grand spring whoopee and the autumns got shorter, assisted by rotten weather. Back in 1990 we had taken more money in October than in September. I put this down to the magnificence of the weather allied to relative prosperity. Those October receipts have never been repeated, but then nor has the October weather. The French have a curious habit, round here anyway, of stopping their incursions into the countryside at the first break in the weather after the summer. No matter how fine it becomes afterwards, once there has been a cold, wet period in October, or even September, the French tourist hibernates. We saw our season getting shorter and the high season being booked later and later. At least there *was* still a high season and we could truthfully argue that we needed more hotel rooms to make the most of the tourists while they are around.

July and August became more and more hectic, because that is when most people take their holidays and we *had* become better known, but we have never recovered our springs and autumns. Even biennial Vinexpo, the Bordeaux wine show, the biggest booze-up in the world, lost its pulling power after 1991. How packed we had been in 1989 when we were full of Californians—the Stratford Winery with their vineyard owners and buyers. That was the famous year when the exhibition centre became so hot that the fire sprinklers in the roof nearly came on. Red wine had to be refrigerated to stop it breaking up. At the end, Stratford's director, Tony Cartlidge (a wheeler-dealer we could really have done with at Commarque ... 'Strikes me you need to refinance the whole set-up and inject some more capital...'), sneaked out dozens and dozens of expensive bottles and gave them to me! Then 1991, with all those charming Greeks trying to break into the French market—Greek wine in France, will the French really go for this? How reluctant they were to leave Commarque, by order of their managing director, because it was too far from Bordeaux, and take up rooms in Sofitel bang next door to the exhibition centre.

'It's so peaceful here after Vinexpo and the food's great ... like real home cooking but with lotsa class!'

Their boss must have paid a gigantic bribe to have got them into Sofitel where there was a waiting list of hundreds. Indeed, every hotel within 100 kilometres of Bordeaux was booked solid that year and people even flew daily from Biarritz to get to the exhibition. The Greeks were all paid up in advance (Sudinter again!) and they were so rich they never even bothered to ask for a refund. Their rooms were rebooked the moment they stepped out of them, so everything was paid for twice that year. And that is what Vinexpo used to do for us. Now it's a shadow of its former self. Oh, it still hums in Bordeaux, but the ripples don't spread to Sauternes like they used to.

* * *

The restaurant was in quite competent hands that year; 1992 was Sébastien's season and Sébastien was 100 per cent reliable during the service. He didn't flap, he didn't crumble, he got on with it and didn't keep calling for help. If there was a group of forty-nine people he could be guaranteed to produce forty-nine even squares of Gratin Dauphinois, forty-nine bundles of *haricots verts* tied up with red and green peppers, to accompany forty-nine Gibelottes de Lapin Sauternaises, Gilles' recipe, dressed out neatly on forty-nine well-warmed plates. Gilles could not be relied on to count forty-nine of anything, but he did produce the Gibelotte and Sébastien could never have done that. When it came to the preparation of dishes, it was better if Georgea did it, but Sébastien was capable of learning. He was always a pleasure to work with and he was assisted by ... Marie-Laure! Her last season before the street entertainment group got going enough to manage without her wages. All in all the restaurant and hotel went well that summer, well that is from the point of view of not giving Georgea so much aggro, not so well from the point of view of fulfilling the forecasts based on 1991 which had been prepared for the bankers. We were not too downcast. This was a hitch year. Our return to the *Guide des Auberges* would set up the hotel again next year and meanwhile there was just what we needed out there on the vines: a huge crop was in preparation. After the lesson of 1991 the vineyard had been pruned less severely, to leave more wood on which more buds would break, but later, and produce more grapes, or more secondary buds if there was another damaging frost. But there was no frost and by July we looked set for the very first time to reach the limit for Sauternes of 25 hectolitres per hectare. We had never been anywhere near this before, even in 1990 when we had made rather too much dry white wine. A passing wine shipper said, 'I hate seeing the vines loaded like this. It always ends in trouble.' But we loved it.

A big crop of decent quality would give us a bulk sale to replenish the rapidly emptying coffers—*and* enough wine left over to bottle and sell expensively like the 1990. We were lumbered with the weedy 1991 and our lovely 1990 was selling out fast. This was all very well, but to keep on an even keel we were obliged to sell it, not to individual customers at a high retail price, but to the excellent shop up on the Place in Sauternes, Le Caveau du Sauternais. It was they who sold it to individual customers at a high price instead of us! They would have taken the whole crop if I had let them. It went very well but that wasn't at all the idea. It was intended to provide *us* with brisk retail sales over two years, while bulk sales each year covered all the vineyard expenses. But no bulk sales in 1992 left a large hole in the edifice which could only be blocked by bottles of 1990.

This was to be, despite appearances in July, another sorry year for Sauternes. Be quite clear that a good year for Bordeaux as a whole can still be a poor year for Sauternes and a poor year for Bordeaux is assuredly catastrophic round here. It's all a question of the lateness of the harvest because of the need to develop Noble Rot. In 1992 there had already been attacks of Botrytis during July and August. It is then Grey Rot, not at all Noble. This disease is damaging and must be treated. The treatment is expensive. No one round here likes doing it, especially in late summer because of the risk of inhibiting the spread of the Noble variety of rot a little later on. In 1992 there was no choice. Premature Botrytis can destroy the whole crop and has done so in the past. We treated. After that, from mid-August onwards, it's too late and you put up with what comes. What came in 1992 was cool, damp weather in September and the Botrytis arrived again, before the grapes were fully ripe. This complicates the issue enormously, for the grapes look quite like nobly rotted ones. But they are more brown than purple, and furrier. The trouble is you can line up a range of grapes, like a museum taxonomist lining up rows of similar but subtly varying insects, in the hope of finding a break in the variation. The taxonomist hopes to find a discontinuity in the arrangement of stripes on the body, width of head in relation to abdomen, shape of legs and so on, which would serve to separate one species from another. I was hoping to find a break in furriness and brownness that I could explain to the *vendangeurs* and say: 'Those are good: keep them. These are bad: throw them away.' But it isn't like that. Just as the appearance varies without a break from 'perfect' Noble Rot to 'perfect' Bad Rot, so does the taste of the grapes. Those that are a little too hirsute and slightly discoloured may well recover with warmth and sunshine to become as noble as you could wish. The noblest rotted grape will go bad if left long enough in the rain. I watch selected plants each year as markers for the development of rot and in 1992 I had one beauty with twelve perfect bunches. Uniformly *pourris pleins* they were, and weighing in at a sugar content equivalent to 12 degrees of alcohol, well ripe, by the end of the third week of September. So prolonged was the cold and wet that six weeks later the grapes were still *pourris pleins*, a few had shrivelled or gone bad, and the rest weighed in now at only 11 degrees! Many others fared even worse as Botrytis got hold when they were at only 7 or 8 degrees. At that level they will never come good. Covered in grey, brown, even black hairs the grapes shrivel as they do when nobly rotted but the juice does not become super-sweet and concentrated; it tastes sour and mouldy, and gives to the wine the dreaded *goût de moisissure* (the taste of rot) of bad Sauternes years. Some of these *goûts* can be removed with bentonite, casein, gelatine and the rest, but the more nasty tastes you remove, the more good ones you take away with them. Finally, you can, if your picking has been careless enough and you have had to add enough chemicals, end up with wine that is free of the *goût de moisissure* and tastes of absolutely nothing at all.

There is only one way to make half-decent Sauternes in bad, or even half-decent, years and that is to redouble the care with which the grapes are picked, scrupulously throwing away those that have been attacked prematurely by Botrytis, that are *piqué*, that have White Rot (*really* awful taste), or are even covered in green and blue mould (never dared try these ones!). The earlier you can start picking, the better, because every day lost is a day nearer the onset of the cold and wet, which is bound to arrive sometime. One of the most important factors making the Crus Classés better than the rest of us is that their *terroir* favours early development; it is relatively frost free, the breaking of the buds, flowering, ripening, are always a week or so ahead of the lower, colder vineyards. So when the autumn damp rolls up from the Ciron the grapes are just that little bit readier to rot nobly and to produce noble Sauternes.

For some châteaux there was another, quite unexpected complication in 1992. The barriers of Europe came down that year and all of a sudden an awful lot of customs men found themselves with nothing to do. French Administration, unable to resist such an opportunity to interfere in a novel kind of way, sent them into the wine producing areas. Roadblocks appeared round Sauternes and they were not there to help hunt down terrorists or even escaped convicts. These roadblocks arrested trailers of grapes on their way to the wine presses. As armed customs men fanned out around the tractors and their astonished drivers, a sample of grapes was solemnly taken. The juice was measured and lo and behold, this being 1992, mischief and skulduggery were uncovered. Châteaux desperate to get something in before all was ruined were picking at illegally low sugar levels. Grapes destined to make Sauternes must not be picked at less than a sugar content equivalent to 13 degrees of alcohol, the minimum alcohol content permitted in the finished wine. Not that that is much good on its own. You have to have residual sugar on top of that; so picking at 13.5 or 14 degrees, although legal, doesn't really help. Except that now we have the *chambres froides* and cheating with excess sugar is more sophisticated than it used to be ... but it might be wise to leave that one alone! Anyway, in 1992 at least one well known château was banned from picking for a fortnight, purely on the basis of what the customs men found at the roadblocks. Serves 'em right, you may say, but it was a hard blow that year. They *should* have been taking more care, but remember my 'control' plant, on which the grapes declined from 12 degrees to 11 between 20 September and the start of November? Waiting didn't help those bunches that year.

Needless to say, we got nowhere near the 25 hectolitres per hectare limit that had seemed likely back in the summer. For the second year running, gambling on a change in the weather and our luck, I waited too long and we lost many, many grapes. I calculate we threw the equivalent of two *tonneaux*, 1,800 litres, down the centres of the rows and the last *tries* were accomplished in a squelch composed not only of mud but also of sodden, squashed flat bunches of grapes. As Flo said, 'This isn't half as much fun as 1990.'

* * *

The writing was on the wall after 1992 but we wouldn't give up yet. Let's try one more year. The *Auberges et Hôtels de Charme* was bound to give us a boost next year and there was the 'Charming Small Hotels Guide', just translated into Spanish, which had brought us a complete hotel-full of Spaniards for the All Saints holiday at the end of October. Perhaps Spain would become the number one supplier of customers with the help of the Pink Guide. It didn't. Spain dipped into recession and the Spanish tourists evaporated as abruptly as they had appeared. Anyway, there couldn't be another wine harvest like 1992 could there? So we changed the year on the forecasts that went with the bank dossiers and Monsieur Jacques Dulong, the charming financial *courtier* who was trying to charm a loan for us, continued his painful search.

Monsieur Dulong was an ex-banker, very patient and he seemed to have contacts. But they disappointed him one and all and he was cross about it: 'Far too many people in this business are *pas sérieux*.' And he considered he had been *mené en bateau* (taken for a ride. Literally, 'led in a boat'). In the course of the next year and a bit I would say Monsieur Dulong was rowed both far and long and got himself into some murky financial waters. He emerged without a penny and it is probably just as well. I'm not sure he hadn't grounded on the shores of that world where money is laundered. In the meantime both he and conventional banking circles were flummoxed by the fact that John and Celia would not act as guarantors for a loan.

'*Mais votre associé* must be a man of substance. Look what he has done already! If he underwrites the loan *and* the bank has a charge on the property the bank cannot lose and will agree to give you the money.' Which is tantamount to saying: 'Your associate is going to get most of this money, so if anything goes wrong' (more wrong!) 'he can give it back to the bank.' John and Celia were trying to get out, not to hang an even heavier millstone around their necks than the one they were bearing already. The banks seemed to find it odd that they were not prepared to take this risk and I had to explain why several times to Monsieur Dulong before he had properly grasped it. Funny isn't it?

After that I learned all sorts of financial wheezes. So did Monsieur Dulong. We talked to people about Revolving Credits, which appeared to reimburse, then reform themselves automatically at amazingly low interest rates; and about Back-to-Back Arrangements, repaid by enormous insurance schemes, for which you also borrowed the money. We never managed to get approved for any of these arrangements. I did get a statement guaranteeing the guarantees set out in a policy, signed by no less than the boss of Generali France, who turned out to have been a customer at Commarque—and had liked it. He liked the idea behind the policy as well and was doing the company no harm by possibly selling it. He didn't succeed. The faceless men in an unknown country, for all this was done through distant intermediaries like 'an international lawyer in Paris', or 'a Swedish financial consultant in the Hague', were never going to accept such a thing. It all depended on stable interest rates for the next fifteen years and you would need to be daft to believe in that. So, Monsieur Dulong was conducted around the high seas and the rest of us got more and more disenchanted and, dare I admit it, cynical.

This was only a sideline at Commarque, even if a time-consuming one. The normal activities went on but those things that should have taken precedence did not. Now as never, I should have been out there marketing Commarque, to produce real figures, not forecasts! Now as never, we both ran round in circles trying to *save* money, rather than generating more. Reducing staff costs by doing more waiting, making Georgea do more cooking by delaying the arrival of the cook. It's not difficult to see why we were going down and hard to see how we could have stopped it, given our strengths and weaknesses. If we stayed as we were, locked in a sort of third-world economy, we would get where we had got to already: nowhere!

The 1993 grape harvest seem to confirm this and put paid to any hopes of a decent set of figures to show a bank. And we really couldn't go on changing the year in order to peddle those ageing forecasts yet again.

There can't have been *another* bad crop, you say. It must be your fault! It was not, but I admit to making it marginally worse by hanging on again, hoping against hope for the change in the weather that might save us. For there was no point, none whatsoever, in making another load of dilute wash, fit only to be sold off as soon as possible for whatever groats the hamstrung *négociants* could still afford! We were learning the story of Sauternes the hard way. Did I not say right at the beginning of this book that 'just occasionally' we are rewarded with 'a rare, golden autumn'? There had been far too many of them in the eighties, a decade like no other there has ever been in Sauternes. Now the balance, firmly against the *viticulteur*, was being restored—bad luck for us but not surprising. So far there had only been three poor years on the trot. That's nothing exceptional in the long and patchy history of this hardest-wine-in-the-world to make. What had been surprising was the rash of pseudo-scientific clap-trap, delivered with all the assurance of perfect ignorance on the telly and elsewhere, about the new, North African climate that was busy installing itself in southern France. The ensuing eighteen months, when the Camargue was nearly washed away, along with several towns in diverse parts of the country, put that one to rest and I hope there were a few blushes.

The autumn of 1993 was as wet as you could have wished, if you didn't fancy the climate of North Africa, but once again small quantities of good wine were made. Those with the nerve to go for it, or with a *chambre froide* in the *chai*, did best But there was a great deal that was thin and weedy, and not only that, unstable. It did its best to referment and become totally unsaleable. Heaven knows prices were low enough already! I thanked my stars for the F22,000 a *tonneau* I got for mine, incredibly quickly. Blessings on that pearl of a *courtier* from Langon, Pilippe Dayres. Anybody buying a vineyard in the region? Let Monsieur Dayres sell your wine for you.

What beats me is why anyone would want to buy wine like mine at any price. I know that if I had kept it, it would not have survived the heat of summer. I suppose it must have been submerged in a great volume, kept very cool, filtered ferociously and maybe even emerged on an unsuspecting market as something else…

If this was such a dodgy year, presumably cheating was rife again, so what of the customs men? There wasn't a sign of them. As the bank manager put it: 'They have been tapped on the kepi.' By which he meant that their hats had been metaphorically pushed over their eyes, with instructions to see no evil.

'They could easily,' went on Monsieur Duperrieu, 'sink the economy of the entire region if they went out and applied the rules strictly. But that wouldn't be in anyone's interest would it?' Tell that to the people in Brussels!

Monsieur Duperrieu has always told me that we live in the correct, the right-thinking, third of France. 'South of the Loire,' he said, 'but not so far south that anarchy prevails. *Midi-moins-le-quart*' (knocking off for lunch quarter of an hour early) 'is one thing, but down there,' and he indicated the south with a dismissive gesture, 'there is *de la magouille* [graft] everywhere.'

What a lovely word *magouille* is, smacking of maggots and rottenness.

North of the Loire is too rigid, he claimed. 'We, on the other hand, try to arrange things for the best, to interpret the regulations in the interests of all.' Here, he sat back and smiled broadly. 'We can claim, quite justifiably, to be the most regulated people in Europe, so a little looseness in the system does no harm.'

Since we are not too far south the customs men did not disappear altogether but they kept their heads, and kepis, out of sight. Instead of attacking the grapes on the open highway they went in for visits to *chais*. Most of the *crus classés* were checked on and, to the delight of many, a certain well known château, well known for frequently delivered sermons about the undesirability of cheating and the need to maintain rigorous standards, was caught, *flagrante delicto*, with its finger in the sugar bowl.

* * *

By now it looked seriously as though the financial expansion necessary to get us out of our third world economy, the *ballon d'oxygène* of which so many of the bank presentations spoke, was never going to happen. Monsieur Dulong presented his last dossier and gave up, not just us but the whole business of loan hunting and financial management, taking up insurance instead. We couldn't help thinking we had finished him off, but I suppose loans were so hard to come by for anyone then that he was just not scoring often enough to live.

We made one last attempt at loan raising, with an Englishman who had advertised his services in a magazine published in England and devoted to property in France.

'Money available for investment in Southwest France,' it said. 'Businesses, Châteaux, Private Houses, all types of property considered.'

Why are people prepared to waste so much time on affairs they have no intention of seeing through? The only answer I can think of in this case is that the man in question saw the possibility of picking up a bargain and reselling it at a profit. Well, he was not going to get Commarque. It may be spiteful but it is difficult to take seriously a financier capable of writing a sentence like this: 'A conception of the scenario by which my company might envisage an involvement in Châteaux [*sic*] Commague [*sic*] could be as follows: monies put in to an agreed level to take out your partner completely only on written agreement by himself as to a lack of debt to himself by the company thereinafter...'

I'm glad he put in the 'thereinafter', which I think means 'after that', otherwise it sounds as though his intention was to 'take out' John with the aid of a hit man.

Are 'monies' more numerous or important than money? They put me in mind of Dominique's little Aumonières, money bags made of pancakes and filled with savoury goodies. 'Monies' sound as though they chink and are lined up in piles on worn, wooden desks. I cannot be sure of this because we never got any of them. Six months of letters, couched in language of aggressive obscurity, came to an abrupt halt when the gentleman announced that his organisation was advancing no more money in France, 'Until the property market which as at the present time is highly uncertain picks up which we think will be at least six months consideration being given of [*sic*] the state of the French economy.' On consideration of which we decided all things being considered that this made a suitable epitaph for our search for 'monies', so we gave up. And if that sounds bitter well that's not how I felt, more relieved really. It's just that I was completely fed up with being polite to all these foul people who might have been (but damn well weren't) about to help us and who wasted so much of my time.

The stuffing had been knocked out of the enterprise by now. The point seemed to have gone. We had put up, willingly, with the hotel and restaurant for the sake of the vineyard. But the price we were paying for it was too high and now the vineyard was no longer paying for itself. Georgea had grown to hate cooking, although she could still manage to joke about it: 'I would work in the vineyard on the hottest day in August in preference to standing in front of the ovens in the restaurant kitchen. The tension there is unremitting. Can I cope with a sixth table when I am already cooking, on my own, for fifteen people? The first order is easy; the second complicates things. When the third arrives I have to choose whether to continue with the third course of the first table or the second course of the second table or should I do the first course of the third table. Then the fourth order arrives. This time it's four people all eating different things. Up until now the tables have chosen menus, all three of them naturally, but nonetheless that's easier than *à la carte*. Now that panicky feeling, which I am convinced is known only to the solitary cook, comes over me. I'd love to creep away and leave the salmon to burn, the magret to dry out and the *pommes forestières* to become a pan of uniform black cubes. The fifth table is nice and simple so I accept my duty as *la patronne*, as usual, I breathe deeply and stay put to see the service through. Things do gradually sort themselves out and are just getting better when that sixth table arrives ... Sometimes in July and August it is as hot here as it is in the vines and at least they won't burn or dry out if I don't work fast enough.'

The reality was not funny. Of course, she had never *liked* cooking. She had done it out of a heroic sense of duty, to help retain the roof over her head. She did it well, for F2,000 a month, never paid throughout the year, because the money simply was not there. Driven by Black Sunday to do *something*, she had ended up doing it all. Must she go on being made to suffer a sinking feeling every morning as she walks across the courtyard to the restaurant? Need supper really be on the table by six forty-five, at the latest, every single day, just so that she can suffer the same sinking feeling at seven thirty as she rushes off, leaving the children to fend for themselves for yet another evening? All for, finally, no more than the privilege of a leaky roof over her head and the prospect of doing it all her life. And yet, and yet ... there was still, there was always, an ambivalence in our attitude, even Georgea's. It has remained, despite everything, impossible to lose that slight, nostalgic, holiday feeling when sitting in the courtyard or watching the setting sun. The feeling of another world elsewhere to which we really belong and must soon return, leaving this idyll, flawed though the reality may be. Oh if this could only go on for ever!

There, there now! There are other gardens, with other sunsets, perhaps more carefree ones.

It was time to admit defeat and sell the place.

Georgea looked distinctly cheerful once the decision was taken and various weights fell away. We no longer needed to worry about what guides thought of us, or come to that what people thought about us, only we are too conscientious to go far with that one. We could shut the place for an evening if it was really impossible to keep open. Previously we had always bowed before of the need to do the impossible. We gave up weddings once and for all, but got one final, disagreeable, family soirée, in which, at about 1.30 am, Georgea tripped over a woman peeing against one of the plane trees in the courtyard. This incident, the antithesis of nostalgic idyll, seemed to epitomise why it was time to leave Commarque!

One weight remained and got heavier: the whole S.C.I., S.A.R.L., overweight, overcomplicated cock-up thrust itself before my dim and reluctant comprehension as never before. Already I had grown sick of statutes, resolutions (leading nowhere, rather like new year's ones), and all the rest of the company apparatus so beloved by those non-lending banks. Then there was the continuous wear and tear engendered by the accounts—S.C.I., S.A.R.L., vineyard, all separately—the taxes each attracted, the *déclarations* of this and that which had to be made at the correct time of year and all the forms that didn't apply but kept on arriving and had to be returned, signed and explained away. Now there was added the problem of what exactly we were selling. Was it the land? The buildings? The company owning them by selling the shares? The business value? The S.A.R.L.? Or what? The consequences of the different possible solutions were important but seemed to me, like so much of this company business, to be quite beside the point and a profound hindrance to a relatively simple matter: setting a price for the whole affair and then finding someone who wanted to pay that price, or something close to it.

As yet another day went up in a mist of queries about the S.C.I. from someone who was thinking of buying it, I yelled out: 'I'm sick of the S.C.I. and damned capital value, current account deficit and all the rest of it month after ruddy month.'

Georgea paused from her ironing and remarked thoughtfully: 'Yes, I suppose it's a bit like me making broth week in, week out, year after year ... You do get sick of it!'

20

Five Yards from the Ciron

Nothing happened for some time and 1994 went on much as all the other years had done. Mandates to sell were signed with various estate agents, whose ideas of the price that ought to be asked for Commarque varied wildly. The English agents seemed more optimistic than the French and they charged for the privilege of being on their books. We couldn't help feeling the French were the more realistic. They *knew* so much more—like how much a hectare of Sauternes was fetching, incidentally about half the price of three years previously! The English agents asked *me* how much a hectare was worth. No wonder we Brits tend to pay through the nose for the right to our place in paradise.

One thing everyone was agreed on: sell the whole thing together. A small vineyard-hotel was more interesting than a small hotel and small vineyard separately. And rich people looking for a place in the sun would like a few vines, even though they would close down the hotel. I was not convinced, having discovered the hard way that the money did not add up. On the one hand it was an enormous set of buildings to buy for a very small vineyard, on the other a very expensive small hotel because of the vineyard attached to it. There would not be that many idiots who would want both, like we had done all those aeons ago. There would be even fewer with the additional money necessary to make it big enough to work. Anyway, out it went in glossy brochures or on badly photocopied pieces of paper, according to the prestige of the agent—to roars of silence.

Just as well you will say, because we were saved in the nick of time, on the threshold of a heart-breaking sale, by the most wonderful and prolific grape harvest.

Not in the least. The decision had been taken. Even a 1990 vintage would be useless because the expensive bottles we needed would not be available to sell until 1996 at the earliest. We, our partners, could not wait that long—even if we had wanted to; but we didn't want to. It was finished and finished it would stay, and no question of heartbreak. In the event it was another lousy harvest. I didn't even bother to wait in the hope of an improvement this time, and if the custom men had come round they would have got me! It is amazing how relatively well it turned out, which does make me think a bit about what goes on. There wasn't much though, an early frost and autumn rain saw to that.

Just after the *vendanges*, with little sign of life on the sale front, a man I know from dinners he had organised in the restaurant came by, and offered to rent the vines from us. He had heard we wanted to get shot of them and he needed more land as his son and daughter were coming in with him. He has a Graves vineyard not far away, and patches of Sauternes dotted about Bommes and Fargues. I explained we were trying to sell the lot and had better say no. He replied that he wouldn't at all mind buying it but he was launching a new company and was not in a position to borrow more money at present. His suggestion about renting the vines did clarify the feeling that we could dispose of them without too much difficulty and this would bring down the price of the buildings into the range of a great many more potential buyers. The agents, we felt, had got it wrong. The continuing silence served to support this view. I consulted them and they all agreed with me. So I let Monsieur Desqueyroux have the vines—and wondered why the agents had not suggested earlier what they now supported so wholeheartedly.

We could now make economies while waiting to sell Commarque. We would have none of the expenses of vineyard management but would still have the income derived from selling the 1994 wine. We should therefore be in pocket for the coming year—or anyway, our long-suffering partner John would be. Heavens knows he had been having a thin time recently.

Monsieur Desqueyroux installed himself and little changed except that instead of the familiar figures of the Saint-Martin brothers pruning the vines, it was the familiar figures of Isabelle and Victor, our ace *vendangeurs*, who did the work for Monsieur Desqueyroux. And naturally we stayed in doors that winter.

In the hurly-burly of recounting our downfall I have not given due place to Isabelle, who had succeeded Joan as Femme de Chambres in 1991. For vigorous endeavour, unfailing cheerfulness and bags of initiative when it came to repairing and making do, Isabelle was great. What's more, she can do anything you like in the vines.

Things still didn't feel different, except that we knew it would not last forever and that set us thinking about where we were going to go and what we might do when we had got there. There was no question of a return to England. For one thing, we did not have remotely enough money to buy a house in that expensive land. For another, we had no intention of abandoning the boys' French education. That has remained something to which we can firmly attach ourselves, when drawing up the balance sheet of this whole affair, and say: '*That* was worth doing, despite all the rest.'

At the start of April Monsieur Desqueyroux wrote me a letter offering to buy the whole vineyard for ... not a bad price. We were on the point of accepting it, after due deliberation of the consequences for the rest of the property, when—wait for it ... we had a frost, and Monsieur D. promptly withdrew his offer! He claimed to have suffered a *perte sèche* (a dead loss) of F100,000 a hectare because of the frost and that Commarque was the only vineyard in the neighbourhood to have been damaged. Calculation showed that Monsieur Desqueyroux reckoned he wasn't going to gather a single grape if he was down by a hundred grand per hectare. But this frost wasn't remotely as severe as that of 1991. Then a brief scout round the area was enough to see that all the frost-sensitive bits had been 'touched', so he was *quand-même* (exaggerating). A few days later I found him mooching in the vines and pointed these things out to him, adding that while the tips of the *mannes* (flowering shoots) were damaged, what was inside–viz. the flowerbuds—were perfectly all right. He looked at me as if I was trying to teach his granny to suck eggs but then looked at the plant beside him, then at the next one and the one after that. They were undamaged as I had claimed, but Monsieur Desqueyroux's offer remained withdrawn, 'In view of the sensitivity of the vineyard revealed by the recent frost.'

However he reached the 25 hectolitres per hectare limit for Sauternes, which is more than we ever did, because 1995 was a good year. Naturally it was; we had rented out the vines so the crop was not ours. At this point Monsieur D. was advised that now was the time to buy, so he made another offer, lower than the first. We weren't so keen on that but it was an offer to buy and the only one we had had. Accepting it meant removing once and for all the vineyard from this old, old property, a vineyard which had extended to 15 hectares not forty years ago. This is not something of which I could be proud, particularly as I am the only *viticulteur* to have made an effort since the 1960s. I thought of what Henri de Vaucelles would say about this betrayal of the southern end of Sauternes. However, the wine will keep the name of Commarque because, in order to make the offer pass muster, I suggested to Monsieur D. that as well as the vines, he might like to buy all the land in the *Appellation Contrôlée* area; land of no interest to anyone not already a *viticulteur* and of little value to the château. He went for this. His son is a *jeune viticulteur*, with priority in the allocation of those hard-to-come-by *droits de plantation*. So after long negotiation, Monsieur D. borrowed the necessary money from his bank and got that government agency in farm sales, SAFER, to agree to buy from us and sell to him (the same day), thus getting avoiding the need to pay a large chunk of notary's fees. Being a government agency, SAFER is exempt from them. But the scheme did not work as well as Monsieur D. had hoped because, being a government agency, SAFER charged him a thumping commission for its kindness in participating in the deal. Also, being a government agency, the complexity of the operation was multiplied several-fold and the timescale extended by a similar amount. Nevertheless, we sold the vines, gave rights of access to them, secured rights of access to all the bits remaining with the château and generally cobbled together the affair *comme il faut*.

So what about the rest of it? And what about somewhere for us to go? The two things hobbled along, apparently going nowhere, until the arrival in the courtyard, unannounced and uninvited, of a local agent whom I had never even approached. I had mistakenly thought that the one and only local agent to whom I had been recommended was all that was needed. Otherwise, wider contacts would be available through big city agents in Bordeaux and even Toulouse. A stupid point of view really, considering their lack of results over the previous months. Jean-François Trescos really started to move things as no one else had done, and that included finding us a place. Very neatly done it was and a great relief to us, and perhaps even more so to the boys.

Our search for housing had been worryingly unsuccessful to say the least. Reckoning on a modest budget, even allowing for a major intervention by Georgea's dad, we went round all the agents in Langon and Bazas. As soon as we announced how many bedrooms we had in mind and how much money we wanted to pay for them, there was a general lifting of eyebrows and pursing of lips. Then a dive into the profoundest recesses of the property files to emerge with everything that had been mouldering there the longest: great crumbling barns in the flood zone of the Garonne near La Réole; properties with beams sticking through the roof and rooms 40 feet long; without water or electricity;, properties fully furnished as they had been when the owners, seemingly a hundred generations away, had moved out or died in situ, twenty or thirty years ago; properties partly modernised in ways too hideous to contemplate; properties enclosed by other properties with but a single window on the outside world; properties where an old lady had lived alone until three, five, eight years ago, in a single room without heating, the walls patched with old newspapers, cardboard over the windows, one tap in the corner and no lavatory. And nearly all a uniform greyish colour, excepting those modernisations in brilliant yellow and green, roof leaks visible on damp ceilings, ancient wiring with the insulation eaten away, foul odours rising from disused and blocked up septic tanks.

Life in these long-dead houses cannot have been much fun towards the end of their previous lives and they were not, they *are* not, the bargains we used to dream of in France. Too many have already been expensively reborn. Those that are left, not far from the (relatively) prosperous city of Bordeaux, tend to be the final rejects. In mounting dejection we in our turn inspected and rejected—to the relief of the children. They started to express affection for Commarque, attachment to their rooms and regrets—muted, but then they were growing up by now—at the prospect of leaving. I find this reassuring. The greater part of their childhoods had been passed there, with the exception of Thomas's. Surely my guilt at our reckless and unsuccessful venture would be unbearable if the children had jumped for joy and shouted: 'Hurray! At last we're leaving this dump!'

It was, in fact, Thomas who spoke out the most clearly in favour of Commarque. He liked France. He had a longstanding French girlfriend and was well on the way to becoming naturalised, which speaks for itself. Francis was the most darkly gloomy about where we were going to drag him next. He would question us periodically, with a sudden access of loquaciousness, about the latest horror we had visited, and then lapse into what looked like glum anticipation of the worst. We could reassure Robert and Edward—anyway Robert was more interested in the potential running tracks round about than in the houses themselves—and William, already halfway from home at boarding school, didn't ask questions and waited in self-sufficient calm—or complete lack of interest, depending on your interpretation—for the problem to be resolved.

Sale *and* purchase were fixed up at almost the same time by Monsieur Trescos. Of course, he knew about Commarque; intimate contact with the grapevine made that inevitable and he arrived with a customer. While I showed them round Trescos took a fancy to the place himself and brought his wife to inspect it that afternoon, disguised as a second customer. But Georgea had guessed before they had even left. He then said: 'I might have a house for you.'

'Where?'

'Right here in Sauternes. Four hundred years old, beautiful situation, four hectares of land.'

'Sounds too expensive for us.'

'Not necessarily.'

'How many bedrooms?'

'Four, five, six—I can't remember exactly. It's a fine property though, magnificent beams.'

'How much is it?'

'Come and look at it first.'

'There's not much point until we know what the owner wants for it.'

'I'm the owner. You'll like it. You can afford it.'

Devious Monsieur Trescos; devious and charming. Stories change from day to day. The ground shifts around him; one point of view for the buyer, a different vista for the seller. Chameleon-like he merges with the background, plays the appropriate role, then reappears in sparkling new colours parading a new customer, or house, or two—there may be three or none—a new description of the house in Sauternes: it has an ancient abbey beside it. It is a luxurious two-bedroomed affair with a great galleried kitchen stretching up to the roof.

'I showed it to a Belgian the other day. He offered me a huge price for it on the spot, but I'm keeping it for you.'

'Why?'

'Because it's what you want. It'll be your next home when I've sold Commarque.'

'But two bedrooms are no use for us.'

'Don't worry about that. It can be arranged. I've got a man from Cannes coming to look at Commarque tomorrow. He's very interested.'

Monsieur Trescos ran so many horses at once he must have had difficulty remembering in which direction they were all supposed to be going. We found his house before he took us to see it. It was Robert and Edward who knew it, from bike expeditions and camping with Gilles. Also, the general direction was inevitable. Sauternes is small, 4 hectares is a lot of land. It could not be within the vineyard area, therefore it must be on the low ground towards the river Ciron.

It didn't look much from the outside: a plain rectangle of stone, mainly covered in elderly rendering. Peeling green shutters on doors and windows, overgrown all round and with an incomplete square of ruined walls beside it, the abbey perhaps? The most interesting features were a brand new and beautifully constructed roof, and the situation. On walking round the back, we found the house was about five yards from the bank of the Ciron.

Monsieur Trescos was amused that we had found it without him and momentarily taken aback when we asked if his wife had liked Commarque. His deviousness worried us, we wanted to show we were not completely gormless. But he hooked us with his house nonetheless. When he flung open the shutters, we saw not four, five or six bedrooms, nor even three, two or one. What we saw was a long, high shell, totally empty save for three immense old beams and one immense new one, supporting the immaculate roof. It smelt dry. It was dry, much drier than Commarque. It smelt really good but that didn't help, given its emptiness. This was hypothetical housing, a creation worthy of Mr Jenkin-Lee.

We turned to Monsieur Trescos with an indignant: 'But it'll cost a fortune to do this up.'

'No, it won't.'

'Well, we can't afford it, on top of what you're asking for it.'

'No! No! You haven't understood. The price is *with* all the work complete.'

'It can't be.' We were incredulous.

'It is.'

It wasn't quite, but it was close enough.

We signed a *compromis de vente* for the house with a long, long, six-month delay before we had to sign the final *acte*. Plenty of time for the work of renovation to be completed and long enough, surely, to get shot of Commarque. A few days later the man from Cannes arrived, spent twenty minutes at the château and made his offer. We accepted it. Now you would think it was all over, a peaceful transition from one life to the next is in prospect. In three months it'll be finished. Why, we could be out of here by April.

That was reckoning without the operation of my 'Broth', that soupy confusion of companies that governs Commarque. It bubbled up on a scale of opacity and futility as yet undreamed of. Here was this very rich man, apparently keen to get his hands on the place as quick as possible in order to start all the works he had in mind. There was us, dying to get out, and John dying to get some francs converted into pounds before the bottom dropped out of the exchange rate, as it had done, in reverse, when we bought Commarque ten years previously. Yet the Broth meant it took over two months to devise a formula whereby the S.C.I. could be transferred satisfactorily to the buyer, a formula which required the vineyard sale to be completed first. And this was the way the sale had to be done—because selling a company attracts much lower legal fees than selling the buildings it owns.

Then nearly three months more were spent getting the documents needed to complete the purchase, following the sale of the vineyard. Actually that's getting ahead. The documents that took so long to obtain only went to complete the bank dossier for the loan this very rich man insisted on having to buy the place: 'Never use your own money to buy property. It leaves you short afterwards to do what you want with it.' But this loan was only a formality. Our buyer was bound to get it, being so rich. Just as well too! Because we are now inextricably bound up with that Machiavellian estate agent Monsieur Trescos and time is marching on. The six-month deadline suddenly looks alarmingly close. The works at 'Magdeleine', down by the Ciron, are coming to a highly satisfactory conclusion but we don't have the money to buy and won't have until Commarque is sold. Has Trescos worked us craftily into a corner? What's he up to? There is a clause in the agreement we signed about going into the house and paying an immense rent if we couldn't complete on time! Will he get back the house with all *our* works added to it? Because *we* have organised the electricity, plumbing, heating—Monsieur Arlic did it of course—that was the deal. We put a protective clause into the agreement, but Trescos might be able to wriggle out of that! Will he accept a partial payment, let us in, then insist on payment in full for all those extras that always crop up when a house is done up? Of which he keeps saying: 'Don't worry about it. We'll see how it all works out at the end. It won't be more than the cost of a good meal when it's all finished.' Etc., etc. But nothing is clear cut, the questions are headed off or side-stepped and there was no way to force the issue. He had our house, and in effect he had our money, locked up in a Commarque committed to his man, who now seemed to be taking an awful long time to get his 'formality' of a loan.

The children were becoming progressively keener on Magdeleine as the work progressed. When the floor was put in upstairs Francis had gone and stood glumly on the bit inside the blue lines marking the positions of the future walls of his room. Six bedrooms and two bathrooms there would be upstairs, a masterpiece of fitting in and all those lovely beams on view.

'Will this just be dirty stone like it is now?' He asked pointing at the outer wall. 'Is that tatty old window staying?'

He had no faith whatever and plainly didn't believe our statements that it would all be new. He came and stood again as the metal rails supporting the inside walls went up.

'Will I get an electric plug so I can use the computer?' Monsieur Arlic is in the process of fitting a good three dozen plugs! 'Do you think there'll be room for my table? The room's pretty small.'

When the walls were finished he looked less gloomy, because now the room looked much bigger than before. When the beautiful, hard-wood, asymmetrical window went in, he sat on the windowsill and was reconciled at last. As the spring days warmed into summer and we thought Commarque was on the point of being sold, we started to lay carpets and asked Monsieur Trescos if he minded us moving things in.

'Not in the least, but make sure you arrange insurance.'

Monsieur Trescos was being extraordinarily helpful. He remarked more than once that each time we met, things went well. There were no misunderstandings. Either he was so devious that the depth of his cunning and trickery were beyond the sight of man, or we had misjudged him. Perhaps he was continually dealing with people as crafty as himself and more ill-intentioned. We might be a refreshing change.

Time at Commarque seemed to be running out. We started to clear up, to throw out. We had to leave ourselves time to move when the final *acte* was signed. The house might only be a couple of kilometres down the road but there would be no removal men to help. If our buyer wanted us out quickly then we must be ready to go. Commarque is very large, with huge outbuildings. Magdeleine is much smaller, with no outbuildings. A ruthless clear out was in progress. A clear out that called up many previous lives for brief review, before the residue of their material clutter was consigned to the bin bags, the bonfire or the rubbish tip at Langon. There were the remains of five childhoods piled high in the enormous wall cupboards and sheds: small bikes, ancient school paintings and notebooks, all the dusty toys and games, a never-completed remote-controlled aeroplane, outgrown pairs of football boots. We drew the line at the 12 kilos of Lego. Surely someone would like that? And we shirked a decision about the electric train. It's still in the attic. Children's clothes that were far too small for any of them now, grown ups' clothes that Georgea and I had carefully kept for ten years and never worn in France, unwanted pots and pans, the relics of sports tried and rejected: Judo (white jackets and baggy trousers, even a few belts of various colours), canoeing (life jackets—wait though!—they might be useful down by the Ciron), they were all inspected—and slung.

Other lives emerged as well, even older ones, that had travelled with Georgea and the removal men from England to France. Space didn't matter then and anyway, ten years ago Georgea had all those near babies to look after, as well as the house to pack up on her own. There was her musical life: books of sixteenth-century lute music in tablature, her transcriptions into modern musical notation, microfilm of more music manuscripts in Italian libraries—the residue of her unfinished MA thesis. Unfinished because of marriage and the arrival of babies. The small remains of my, even older, academic life appeared too: reprints from learned journals, like the Philosophical Transactions of the *Royal Society of London B.—Biological Sciences* or *The Journal of Insect Physiology*, signed 'best wishes Mike' or 'Robert' or 'Stan'. Where are they all now? Doing pretty well most of them! I know 'Mike' is a professor at Imperial College and 'Robert' has recently been awarded his Doctorate of Science. 'The Cockroach Integument: PAS-Positive Granules and their possible relationship with Phenol Storage'. (What on earth was that about?)—Viles and Mills. Yeah! Dick Mills of Tulane University, New Orleans, who swaggered through the Oxford Zoology department with his students behind him like the hoods of some latter-day Chicago gangster. But all that was so long ago! Into the bin bag with the lot of them, alongside Edward's broken *Star Wars* monsters.

The children seemed quite unmoved by this, unsentimental, as philosophical as the *Phil. Trans. B.* Though Edward has since confided that he misses the wall against which he practised football and regrets having thrown away *all* his little men. But they went, and all of a sudden just about everything had either been thrown away or moved to Magdeleine. Commarque was looking bare. Our beds, the kitchen table, the telly were still there, but our hearts were down by the river and Thomas installed himself to guard it all. Monsieur Trescos thought it an excellent idea, but his six-month deadline was only a matter of weeks away. At this point we found out that our buyer had made a fatal mistake. He had announced that he wanted to reopen the hotel, by no means part of his original plans, much smarter, of course, and without a restaurant. Into the S.C.I. Broth went the S.A.R.L. and the whole unsavoury mess went bubbling up again. His bank started to ask questions, the kind of questions I had heard before. I knew the symptoms, those I described in the last chapter. The very rich man seemed never to have encountered them before—lucky him! The bank back-peddled like fury, imposed condition after condition, until finally the objective was achieved: the very rich man told the bank to get stuffed. Now it was no longer clear whether he would get Commarque. Other lines to other agents were reopened. Monsieur Trescos showed round a steady trickle of new customers and expressed renewed interest on his own behalf. While behind the scenes he was wheeling and dealing to get other banks to look at his original man. For all this goes with the house deal and he did not want to lose it. Heaven knows how it will end, but I back Trescos against all the others. He puts so much more into it.

We don't live in Commarque now. Isabelle and Victor are looking after it though. They are guarding it with their alarmingly blue-eyed husky Shere-Khan. We are down at Magdeleine but I go to Commarque every day. We aren't renting the house either. We bought it! Fearing the worst from Monsieur Trescos to the very end, we asked John if we could have all our share of the money from the sale of Commarque out of the first slice, the vineyard slice. Otherwise we felt we would lose our house over which we had laboured so long: decorations, kitchen, skirting boards, concrete floor, trenches, cables, months we had spent learning loads of new tricks, and look how well it had turned out! And John said: 'Go for it! You can't miss it now.' Bless him!

A few days from the deadline, when the notary had just announced that he couldn't possibly give us an appointment to sign the *acte* for at least two weeks, Monsieur Trescos said: 'Move in whenever you like. Don't lose a moment's sleep over it! Of course, I won't charge you rent.'

And when the *acte* was signed and we held our breaths over the extras, not a word was mentioned about them. There were no supplements, no catches and Monsieur Trescos went cheerfully on his way with a charmingly elegant wish for our future happiness in his former house. The architect who had come to witness the completion of the works and the state of the house whistled through his teeth when the costs were totalled and he was told the selling price and said: 'All that for so little?'

* * *

There is a black carpet downstairs at Magdeleine which shows all the bits of dirt. Georgea hoovers it two or three times a day. This is not obsessive behaviour. It is partly a reaction to having something truly hers, more truly hers than Commarque ever was. Anyway, however much you hoovered Commarque it still looked tatty. Also, she doesn't have to put quite all her energy into cooking these days. We wonder how we did it now, all that work at Commarque and already it seems so long ago. Some of it feels as old as the oldest lives we discarded when we left the château. It is so disconnected from what went before as to feel unreal, more like a vivid dream. But here we are by the Ciron and how could we have got there without having passed by Commarque? So, it must have happened. And every day I am jerked back to the unsold reality of those long walls, that green and shaded courtyard. All the people we met and the things that happened are therefore real and may legitimately be trotted out and used to bore our friends and grandchildren in years to come.

Like Black Sunday and the First Winter, Monsieur Saint-Martin, Gilles, Mr Jenkin-Lee and granny macs.

Like the time I glanced across at the *chai* and saw the roof lifted at the lower end by the huge broken stump of a main beam thrusting up from the inside. Rotted through and snapped it was, poised precariously 2 feet above hundreds and hundreds of bottles of Château of Commarque, hot from the previous day's *mise en bouteille* … a desperate five minutes with iron bars, then Monsieur Arlic, thank the Lord for Monsieur Arlic, to the rescue.

Like the time Francis, carrying out his daily duty of cleaning the swimming pool, stuck his hand into the skimmer box to lift out the basket and grabbed hold of a snake, neatly coiled up inside. He was very quick. He let go in a flash, faster than the snake could uncoil himself and get at him. The snake shot out of the skimmer into the middle of the pool and intrepid Francis caught it neatly in the net, used more commonly for leaves and beetles, and flung it far into the bushes below the vines.

Like the huge hailstorm that ripped through Sauternes in July 1989, passing in two corridors. Commarque was between them but nonetheless all the cars parked outside had their roofs dented and the restaurant, well filled that night, was like a lake…

And all those people, like the charming Pamela Prior of Château Loudenne in the Médoc. She will not take it amiss if we say, our Margaret Thatcher look-alike. She terrified the children, watching beside the swimming-pool, with her perfectly vertical dives in just over a metre of water, and whose friend, a stout middle-aged lady, reduced them to hysterics with her rubber ring and bathing cap.

Like Tony Cartlidge of the Stratford Winery in California talking to Edward who was showing him his magic stick.

'It breaks wood, it breaks metal, it breaks bricks, it breaks concrete.'

'Ah,' says Tony, earnestly looking down at him, 'but does it break wind?'

Like the German lady who telephoned to ask us to send on a couple shirts she had left in her room and, very anxious not to be a nuisance, asks, 'Do you haf vays of making me pay?'

'Oh! Ja! Ja! Ve haf vays…'

Like Christine, a waitress of erratic habits and brief career at Commarque, whose screaming telephone quarrels with her boyfriend were clearly audible from the far end of the vines.

Like the painfully shy English lady who left her window open in a storm and needed a dry mattress. Thomas and I arrive puffing at the top of the stairs to her bedroom to put the mattress in place, and find her standing stark naked in the middle of the room.

Like the football match, staff versus customers. The staff includes Thomas, Francis and Robert, fit as fleas and stone cold certain of running the opposition into the ground in the second half. They are roundly defeated by a team of large, middle-aged gentlemen who have been overeating for days. One of them, it is disclosed afterwards, has been a semi-pro in the National B division. The staff fail dismally to avenge this defeat in the return match the following year, even with me as referee.

Like the rep for a well-known ice-cream firm who was so persistent that we used to hide in the cellar whenever her old Renault Four appeared in the courtyard. Not to mention the frozen food rep who insisted on going through every single item in his fifteen-page catalogue and sent me soundly to sleep.

Like Jimmy Bolton and his riveting games for children in the swimming-pool. Like the Donoghues of the eccentric aperitifs; the Linley-Adams, who were the first to buy the dry white wine in quantity—for their daughter's wedding; the Bindoffs, who brought rolls and rolls of wire for the new vineyard planting that never happened; and the Bossoms, whose postcard, sinfully peeked at, read, 'Château Commarque is as wonderful as ever!' The Züblers, invisible in their Porsche, beneath two large dogs peering through the windscreen; like Monsieur Marty and the gifts of Swissair umbrellas; the Belgian School of Hotellery 'Stella Maris'; the longest ever stayer, Madame Boisserie, plus baby; Dr Bernard Green, New York psychologist, who had the secrets of every person in the hotel before he left; the Drs Girard from Langon—our biggest ever wedding; wine merchants Terry Herbert and David Milburn …

Like ... like ... Monsieur Astié who left a note pinned to our bedroom door on the night of a violent storm (and we *never* leave the front door unlocked!): 'Cher Monsieur. It's midnight, and it's raining in room four. I rang in the restaurant but nothing happened. I came to the house and knocked but no one answered. I have said "hallo" to the hamsters and I'll see you in the morning at breakfast. Bonne Nuit.'

There's all that and more stored up, to be got out, dusted off and laughed over for ever. Unless Georgea wants to forget it all so much that she finds herself with the same selective amnesia as that favoured by Francis for the first day at school.

Afterword

One problem we haven't quite sorted out yet is how to make a living. There was enough money for this lovely house but nothing left over! A bit of language teaching? What about a spot of translating into English? I have tried to start a little specialist translating service: wine, vineyards, tourism, that sort of thing. There's enough hopeless English and sheer rubbish written round here to merit something like that. The difficulty is to persuade people just how badly they are doing. I call my service PRATS—aren't we getting droll? It's perfectly serious in French though. Someone even said, 'What a nice name', and it stands for <u>P</u>ublicité, <u>R</u>éception (receiving visitors), <u>A</u>nglais, <u>T</u>raduction (translation), <u>S</u>auternais. It hasn't exactly got going yet. In an idle moment I looked up 'prat' in the dictionary, having hitherto only known it as a mild term of abuse. It means 'the buttocks'. Hence the dictionary went on to say, the word 'pratfall'—'a fall on the buttocks' or ... 'a humiliating failure'! This could have been the cue for retirement, but we haven't got a pension. Monsieur Trescos is interested in the idea that I look after his English customers... That would be a turn up, wouldn't it?!